A DICTIONARY OF

FRENCH USAGE

FOR ALL ENGLISH-SPEAKING USERS OF FRENCH

DONALD CHRISTIE

IMAGES
PUBLISHING

Published in Great Britain 1995 by
Images Publishing (Malvern) Ltd.,
Upton-Upon-Severn,
Worcestershire.

British Library Cataloguing in Publication Data

A catalogue record for this book is available
from the British Library

ISBN 1 897817 50 9

Set in Times New Roman 9 pt

Designed and Produced by Images Publishing (Malvern) Ltd.
Printed and Bound in Great Britain by Bookcraft, Bath, Avon.

CONTENTS

SYMBOLS AND ABREVIATIONS

1. *qlqn (quelqu'un)* = sn (someone);   *qlqch (quelque chose)* = sth (something) – **note**: these indicate any noun (person = *qlqn*: thing = *qlqch*) can be used in the same manner as shown by the example.

2. masc (m) = masculine;   fem (f) = feminine;   sing = singular;   plur = plural.

3. adj = adjective;   adv = adverb;   conj = conjunction;   prep = preposition;   pron = pronoun.

4. **Tenses** – Imperf = imperfect (endings **always**: *-ais, -aios, -ait, -ions, -iez, -aient*). Fut = future (stem **always** ends in *-r-* followed by: *-ai, -as, -a, -ons, -ez, -ont*). Past hist = past historic/preterite. Imperat = imperative. Pres subj = present subjunctive. Imperf subj = imperfect subjunctive. Pres part = present participle. Past part = past participle. Condit = conditional. **Note**: participles can take plural and feminine forms unless otherwise stated.

5. aux = auxiliary. **Note**: the auxiliary is *avoir* unless otherwise stated. If the verb is reflexive, the auxiliary is *être*.

6. The symbol ¶ refers to the Grammar Section.

7. eg: = for example (exempli gratis);   ie: = that is to say (id est);   ff = following pages, paragraphs, etc.

8. In relation to 'correspondence': inst = instant (of current month);   ult = ultimo (of last month).

9. / = a stroke between words or phrases indicates an alternative;

10. * = an asterisk. This indicates an explanatory note.

11. **Note**: where a table is continued on to the next page in the Grammar Section, the dividing line of this table, between pages, is grey and is not the solid black line denoting a table's completion.

12. **Note**: a single word in brackets (eg: *ne*) in a French example means that the inclusion of this word is optional.

INTRODUCTION

This book is designed to help all those whose native language is English and who learn, teach or use French. It is not a dictionary as such, nor a grammar/course book – but it is a work of reference; a 'dictionary of usage'. Its purpose is to provide answers to problems of syntax and grammar, giving, in a readily available form, what might not be found in either a grammar/course book or a dictionary.

Throughout the book there are ample translated examples by way of explanation. Individual words selected for entry are whose which many year's experience have suggested as most likely to cause problems for English speaking users of French.

Although not every possible problem can be foreseen, nor every question answered, it is hoped that the user will find the information wide and varied enough to prove of real value.

The book is divided into two sections. The first part is the Reference Section which is alphabetically arranged and contains individual words and some shorter articles on points of usage and grammar. The second part is the Grammar Section with longer articles on the parts of speech.

In the Reference Section, English entries are introduced in **bold type**, French in ***bold italics***, cross references are also introduced in **bold type** or ***bold italics***. References to articles in the Grammar Section are in CAPITALS followed by the ¶ symbol and the number of the paragraph in the article. The Grammar Section is divided into articles on adjectives, adverbs, articles, conjunctions, nouns, numbers, prepositions, pronouns and verbs.

It is perhaps useful to know the main reasons as to why some words have been selected for entry in the Reference Section, and to know why others have not. Verbs have been included where they are most likely to be mis-translated or mis-spelt, where they serve as examples for the conjugation of the group to which they belong or where they present spelling difficulties (eg: verbs which take or change accents in the stem). Those verbs which present problems of idiomatic usage and those which are commonly used in popular and useful idioms, are also included. However, the majority of verbs listed are those which present problems of prepositional usage (either before an infinitive or before an indirect object). It is important to realise that English usage is no safe guide to the prepositions used in French and, moreover, a verb which is transitive in English may be intransitive in French (and vice versa). In examples of verb usage, the verb *faire* = to do, is used to show the correct construction when an infinitive follows another verb. For example, *vouloir faire* = to wish to do, means that *vouloir* is followed by an infinitive without any intervening preposition (eg: *vouloir manger* = to wish to eat). Similarly, *décider de faire* = to decide to do, means that the English 'to' is translated by *de* in French (eg: *décider de parler* = to decide to speak), whereas, the verb *obéir* = to obey, requires the preposition *à* to translate the English 'to', etc. **Note**: *demander qlqch* = indicates that no preposition is needed to translate the English, to ask for something. If a verb is irregular in any way its conjugation is given, or reference is made to another verb similarly conjugated.

Verbs with prefixes which are conjugated like their base verb require no other explanation (eg: *refaire* = to re-do) and a few obsolete or very rare verbs have been omitted. In the conjugation of individual entries, the conditional tense is not given as this is **always** formed from the stem of the future + the endings of the imperfect (both of which are given). Compound tenses are not given as these can **always** be formed according to the rules given in the article VERBS in the Grammar Section. The 3rd person singular and plural of the imperative is not always given either, as these are **always** taken from the present subjunctive. The auxiliary is **always** *avoir* unless otherwise stated and if a verb is reflexive the auxiliary is *être*. (**Note**: the conjugation of regular verbs is dealt with fully in the Grammar Section.)

Adjectives have been selected where they are either important or present any special problems of usage. (**Note**: the article ADJECTIVES in the Grammar Section gives the rules for forming feminines and plurals, their position and comparison, and those which are irregular.) Adverbs are included (with their adjective) in the Reference Section and many other common adverbs are listed separately – where necessary in both French and English entries. Prepositions have been selected only if they are important and they are entered in both French and English, together with examples of their use. (**Note**: the article PREPOSITIONS in the Grammar Section fully explains their use after individual verbs or adjectives.) Other parts of speech in everyday use (eg: relative pronouns, impersonal pronouns and those nouns which present particular problems of gender and usage) have also been included in the Reference Section.

To conclude, the longer articles in the Grammar Section comprehensively explain the regularities, the rules and the above irregularities and problems referred to in the Reference Section, as simply and effectively as possible, and will hopefully prove a beneficial guide for any English speaking user of French.

Reference

A

à, preposition: meaning and use

i.   *à* = **at**: *à la maison*, **at** home; *à quelle heure?* **at** what time? *à cent francs*, **at** 100 francs; *être à Douvres*, to be **at** Dover

ii. *à* = **to**: 'to', **dative**: *il le donne à son frère*, he gives it **to** his brother: 'to', **direction**: *aller à la gare*, to go **to** the station: 'to', **before infinitive**: *il est à craindre*, it is **to** be feared = (it is to fear); *consentir à le faire*, (to) consent **to** do it. See **to**

iii. *à* = **in**: *à Londres*, **in** London; *à l'ombre*, **in** the shade; *à la main*, **in** my/his/their, etc, hand (see ***main***); *réussir à faire qlqch*, to succeed **in** doing sth

iv. *à* = **on**: *à la télé*, **on** TV; *à la Bourse*, **on** the stock exchange

v.   *à* = **by means of**: *à pied*, **by** foot; *à la nage*, (**by**) swimming; *à bicyclette*, **by** bicycle (**but**: *en auto, par le chemin de fer*, etc: see **by**)

vi. *à* = **for**: *une table à thé*, a table **for** tea (a tea table)

vii. *à* = **with** (descriptive): *à la barbe blanche*, **with** the white beard (see **with**); *pêcher à la ligne*, to fish **with** a line, to angle; *un bateau à vapeur*, a steamship (ship **with** steam); *un bateau à voiles*, a sailing ship (ship **with** sails)

viii. *à* = **from**: *emprunter à*, to borrow **from**; *acheter à*, to buy **from** (see ***acheter***)

ix. *à* = **about**: *penser à qlqn*, to think **about** sn (see ***penser***)

x.   *à* = **of**: *demander à qlqn*, to ask **of** sn

xi. *être à* = **to belong to**: *c'est à moi*, it belongs to me; *ce livre est à Jean*, this book belongs to John/is John's. See ADJECTIVES ¶10. See also usage with individual verbs listed throughout, especially: ***aider, acheter, avoir, commencer, demander, dire, inviter, penser, permettre, promettre, se mettre, réussir***

xii. *à* **combines with the definite article thus**: *à + le = au* (*à l'* and *à la* do **not** alter) *à + les = aux*, eg: *au garçon*, to the boy; *à l'homme*, to the man; *à la maison*, to the house/at home; *aux enfants*, to the children

xiii. *à* **as used before countries, towns, etc**: see **Countries**.

abattre, to pull down. Like ***battre***.

able: to be able to: see ***pouvoir, savoir***.

abondant, -e, adjective: *abondant en*, abounding in, rich in. Adverb: ***abondamment***, abundantly, in abundance.

about

i.   **near to**: *auprès de, près de*

ii. **around**: *autour de*

iii. **concerning**: *au sujet de, à propos de:* **about nothing**, *à propos de rien*

iv. **approximately**: about ten men, *environ dix hommes;* about here, *près d'ici;* about two o'clock, *vers les deux heures;* about one o'clock, *vers une heure;* about midday/midnight, *vers midi/minuit* (**but** *vers le/les midi, le/les minuit* are also used)

v. **to roam about the town/the streets**, *errer dans la ville/par les rues*

vi. **to think about** (keep in mind), *penser à:* think about it, *penser-y.* (See *y.*)

vii. **to think about** (consider = weigh merits of, judge), *penser de* (see *penser*)

viii. **to be about to do sth**, *être sur le point de faire qlqch* **or** *être près de faire qlqch.*

above: preposition: *au-dessus de, par-dessus, sur.* **Adverb**: *en haut, là-haut, au-dessus:* above all, *surtout;* above everything, *par-dessus tout;* above all things, *sur toutes choses;* from above, *d'en haut.* See *dessus.*

aboyer, to bark: *y* becomes *i* before *e*-mute, and in the future and conditional stem, like *employer:* bark **at**, *aboyer à, après, contre.*

abréger, to abridge, abbreviate. Like *protéger,* eg: *j'abrège, je abrégerai.* (**Note** accents.)

absent, -e, adjective: *absent de,* absent from. Adverb: *distraitement,* absently, absent-mindedly.

absoudre, to absolve. Pres: *absous, absous, absout, absolvons, absolvez, absolvent.* Imperf: *absolvais, -ais, -ait, -ions, -iez, -aient.* No past historic. Fut: *absoudrai, -as, -a, -ons, -ez, -ont.* Imperat: *absous, absolvons, absolvez.* Pres subj: *absolve, absolves, absolve, absolvions, absolviez, absolvent.* No imperfect subjunctive. Pres part: *absolvant.* Past part: *absous, absoute, absous, absoutes.* Aux: *avoir.*

s'abstenir, to abstain, forbear, refrain (from = *de*). Like *tenir,* but because reflexive, auxiliary = *être.* Past part: *abstenu(e)(s).*

Abstract Nouns: when used in a general sense, are normally preceded by the **definite article**: he loves justice, *il aime la justice;* happiness must be shared, *le bonheur doit être partagé.* **But** where otherwise qualified, or the sense requires it, and in idiomatic phrases, this does not apply, eg: beyond all hope, *au-delà de toute espérance;* full of hope, *plein d'espoir.*

abstraire, to abstract. Like *traire: s'abstraire,* to withdraw into oneself.

abuse

i. **to insult**: *insulter, dire du mal de*

ii. **misuse** sn or sth: *abuser de qlqn* or *qlqch.*

Accents: there are **three** accents: acute ', grave ` and circumflex ^. **Accents can be used on vowels only**: *é* is the only form of accented *e* at the end or beginning of a word with the exceptions of *être, êtes* and *ès* (see separate entry). **Except** for *ès, è* is **always** found inside a word and is usually followed by a single consonant plus mute (unaccented) *e*, *eg: mène, mènent, promèneront*. **The grave accent** appears on other vowels, usually to distinguish two otherwise identically spelt words, eg: *où*, where – *ou*, or; *là*, there – *la*, the: *ê* sometimes replaces *è: il arrête*. Usually this occurs where there was once an *s* (often still present in the English equivalent), eg: *forêt*, forest; *arrêter*, arrest. **Note** the circumflex on the possessive pronouns, *le nôtre, le vôtre* (formerly *le nostre, le vostre*) = our, your (**not** on the adjectives *notre, votre*). The circumflex also distinguishes the masculine **singular** (only) of the past participle of *devoir* – *dû*, from the partitive article *du* = of the, some. See *devoir*. See also **cedilla**.

accepter, to accept, to consent: to consent to do, . . . *accepter de faire* . . .; to accept/agree to have dinner with sn, *accepter à dîner avec qlqn* **or** *chez qlqn*.

accommodate: to put up, to house, *loger*. See next entry.

accommoder, to adapt, to arrange, to put in order: *s'accommoder*, to put up with sth; *s'accommoder de qlqch*, to adapt oneself to; *s'accommoder à*, to 'go along with' (arrange to fit in with), eg: *s'accommoder avec vos plans*, to fit in with your plans.

accourir, to run up, to come running: *accourir faire qlqch*, to run up to do sth. Like *courir*, but auxiliary = *être* when describing the state or condition of having run up: aux = *avoir* when describing the action itself, eg: *il est déjà accouru*, he has already run up; *ils ont accouru le féliciter*, they ran up to congratulate him.

accroître, to accrue, to increase. Like *croître*, but sometimes the circumflex is **only** retained before *-t*, eg: *accroît, accroîtrai, accrûtes*.

acheter, to buy: to buy sth from sn, *acheter qlqch à qlqn*. Conjugated like *mener*, with *-èt-* in stem before endings starting with *e*-mute and in the future stem, eg: *j'achète, j'achèterai*.

achever, to finish: finish doing sth, *achever à faire qlqch*. Conjugated like *mener*, with *-èv-* in stem before *e*-mute endings and in the future stem, eg: *j'achève, j'achèverai*.

acquérir, to acquire. Pres: *acquiers, acquiers, acquiert, acquérons, acquérez, acquièrent*. Imperf: *acquérais, -ais, -ait, -ions, -iez, -aient*. Fut: *acquerrai, -as, -a, -ons, -ez, -ont*. Past hist: *acquis, acquis, acquit, acquîmes, acquîtes, acquirent*. Imperat: *acquiers, acquérons, acquérez*. Pres subj: *acquière, acquières, acquière, acquérions, acquériez, acquièrent*. Imperf subj: *acquisse, acquisses, acquît, acquissions, acquissiez, acquissent*. Pres part: *acquérant*. Past part: *acquis, acquise, acquis, acquises*. Aux: *avoir*.

actif, active, adjective: *actif à*, active at, busy with.

Active Voice: see VERBS ¶8.

acute: see **Accents** above.

ADJECTIVES: see Grammar Section.

admettre, to admit. Like *mettre*.

adresse, noun (fem): address (place of residence, etc), dexterity (**note** spelling: one *d*).

adresser, to address (an envelope), direct: *adresser qlqn*, to speak to sn.

s'adresser

    i. **to be directed**: *c'est à vous que ces mots s'adressent*, it is to you that these words are addressed

    ii. **to apply oneself**: *il s'adresse à la tâche*, he applies himself to the task. (**Note**: only one *d* in French.)

advenir, impersonal verb: to come to pass, to take place, to happen. Conjugated like *venir* **but** in third person singular only, eg: *il advient*, it comes to pass, it happens; *advienne que pourra*, come what may.

ADVERBS: see Grammar Section.

s'affairer à faire qlqch, to busy oneself doing sth.

affamer, to starve: *être affamé de qlqch*, to be starved of sth.

affecter de faire qlqch, to pretend to do sth.

affirmer qlqch à qlqn, to affirm, aver sth to sn: *affirmer avoir fait qlqch*, to affirm having done sth.

after: *après:* **after** a minute/hour, *au bout d'une minute/heure;* to follow after, *venir après, suivre:* **after** (in imitation of/according to), *d'après;* to ask after sn, *demander après qlqn;* after the war, *après la guerre;* after dinner, *après dîner* (also as adjective: after-dinner, *après-dîner*): **after** (at the end of a period): at the end of (the year), *au bout de (l'année);* following after, *à la suite de.*

age: he is twenty (years old), *il a vingt ans**, etc; how old are you? *quel âge avez-vous?* a man of twenty, *un homme de vingt ans*;* aged six, *âgé de six ans** (**ans* must **not** be omitted); a woman of about forty, *une femme d'une quarantaine d'années* (see *an*, *année*).

agir, to act, do, behave: *s'agir*, impersonal: *il s'agit de (faire) qlqch*, it is a question of doing sth; *de quoi s'agit-il?* what is it about?

agree: *s'entendre, être d'accord, consentir à:* agreed! *d'accord!* Do **not** confuse with *agréer* – see below.

AGREEMENT

    i. **of adjectives with nouns**: see ADJECTIVES ¶5

    ii. **of verb with subject**: see VERBS ¶6, ¶9 (end)

    iii. **in relative clauses**: PRONOUNS ¶42, ¶43

    iv. of the **past participle**: see VERBS ¶44 and PRONOUNS ¶6.

agréer, to accept, approve (sth): to suit sn, *agréer à qlqn*. Regular *-er* verb, the stem *agré-* remains unchanged throughout: *j'agrée, j'agréais, j'agréerai, agréant, agréé*, etc. For use in formal endings of letters, see **Correspondence**.

ahead (of): *en avant (de);* straight ahead, *tout droit*.

aide, **masculine** = male assistant: **feminine** = female assistant, assistance.

aider, **to aid, to help**: *aider qlqn à faire qlqch*, to help sn do sth; *il aide son frère à trouver le chien*, he helps his brother find the dog: **contribute to**: *il aide au succès de leurs entreprises*, he contributes to (helps with) the success of their undertakings: *s'aider à*, make use of: *il s'aide d'une loupe*, he makes use of (helps himself with) a magnifying glass.

aïeul, -e, grandfather, grandmother: plur = *aïeul(e)s*. **Note**: *aieux*, masc = ancestors.

ailleurs, adverb: elsewhere: *il se trouvait ailleurs*, it was somewhere else; *il est ailleurs*, he is distrait (absent-minded); *il vient d'ailleurs*, he comes from somewhere else; *partout ailleurs*, everywhere else; *par ailleurs*, besides, moreover, from another viewpoint.

aimable, kind, amiable: *envers, pour, avec qlqn*, towards sn: in letters: *vous êtes bien aimable de m'avoir écrit*, you are very kind to have written to me/it was very kind of you to write to me.

aimer, to love, to like: *aimer bien*, to like; very much; *aimer faire* **or** *aimer à faire qlqch*, to like to do/like doing sth; *il aime que l'on flatte* (with subjunctive), he likes to be flattered.

ainsi, thus: *ainsi que*, as well as, like; *ainsi de suite*, and so on.

aise, **adjective**: pleased, eg: *je suis bien aise de vous voir*, I'm very pleased to see you. Also as **noun** (fem) = comfort.

aisé, aisée, adjective: easy, natural (= unaffected), well-to-do: *peu aisé(e)*, badly off; *plus qu'aisé(e)*, of independent means; *aisé à faire quelque chose*, easy to do sth.

s'alarmer de qlqch, to take alarm at/be alarmed by sth.

alentour, adv: around: *errer alentour*, to roam around; *d'alentour* (**adj** phrase), neighbouring; *les alentours* (**noun**: masc plur) *d'une ville*, the surroundings/ neighbourhood of a town.

all (adjective and pronoun): the whole/every: see *tout*. All = everyone, *tout le monde* (**always** masc sing, so singular verb and masc sing complement/adjectives); everyone is here, *tout le monde est ici;* everyone is pleased, *tout le monde est content.*

aller, to go: one of the two really irregular *-er* verbs (the other is *envoyer*): also used to make immediate future as in English: *nous allons partir*, we are going to leave; *aller faire qlqch*, to go and do/to be going to do sth. Pres: *vais, vas, va, allons, allez, vont*. Imperf: *allais, -ais, -ait, -ions, -iez, -aient*. Fut: *irai, iras,* *ira, irons, irez, iront.* Past hist: *allai, allas, alla, allâmes, allâtes, allèrent.* Imperat: *va* (**but** see VERBS ¶19), *allons, allez.* Pres subj: *aille, ailles, aille, allions, alliez, aillent.* Imperf subj: *allasse, allasses, allât, allassions, allassiez, allassent.* Pres part: *allant.* Past part: *allé, allée, allés, allées.* Aux: *être.*

along: along the street, *le long de la rue;* all along, *tout le long (de);* along (= beside) the river, *le long du fleuve;* you can go along here, *on peut aller par ici;* along this path, *par ce sentier.*

alors que, when, at a time when, whereas, now that: subordinating conjunction, with the following clause in the indicative: *alors qu'il est ici,* now that he is here. (See CONJUNCTIONS ¶4.)

ambitieux, ambitieuse, adjective: ambitious: *de qlqch,* for sth.

amener, to lead, induce: *amener qlqn à faire qlqch,* to induce sn to do sth. Like *mener.*

à mesure que, subordinating conjunction, with following clause in the indicative: as, in proportion as, according as: *à mesure qu'il mange il grandit,* as (according as/to the same extent that) he eats, he grows; *au fur et à mesure,* as fast as, one after the other. See CONJUNCTIONS ¶5.

amuser, to amuse: *s'amuser de qlqch,* to enjoy oneself with/by with sth; *à faire qlqch,* with/by doing sth; *s'amuser aux dépense de qlqn,* to make fun of sn.

an = (masc): *année* = (fem): year: **note:** *an,* is used after a cardinal number, eg: *il a vingt ans,* he is twenty (he has twenty years): *an,* is **also** used in dates: *en l'an 1995,* in the year 1995 (see NUMBERS ¶1 end) **and** *le jour de l'an,* New Year's Day; *le nouvel an,* the New Year. **In all other cases use** *année: cette année,* this year; *quelques années avant,* several years earlier; *une année scolaire,* a school year; *la première année de sa vie,* the first year of his /her life; *la dernière année de la guerre,* the last year of the war; *l'année dernière/prochaine,* last/next year; *pendant toute l'année,* during all/throughout the year.

ancien, ancienne: old, ancient: **before** the noun = former: *un ancien soldat,* an old (former) soldier; *l'ancienne Grèce,* ancient Greece. **After** the noun = ancient, old: *une maison ancienne,* an old house; *les coutumes anciennes,* ancient customs.

août, August (month). Pronounced 'oo': the final *-t* should **not** be sounded: spelt **without** capital. Both these rules are sometimes broken.

apercevoir, to perceive (with the eyes): *qlqn/qlqch faire qlqch,* sn/sth doing sth; *s'apercevoir de qlqch,* to notice sth/remark on sth (mentally). Like *recevoir.*

apparaître, to appear. Like *connaître.* Aux: *être* (state): *avoir* (action). See *disparaître.*

appartenir (à), to belong (to): *il lui appartient de faire qlqch,* it behoves him to do sth. Like *tenir.*

appeler, to call. Regular *-er* verb, **but** the *-l-* is doubled *(-ll-)* before all *e*-mute endings, eg: *j'appelle, ils appellent* and in future stem, *appellerai:* **but** past participle, *appelé: s'appeler*, to be called; *je m'appelle*, I am called/my name is; *comment vous appelez-vous?* what is your name? *appeler qlqn à faire qlqch*, to call, invite, summon sn to do sth; *vous appelez cela vivre?* do you call that living? *en appeler à qlqn/qlqch*, to appeal to sn/sth; *appeler d'un jugement*, to appeal against a judgement.

apport, il apport = it is evident, it follows (**legal term**).

apprendre, to learn, to teach, to inform: *apprendre à faire qlqch*, to learn to do sth; *apprendre qlqch à qlqn*, to teach sn sth; *apprendre à qlqn à faire qlqch*, to teach sn to do sth; *apprendre qlqch à qlqn*, inform sn of sth. Like **prendre**.

approcher, to approach = to bring sth close to, eg: *approcher la chaise de la table*, to bring the chair close to (up to) the table.

s'approcher, to approach = to draw near: *s'approcher de qlqn/qlqch*, to draw near sn/sth.

après, after, later, afterwards, behind: *après dîner*, after dinner (= 'after to dine'); *après avoir fait qlqch*, after having done sth (see PREPOSITIONS ¶6); *après qu'il l'avait fait*, after he had done it; *crier après qlqn*, to be in pursuit of sn; *je le ferai après*, I shall do it afterwards/later; *il est après moi en classe*, he is behind me in class.

après-midi, masc (rarely fem): afternoon. 'Good afternoon!' = *'Bonsoir!'* (one word).

arguer, to accuse, argue, infer. Regular *-er* verb, pronounce the *-u*.

armer qlqn de qlqch, to arm sn with sth: *s'armer de qlqch*, to arm oneself with sth.

arracher qlqch à qlqn, to snatch sth from sn.

arranger, to arrange: *s'arranger avec qlqn*, to come to terms with sn; *cela peut s'arranger*, that can be put right/managed.

arrêter, hinder, prevent, arrest, stop: *arrêter qlqn/qlqch*, to stop, arrest sn/sth; *s'arrêter*, come to a stop, stay, remain; *s'arrêter de faire qlqch*, to stop doing sth; *s'arrêter à faire qlqch*, to stop in order to do sth. Regular *-er* verb: accent and single *t* unchanged throughout: *j'arrête, j'arrêterai, arrêté*.

arrière, **noun** (masc): the rear, back part: **preposition/adverb**: back, behind, aft: *en arrière*, behind, backwards, behindhand, in arrears; *en arrière de qlqch* (**also**: *derrière qlqch*), behind sth.

arriver, to arrive, to happen, to approach: *ils sont arrivés dans la ville*, they have arrived in the town; *qu'est-ce qui est arrivé?* what has happened? *arrive que pourra*, happen what may; *quoi qu'il arrive*, whatever may happen, in any case; *tout arrive comme prédit*, everything is happening as foretold; *nuit arrive*, night approaches. Aux: *être*.

s'arroger, to arrogate to oneself, to assume (take on): **no** agreement of past participle.

ARTICLES: see Grammar Section.

as: as always, *comme toujours:* as I do (= like me), *comme moi:* as = since/because, *puisque/parce que:* as much/many as, . . . *autant que* . . .: in proportion as, *à mesure que:* as = while, eg: as I was talking, *pendant que* (or *tandis que, alors que, comme*) *je parlais:* not so good as, *pas si bon que:* as it were (= 'so to speak'), *pour ainsi dire:* such as/like = *tel/telle/tels/telles que*, eg: a house such as/like mine, *une maison **telle** que la mienne* (note **agreement** of *telle*): as if, *comme si:* as far as (up to), *jusqu'à:* as long as, *tant que:* as soon as, *aussitôt que, dès que:* as well as, *ainsi que:* dressed as (a soldier), *habillé en soldat:* to chose as friend/assistant, *choisir pour ami/aide.* See *comme, dès, tel.*

ask

    i.   **to beg,** *prier:* sn to do sth, *prier qlqn de faire qlqch*
    ii.   **to request,** *demander* (**not** so peremptory as English 'demand': see **demand** and *demander*)
    iii.   **to ask** (sn to dinner, to stay, etc), *inviter (qlqn à dîner, à rester,* etc)
    vi.   **to ask a question** (of sn), *faire/poser une question (à qlqn)*
    v.   **to question sn,** *interroger qlqn*
    vi.   **to ask about,** *s'informer de (qlqn/qlqch).*

assaillir, to assail, to assault, to attack. Pres: *assaille, assailles, assaille, assaillons, assaillez, assaillent.* Imperf: *assaillais, -ais, -ait, -ions, -iez, -aient.* Fut: *assaillirai, -as, -a, -ons, -ez, -ont.* Past hist: *assaillis, assillis, assaillit, assaillîmes, assaillîtes, assaillirent.* Imperat: *assaille, assaillons, assaillez.* Pres subj: *assaille, assailles, assaille, assaillions, assailliez, assaillent.* Imperf subj: *assaillisse, assaillisses, assaillît, assaillissions, assaillissiez, assaillissent.* Pres part: *assaillant.* Past part: *assailli, -e, -s, -es.* Aux: *avoir* .

asseoir, to seat: a very irregular verb: some tenses have two forms (in the future and conditional, three – see end of this entry) of which the first given is the most usual. Pres: *assieds/assois, assieds/assois, assied/assoit, asseyons/assoyons, asseyez/assoyez, asseyent/assoient.* Imperf: *asseyais/assoyais, -ais, -ait, -ions, -iez, -aient.* Fut: *assiérai/assoirai, -as, -a, -ons, -ez, -ont.* Past hist: *assis, assis, assit, assîmes, assîtes, assirent* (one form only). Conditional is formed with both future stems + usual imperfect endings: *assiérais/assoirais,* etc. Imperat: *assieds/assois, asseyons/assoyons, asseyez/assoyez.* Pres subj: *asseye/assoie, -es, -e, -ions, -iez, -ent.* Imperf subj: *assisse, assisses, assît, assissions, assissiez, assissent* (one form only). Pres part: *asseyant/assoyant.* Past part: *assis.* Aux: *avoir,* eg: *j'ai assis,* I have seated. *s'asseoir,* reflexive form = to sit: has the same forms throughout **but** with reflexive pronoun. Past part: *assis, -e, assis, assises.* Aux: *être,* eg: *je me suis assis* (or *assise* if *je* is feminine) = I have sat down; sit down! *asseyez-vous!* In a third form, future and conditional have the stem *asseyer-.*

assidu, assidue, adjective: assiduous, diligent. Adverb: ***assidûment***, assiduously, diligently.

assister, to assist: *qlqn de qlqch*, sn with sth; *assister à qlqch*, to be present at sth.

assurer, to assure, to ensure: *assurer qlqn de qlqch* **or** *assurer qlqch à qlqn*, to assure sn of sth.

attaquer, to attack: *qlqn*, sn; *s'attaquer à qlqn/qlqch*, to make an attack on sn/sth.

atteindre *qlqch*, to reach/affect/hit sth: *atteindre à qlqch*, to attain/accomplish sth. Conjugated like ***craindre***.

attendre, to wait for*, to await (*no preposition in French): *il attend son ami*, he waits for his friend; *nous attendons qu'ils reviennent*, we wait for them to return (= wait that they return – subjunctive); ***s'attendre à***, to expect; *je m'attendais à vous voir*, I expected/hoped to see you/counted on seeing you; *il s'attend à ce qu'il revienne*, he expects he will return (= that he may return – with subjunctive).

attendrir, to soften: *s'attendrir sur qlqn*, to feel compassion for sn, soften towards sn; *s'attendrir sur qlqch*, to relent about sth.

attenter, to make an attempt: *attenter à la vie de qlqn*, to make an attempt on the life of sn.

atterrir
    i.   to land, to alight (= come down or go on to land)
    ii. to make for land, make for port
    iii. to silt up.
Auxiliary ***avoir*** for action, ***être***, for state resulting from action.

attester *avoir fait qlqch*, to testify having done sth.

attraire, to cite (in court of law). Like ***traire***.

aucun, aucune
    i.   **adjective** = any: used with *ne* before the verb: *aucune rose n'est plus belle*, not any (= no) rose is more beautiful; *je n'ai vu aucun de ces livres*, I have not seen any (I have seen none) of these books
    ii. **used without a noun** = indefinite pronoun: *je n'ai vu aucun d'eux*, I have seen none (not any) of them (or *aucune d'elles*, not any of them: (fem). When used without verb *ne* is not used, eg: *–Vous avez visité ces villes? –Aucune!* 'You have visited these towns?' 'Not any of them!' **Used nearly always in the singular.**

au-dehors, outside, out of doors. See ***dehors***.

au-dessous, au-dessus, see ***dessous, dessus***.

augmenter, to augment, increase (sth): auxiliary: ***avoir***. To become greater, auxiliary: ***être***.

aujourd'hui, today, nowadays: *aujourd'hui même*, this very day.

auparavant, adverb: before: *un mois auparavant*, a month before; *vous pourrez y aller, mais, auparavant, il faut faire qlqch*, you will be able to go, but first you must do sth.

auprès, adverb: near, near it: *il faut qu'on soit* (**or** *il faut être*) *auprès pour le voir*, one must be near (it) to see it. See **auprès de**, preposition, below.

auprès de, preposition

    i.   **near**, close to: *il demeure auprès de l'église*, he lives near the church

    ii. **compared with**: *ton malheur n'est rien auprès du mien*, your misfortune is nothing compared with mine

    iii. **in the eyes of, in the opinion of**: *il est fort bien auprès du patron*, he is well thought of by the boss (= 'he is very well in the opinion of the boss').

auquel = *à* + *lequel*, to whom, to which: see PRONOUNS ¶35, ¶40.

aussi

    i.   **adverb = as, to the same extent as, also**: *il est aussi riche que son frère*, he is as rich as his brother; *il court aussi vite que vous*, he runs as quickly as you: = **too, also, as well**: *il sait lire et son frère aussi*, he can read and his brother also/too; *Jean était là, et Jeanne aussi*, John was there, and Joan also/as well/too; *il faut aussi dire que* . . ., it must also be said that . . .; *aussi bien est-il* trop tard*, besides, it's too late (*note the inversion when *aussi bien* means 'besides' = in the sense of 'moreover'): *aussi bien que*, as well as, eg: *les femmes peuvent le faire aussi bien que les hommes*, the women can do it as well as the men.

    ii. **conjunction** = therefore, hence and so, as a consequence: *il travail bien, aussi est-il* très riche*, he works well, therefore (and so) he is very rich (*with *être*, the subject and verb are inverted); *il est cruel, aussi chacun le haït*, he is cruel, so everyone hates him.

autant, as many/much as: *il y avait autant d'hommes que de femmes dans la salle*, there were as many men as women in the room; *il a autant que moi*, he has as much as me (as I have); *ce vase ne vaut pas autant que l'autre*, this vase is not worth as much as the other; *d'autant que*, considering that.

autoriser *qlqn à faire qlqch*, to authorize sn to do sth: *s'autoriser de*, to justify oneself on the authority of.

autre

    i.   **adjective** = other, different: *un autre homme et une autre femme*, another man and another woman: in the plural, *d'autres: j'ai eu d'autres idées*, I have had other ideas; *d'autres livres se trouvent sur la table*, other books are on the table; *ma maison est tout* autre*, my house is quite different (*for agreement of *tout* used before *autre* see **tout** ii); *l'autre jour*, the other day

    ii. **pronoun** (a) **another, others**: *un(e) autre l'a fait*, another (sn else) has done it; *voici un(e) autre*, here is another (agreeing in gender with whatever is referred to); *il faut aider les* autres*, it is necessary to help others (**les* is necessary unless a quantity is referred to: *il a beaucoup d'autres, il a bien d'autres,* he has many others. **Note** that usually after *bien* the partitive article is used, **but** *bien d'autres* is an idiomatic exception): the partitive article is needed if 'of the' is meant, eg: *il a beaucoup **des** autres,* he has many **of the** others; *j'ai vu beaucoup de grandes villes, entre autres Paris et Rome,* I have seen many great cities, among others Paris and Rome (*les* is not needed after *entre* unless meaning 'among **the** others'). When 'another' implies 'another of them' or 'of that sort', *en* must be used: *mon habit est usé, il me faut **en** acheter un autre,* my coat is worn out, I must buy another; *hier j'ai trouvé un des livres perdus et aujourd'hui j'**en** ai trouvé un autre,* yesterday I found one of the lost books and today I found another (b) ***nous autres*** = 'we' when speaking of 'us' as a group, class, nation, etc: similarly, *vous autres Français,* you French people (c) **note:** *d'autre* ***part,*** besides, on the other hand, moreover: *autre part,* elsewhere: *de temps à autre,* from time to time.

autrui, singular indefinite pronoun = others: *il faut chercher le bien d'autrui,* one must seek the good of others; *il ne faut pas faire mal à autrui,* one must not do wrong to others. Only rarely used as subject or direct object: *autrui ne nous rendra pas ce que nous donnons autrui,* others will not give back to us what we give others (**not** '*à l'autri*'). (Sometimes considered as a noun.)

Auxiliary Verbs: are used to form **compound tenses**: see VERBS ¶20ff. In French both ***être*** and ***avoir*** are used: *je suis allé,* I have gone; *j'ai parlé,* I have spoken. **All reflexive verbs** are conjugated with ***être:*** verbs also take ***être*** if the action essentially effects a change of position or condition (*aller,* to go from one place to another: *devenir,* to become sth else: *mourir,* to die, changing one's condition). All other verbs take ***avoir:*** including verbs which may describe an activity which does not necessarily produce a change of position or condition, eg: ***marcher,*** to go (*ma montre a marché bien,* my watch has gone well). If a verb has, or can have, a **direct object**, the auxiliary will be ***avoir.*** See ***avoir*** below. (Non-reflexive verbs conjugated with ***être*** are individually entered: those conjugated with ***avoir*** are not listed unless likely to cause doubt, such as ***courir.***) **A few verbs may use both auxiliaries according to their meaning**: see ***accourir*** for an example. See also VERBS ¶10, ¶20ff.

avancer, to advance. Like ***placer,*** with *ç* before endings starting with *a* or *o,* eg: *nous avançons, j'avançai.*

avant

    i.   **preposition**: before, in front of, usually in time: *avant la guerre,* before the war; *quelques jours avant,* several days before; *avant d'aller,* before going. **Also of position**: *avant la maison,* before the house (but ***devant*** is more usual in this sense): **of degree**: *l'amour avant la richesse,* love before wealth

    ii. **adverb**: *aller avant,* to go ahead, forward; *en avant!* forward march! *plus avant,* farther forward (position)/further forward (state)

    iii. **invariable adjective**: *les roues avant,* the front wheels

    iv. **noun**: *l'avant* (masc) *d'un bateau,* the forepart of a ship; *un avant,* a (football) forward.

avant que, subordinating conjunction: see **before,** and CONJUNCTIONS ¶5.

avenir, the future: *à l'avenir,* in the future, henceforth. **But,** when referring to the future tense, *le futur, au futur,* is used. The old verb *avenir* = to come to pass, to happen, is now replaced by *advenir.*

s'aventurer à faire qlqch, to venture, risk doing sth.

avertir qlqn de qlqch, to warn sn about sth: *avertir qlqn de faire qlqch,* to advise, admonish, warn sn to do sth.

s'aveugler, to blind oneself: *s'aveugler sur qlqch,* to turn a blind eye to/to shut one's eyes to sth.

aveugle, adjective: blind. Adverb: ***aveuglément,*** blindly (**note**: with accent).

aveuglement, noun (masc), (**without accent**): mental blindness, ignorance (**note**: blindness of sight = *la cécité*).

aviser, to perceive, to warn: *aviser qlqn de qlqch,* to warn sn about sth; *aviser à faire qlqch,* to deal with, see about sth; *s'aviser de faire qlqch,* think about doing sth (take it into one's head to do sth).

avoir, auxiliary verb: 'to have'. Used to form compound tenses in all verbs except reflexive verbs and verbs of change of position or condition: for these, see *être,* eg: *j'ai parlé,* I have spoken; *il aura fini,* he will have finished. (See **Auxiliary Verbs** above.) **Very irregular.** Pres: *ai, as, a, avons, avez, ont.* Fut: *aurai, auras, aura, aurons, aurez, auront.* Imperf: *avais, avais, avait, avions, aviez, avaient.* Past hist: *eus, eus, eut, eûmes, eûtes, eurent.* Imperat: *aie, ayons, ayez.* Pres subj: *aie, aies, ait, ayons, ayez, aient.* Imperf subj: *eusse, eusses, eût, eussions, eussiez, eussent.* Pres part: *ayant* (invariable). Past part: *eu, eue, eus, eues.* Compound tenses of *avoir* are formed with itself and its past participle – *eu,* eg: I have had, *j'ai eu;* I had had, *j'avais eu,* etc. Note these idioms: *en avoir à/contre qlqn,* to have a grudge against sn; *avoir à faire qlqch,* to have to do sth; *avoir qlqch à faire,* to have sth to do; *avoir beau faire qlqch,* to do sth in vain, eg: *vous avez beau dire cela,* it's no good/a waste of time your saying that; *avoir l'air de faire qlqch/d'être qlqch,* to seem to do/be sth; *avoir l'air content(e)*,* to seem pleased; *vous avez l'air fatigué(e)*,* you seem/look tired (*usually the adjective agrees with the person or thing, not with *air,* but usage varies). And: *avoir besoin de qlqch/de faire qlqch,* to need sth/to do sth; *avoir faim,* to be hungry; *avoir froid/chaud,* to be cold/hot (**note**: of persons, *froid* and *chaud* are nouns: **no** agreement); *avoir honte,* to be ashamed; *avoir peur,* to be afraid; *avoir sommeil,* to be sleepy; *avoir soif,* to be thirsty; *avoir tort,* to be wrong.

-ayer, **verbs**: verbs with infinitive ending in *-ayer* are regular, conjugated like ***parler,*** retaining *-y-* throughout: **but** the '*y*' at the end of the stem may be changed to

'*i*' before *e*-mute endings and in the future stem (as in -*oyer* verbs). Both forms are correct. See *payer*.

B

balayer, to clean with a broom *(un balai)*, to sweep. Regular -*er* verb but can (optionally) change the -*y*- to -*i*- before *e*-mute endings, and in the future stem: see *payer*.

bas

    i. **noun** (masc): bottom, stocking
    ii. **adjective**: *bas, basse* = low, shallow, vile, base: *mer basse*, low tide
    iii. **adverb**: *bas* = low, low down, down: *en bas*, below, downstairs; *à bas* . . .! down with . . .!

battre, to beat. Like *vendre*, **except** only one -*t*- in the singular of present and imperative. Pres: *bats, bats, bat, battons, battez, battent.* Imperf: *battais*, etc. Fut: *battrai*, etc. Past hist: *battis*, etc. Imperat: *bats, battons, battez.* Pres subj: *batte*, etc. Imperf subj: *battisse, battisses, battît, battissions, batissiez, battissent.* Pres part: *battant.* Past part: *battu, battue, battus, battues.* Aux: *avoir.* (**Example verb** for other verbs in -*attre*.)

se battre, to fight: *contre* **or** *avec qlqn*, with sn; *ils se battent*, they are fighting (together). Reflexive – auxiliary: *être*.

be: see *être*.

beau, **adjective (comes before the noun)**: beautiful, handsome, fine, etc. **Note**: before vowel and *h*-mute, masc sing = *bel:* fem sing = *belle:* masc plur = *beaux:* fem plur = *belles: un beau jour*, a fine day; *un bel ouvrage*, a fine work; *un bel habit*, a nice coat; *une belle fleur*, a beautiful flower; *de beaux ouvrages*, fine works; *les belles fleurs*, the beautiful flowers. **Note also**: *beau*- and *belle*- before a relative = -in-law, eg: *beau-frère*, brother-in-law; *belle-mère*, mother-in-law. **Adverbial phrases**: *tout beau*, gently; *avoir beau*, in vain; *avoir beau faire*, to do sth in vain; *j'ai beau parler*, I speak in vain, it's useless my speaking; *de plus belle*, more and more; *l'échapper belle*, to have a narrow escape. As **noun** (masc): *le beau*, beauty, excellence: *faire le beau*, parade oneself (masc).

beaucoup, a lot, many, much: *beaucoup de livres* (note the *de*), a lot of books/many books; *il y a beaucoup d'eau ici*, there is a lot of water here; *après beaucoup d'années*, after many years (compare use of *bien*, below); *nous en avons beaucoup*, we have a lot of it (*de* is included in the *en*). The partitive article, *du, de la, de l'* or *des*, must be used instead of *de* if the idea 'of the' has to be expressed, eg: *j'ai bu beaucoup de l'eau*, I have drunk a lot **of the** water. When the **subject of a verb**, *beaucoup* requires the verb in the **plural** and adjectives **agreeing in number and gender**, eg: *beaucoup des femmes étaient contentes de travailler dans les champs*, a lot of the women were content to work in the fields: **but**, if the adjective refers to *beaucoup*, that is, to 'a lot' or 'many', rather than to what makes up 'many', the adjective remains masculine singular, eg: *beaucoup de fleurs sera plus décoratif*, a lot of flowers will be more decorative. **Note**: *beaucoup* cannot be qualified by another adverb (eg: by *très*) **except** *pas*: *pas beaucoup*, not many. In cases like: *il y en a encore beaucoup*, there are still many/many more of them: *encore* qualifies *il y a*. See **many, much**.

beautiful: see *beau*. Adverb: *admirablement*, beautifully.

because: *parce que*: because he is rich, *parce qu'il est riche*; because of, *à cause de*; because of his riches, *à cause de ses richesses*.

before (place or position – before/in front of): *devant*: there is a tree before/in front of the house, *il y a un arbre devant la maison*: **before**, in the presence of, *devant, par devant*: they pass before the king, *ils passent devant le roi*: **before** going out, *avant de sortir*; before you go upstairs, *avant que vous montiez* (with subjunctive): **before**/earlier than, *avant*: before tomorrow, *avant demain*; several days before (earlier), *quelques jours avant*; an hour/before (that), *une heure auparavant*: **before**/already, *déjà*: he had done it before/he had already done it, *il l'avait fait déjà*. The two words, *avant* and *devant* are to some extent interchangeable: the distinction between time and place is **not** absolute. See also *avant, devant*.

Belge, **noun**: Belgian of either sex: **adjective**: *belge* (masc or fem).

below, beneath: **preposition**: *sous, au-dessous de*: to crush sth beneath one's feet, *écraser qlqch sous ses pieds*. **Adverb**: *dessous, au-dessous*: the bird is in the tree, the cat is waiting below, *l'oiseau est dans l'arbre, le chat attend au-dessous*. See *dessous*.

bénir, to bless: like *finir* – except **two** past participles – *béni, bénit*. The second form used for things blessed or consecrated in religious rites, eg: *l'eau bénite*, holy water ('blessed water').

beside: besides, at the side of, *à côté de, auprès de*: beside, other than, *en dehors de*: besides, I don't want to, *d'ailleurs/de plus/en outre, je ne veux pas* (see also *aussi* i.): **beside** = along the side of, *le long de*: to be beside oneself with fear, *être hors de soi de peur, être fou de*: **besides** = moreover: besides it must be said that, *d'ailleurs/en outre/de plus, il faut dire que*.

besoin, masc: need: *avoir besoin de qlqch*, to have need of sth; *avoir besoin de faire qlqch*, to need to do sth; *au besoin*, in case of necessity. See also **want**.

better

   i. **adjective**: *meilleur, meilleure, meilleurs, meilleures*: he has written a better book, *il a écrit un meilleur livre*; my health is better, *ma santé est meilleure*. **Note**: **earlier**: *de meilleure heure*: **best**: *le meilleur, la meilleure*: these houses are the best, *ces maisons sont les meilleures*; the best of it is that, *le meilleur est que*; the next best is, *le meillleur après est* (agrees in gender if speaking of a noun: remains masc if speaking of some circumstance, event, or state of affairs, etc)

   ii. **adverb**: *mieux*: he is better (in health), *il va mieux*; it is better to do sth, *il vaut mieux faire qlqch*. See *valoir*.

bien

    i.   **adverb**: well, very, a lot, much: *il l'a bien fait*, he has done it well; *merci bien*, thanks a lot, thanks very much; *très bien*, very well (often used where we would say 'Very good'); *c'est bien*, that's all right; good! *eh bien!* well! well now/then! *il est bien gentil*, he is very kind: **bien de** *(du, de la, des):* a lot of/much (alternative to *beaucoup* in this sense, **but** notice use of partitive article), eg: *après bien des années*, after many years; *il y avait bien du monde dans la salle*, there were a lot of people ('much of the world') in the room: **but** (exceptionally) *bien d'autres*, many others; *il faut bien*, it is necessary (or I/you/we, etc, must – impersonal phrase); *vouloir bien*, to be willing, eg: *je veux bien*, I'd like to, gladly; *aussi bien que*, as well as. In **compound tenses** *bien* is normally placed between the auxiliary and the past participle: *il avait bien pu le faire*, he was well able to do it: when an **infinitive** follows the verb *bien* precedes it: *je voudrais bien apprendre*, I should much like to learn. **Comparative** of *bien*, well = *mieux*, better. **Superlative**: *le mieux*, best (adverb, invariable). See also **many, much, better**

    ii. **noun**: *(un) bien*, an advantage, welfare, well-being: when in plural: goods, etc: *tous ses biens*, all his goods/possessions; *faire du bien*, to do good; *dire du bien de*, to speak well of; *vouloir du bien à qlqn*, to wish sn well, to take an interest in sn's (welfare)

    iii. **conjunction**: *bien que* = although: followed by clause in the subjunctive: *il ne le fait pas, bien qu'il puisse le faire*, he does not do it, although he can do it; *il ne paye pas, bien qu'il soit riche*, he does not pay, although he is rich (**or** *bien que riche*, although rich). See CONJUNCTIONS ¶5.

better = someone who wagers = *parieur, -euse*.

bienséant, -e, adjective: seemly: *à faire qlqch*, to do sth.

bienveillant, -e, adjective: friendly, benevolent: *à l'égard de, envers, pour, qlqn*, towards sn.

big: **larger than normal** = *gros, grosse:* the cat catches a big mouse, *le chat attrape une grosse souris:* **big as compared with other things** = *grand, grande:* the elephant is a big animal, *l'éléphant est un grand animal:* **big** = **tall**: a tall man, *un homme grand* (with *grand* following noun). **Note**: *grand* before a noun may mean 'great, renowned': *un grand général*, a great general. See *grand*.

blâmable, adjective: blameable: *de qlqch*, for sth.

blâmer, to blame: *qlqn de qlqch*, sn for sth.

blesser, to wound: *être blessé de qlqch*, to be wounded by (offended at) sth; *se blesser avec qlqch*, to wound oneself with sth; *se blesser de qlqch*, to take offence at sth. (**Note**: to bless = *bénir*.)

boire, to drink. Pres: *bois, bois, boit, buvons, buvez, boivent*. Imperf: *buvais, -ais, -ait, -ions, -iez, -aient*. Fut: *boirai, -as, -a, -ons, -ez, -ont*. Past hist: *bus, bus, but*, *bûmes, bûtes, burent.* Imperat: *bois, buvons, buvez.* Pres subj: *boive, boives, boive, buvions, buviez, boivent.* Imperf subj: *busse, busses, bût, bussions, bussiez, bussent.* Pres part: *buvant.* Past part: *bu, bue, bus, bues.* Aux: ***avoir***.

bon

    i. **adjective**: good: fem = ***bonne*. Comparison**: *meilleur(e)(s)*, better. **Superlative**: *le/la/les meilleur(e)(s)*, best. Normally precedes the noun it qualifies: *une bonne idée*, a good idea; *une meilleure idée*, a better idea; *la meilleure idée*, the best idea; *être bon à qlqch*, to be good for/fit for sth; *vous êtes bon de faire qlqch*, you are good to do sth (eg: *de nous inviter*, to invite us); *trouver bon de faire qlqch*, to find it good to do sth; *il est bon pour 1.000 francs*, he is good for 1,000 francs

    ii. **noun**: *un bon* = a good, a benefit, an advantage, a good man, etc: to do good, *faire du bon*. **Note**: *bonne*, noun (fem) = a maid-servant, nursery-maid, servant, good woman.

both: **adjective**: *tous/toutes (les) deux:* he has bought both books, *il a acheté tous les deux livres*. **Pronoun**: he has bought both, *il a acheté les deux* (**without** *tous*) or *il a acheté l'un(e) et l'autre*: **both . . . and . . .**: *et . . . et . . .*, eg: both the boy and the girl, *et le garçon et la fille* (**but** the first *et* is usually omitted except mainly in literary French).

bouder, to sulk: *bouder contre qlqn*, to be sulky with sn; *bouder à qlqch*, to be afraid of sth/shirk from sth.

bourrer, to stuff, to pad, to cram: *bourrer qlqn/qlqch de*, to cram sn/sth with.

bouillir, to boil. Pres: *bous, bous, bout, bouillons, bouillez, bouillent.* Imperf: *bouillais, -ais, -ait, -ions, -iez, -aient.* Fut: *bouillirai, -as, -a, -ons, -ez, -ont.* Past hist: *bouillis, bouillis, bouillit, bouillîmes, bouillîtes, bouillirent.* Imperat: *bous, bouillons, bouillez.* Pres subj: *bouille, bouilles, bouille, bouillions, bouilliez, bouillent.* Imperf subj: *bouillisse, bouillisses, bouillît, bouillissions, bouillissiez, bouillissent.* Pres part: *bouillant.* Past part: *bouilli, -e, -s, -es.* Aux: ***avoir***.

braire, to bray. **Only** found in the following persons and tenses. Pres: *il brait, ils braient.* Fut: *il braira, ils brairont.*

brave, courageous = *courageux, -se*. See below, ***brave*** ii.

brave, **adjective**

    i. **before noun = worthy**: *un brave homme*, a worthy man, a 'good chap'; *mon brave*, 'old chap', 'my good fellow', etc

    ii. **after noun = brave, courageous**: *un homme brave*, a brave man: **but** *courageux* is more usual. Adverb: ***bravement***, bravely, stoutly, well.

brillant, -e, shining, bright: *de qlqch*, with sth.

brouir, to blight, blast, dry up. **Only** found in third persons singular and plural. Pres: *il brouit, ils brouissent.* Imperf: *il brouissait, ils brouissaient.* Other tenses like ***finir***.

bruire, to rustle, to rattle. **Only** found in the following persons and tenses. Pres: *il bruit, ils bruissent.* Imperf: *il bruissait, ils bruissaient.* Pres part: *bruissant.* Pres subj: *qu'il bruisse.*

brûler, to burn: *brûler du bois*, to burn wood; *brûler de faire qlqch*, to burn to do sth (want very much to do sth); *être brûlé*, to be ruined ('undone'), found out.

but: conjunction: *mais:* but for you = except for you, *sans vous;* he is but a child, *il n'est qu'un enfant* **or** *il est seulement un enfant.*

by

    i. **by** = *de:* near by, *près de, à côté de;* near (me), *auprès de (moi);* see **auprès de**: longer by two metres, *plus long de deux mètres;* a book by Dumas, *un livre de Dumas;* by day/night, *de jour/nuit;* this watch is fast by five minutes, *cette montre avance de cinq minutes*

    ii. **by** = *à:* he recognised me by my voice, *il m'a reconnu à ma voix;* by the dozen, *à la douzaine;* by weight, *au poids;* by foot, *à pied;* by bicycle, *à bicyclette* (popular: by bike, *à vélo*)

    iii. **by** = *en:* by doing sth, *en faisant qlqch;* by car, *en voiture;* by rail, *par* (or *en) (le) chemin de fer*

    iv. **by** = *par:* by air, *par avion;* by way of (= via) Lyons, *par Lyon*

    v. **by** = *sur:* a room ten metres by five, *une chambre dix mètres sur cinq* (see **Dimensions**)

    vi. **by** = *près:* close by the station, *près de la gare*

    vii. **by oneself** = alone, *seul; tout seul* (see **seul** and **tout**).

C

ça, an abbreviation of *cela*: see PRONOUNS ¶21, ¶22.

çà, with accent: adverb: used **only** in *çà et là*, here and there **or** as an interjection = Ah!

cacher, to hide: *qlqch à qlqn*, sth from sn; *se cacher de qlqn/qlqch*, to hide (oneself) from sn/sth.

calé en français, well up in French.

camarade, un **or** *une*: male or female pal, chum, comrade.

can (verb = to be able to): see *pouvoir*.

Capital Letters: used less than in English, but there is a tendency to use them more often; should not be used for adjectives of nationality, **but** are used for national nouns: *un homme anglais*, an English man; *un Anglais*, an Englishman: should not be used for the names of months or days of week (though they often are): as in English, capitals are used with proper nouns, names of persons and places, **but** not used with titles used before names: *le docteur Brun, la mer Rouge:* nor used with such words as 'street', 'boulevard', etc, **but** are used with a name: *la rue de Rivoli*. Otherwise used as in English. See *Monsieur*.

Cars: when called by their make, are feminine, eg: *une Renault*.

causer, to chat, speak, talk: *causer avec qlqn de qlqch*, to talk (chat) with sn about sth. **Note**: *causer* also means **to cause**.

ce

    i. **demonstrative pronoun**: see PRONOUNS ¶23 – 36. For *ce* = it before *être:* see also **it**

    ii. **adjective** (used with a noun) = this, that, these, those: changing in form to agree with the following noun it qualifies: masc sing = *ce* **or** *cet* before a vowel or *h*-mute (*ce* adjective is **never** elided to *c'*): fem sing = *cette:* masc and fem plur = *ces* (**no** special fem plural form): *ce garçon: cet homme: cet arbre: cette femme: cette eau: ces garçons/hommes/ arbres/femmes/eaux.* There is no difference between 'this' and 'that' in the singular, or between 'these' and 'those' in the plural. Where it is necessary to indicate which is intended: *-ci* (= here) and *-là* (= there) can be added, eg: *ce livre-ci et ces crayons-là,* this (here) book and those (there) pencils. Both these suffixes are invariable. (Compare *celui, celle,* PRONOUNS ¶20.) For *ce que,* that which: see PRONOUNS ¶35.

ceci, invariable demonstrative pronoun = this: see PRONOUNS ¶21.

céder, to cede, concede, abandon, yield: *céder à,* give way to. The *é* becomes *è* before *e*-mute endings, eg: *cède, cèdes, cèdent:* **but** *é* is retained elsewhere, including in the future stem: *je céderai, je céderais*.

cedilla: the sign (ç) put under '*c*' before '*a*', '*o*' or '*u*' when it sounds like '*s*', and thus used in verbs like *placer* before endings starting with '*a*' or '*o*', eg: *plaçant, plaçons*.

ceindre, to gird, to encompass, surround: sn/sth with sth, *de qlqch*. Like **craindre**.

cela, demonstrative invariable pronoun = that: often abbreviated to *ça:* see PRONOUNS ¶21iii and iv and see *ça* above.

célébrer, to celebrate. Like *céder*, with *-èbr-* before *e*-mute endings, **but** keeping *célébr-* in future stem, eg: *je célèbre, ils célèbrent, je célébrerai: être célébré par qlqch,* famous for sth; *célébré pour avoir fait qlqch,* famous for having done sth.

celer, hide, conceal: sth from sn, *qlqch à qlqn*. Like **mener** with *è* before endings in *e*-mute and in the future stem, eg: *cèle, cèlent, cèleront*.

celui, demonstrative pronoun: see PRONOUNS ¶20.

cent, hundred: use when multiplied: see NUMBERS ¶1.

-cer, **verbs**: see *placer*.

certain, -e, adjective: certain, sure. Adverb: *certainement*, certainly.

certains, -es, plural indefinite pronoun (usually masc) = certain people: used

> i.   **as subject**, eg: *certain(e)s disent que c'est vrai,* some (people) say it is true
> ii. **after a preposition** following the subject: *elle, avec certain(e)s, le fait souvent,* she, with certain others, often does it.

cesser, to cease: *de faire qlqch,* from doing sth. In the negative, when followed by an infinitive, *pas* is dropped, eg: *elle ne cesse de parler,* she never stops talking.

chacun, chacune, indefinite pronoun: has **no** plural = each one, everyone: *chacun pense uniquement à soi,* everyone thinks uniquely of himself; *chacune de ces femmes a dit oui,* each one of these women said yes; *après chacun des films,* after each one of the films.

changer, to change. Like *manger.* Aux: *avoir* when meaning 'to change' sth: *être* if meaning 'to become different'.

charger
> i.   to load, put upon, commission: *qlqn de faire qlqch,* sn to do sth; *se charger de faire qlqch,* to take upon oneself (to do sth).
> ii. **to charge** (the enemy), *charger (l'ennemi).* Like *manger.*

charitable envers qlqn, benevolent towards sn.

chaud, **noun** (masc): heat: see *avoir* and **Weather. Adj:** *chaud, -e,* hot.

chaussée, fem: the roadway (as used for vehicles). See **Road.**

chemin, masc: the way, the route, path, eg: *le chemin le plus court pour aller à la gare,* the shortest way to go to the station. See **Road.**

cher, chère, adjective: dear, beloved, expensive: *mon cher,* 'old chap'. Used as invariable adverb in such phrases as: *ça coûte cher,* that's expensive.

chercher, to seek, to look for: *chercher le livre,* to look for the book (**no** preposition); *chercher à faire qlqch,* endeavour to do sth.

chez, preposition: at the house/home/workplace, etc, of: according to the customs/opinions of: *chez Jean et chez moi,* at John's house and mine; *chez les Français,* according to the customs of the French, among the French, with the French; *chez Pascal,* in the writings of Pascal; *chez Saint Paul,* according to St Paul.

Christmas: *(la) Noël:* **but** Happy Christmas, *joyeux Noël.* See **Feasts and Festivals.**

-ci and *là:* see ADJECTIVES ¶11 and PRONOUNS ¶20.

circumflex: see **Accents.**

clock times: see **Time.**

clore, to close, to shut, enclose, shut off. Used **only** in the following persons and tenses. Pres: *je clos, tu clos, il clôt (ils clorent* (rare)). Fut (rare): *cloirai,* etc. Condit (rare): *cloirais,* etc. Imperat: *clos.* Pres subj (rare) *close,* etc. Pres part:

(rare) *closant.* Past part: *clos, close.* Aux: **avoir**: *clore une séance,* to close a meeting/sitting; *clore un marché,* to close a deal.

Collective Nouns: a collective noun for agreement purposes is **singular**: the government is new, *le gouvernement est nouveau;* a crowd of people is in the street, *une foule de gens est dans la rue;* a great many of the apples are bad, *une grande quantité des pommes est mauvaise.* This rule is **not** always adhered to when the collective is followed by a plural noun, eg: a great number of the soldiers have fallen on the battlefield, *un grand nombre des soldats sont tombés sur le champ de bataille* (see NOUNS ¶6).

Colour: adjectives of colour (with those of shape and taste) **follow** the noun: a blue dress, *une robe bleue.* Normally the adjective agrees with its noun in gender and number, but if one colour qualifies another the combination is invariable: her light blue eyes, *ses yeux bleu clair;* an apple-green dress, *une robe vert pomme.* Colours of some named noun, eg: *argent, cerise, marron, or, orange, poivre* (silver, cherry, chestnut, gold, orange, pepper) **remain invariable**, eg: orange ribbons, *des rubans orange* (= *rubans de la couleur d'orange,* ribbons of the colour of orange). Colour adjectives (agreeing) and colour nouns used as adjectives (invariable) may occur together, eg: white and chestnut (coloured) cloths, *des étoffes blanches et marron.*

combattre, to fight, to give battle: *combattre l'ennemi,* to fight the enemy; *combattre un incendie,* to fight a fire. Like **battre**.

combien, how much? how many? *combien de pommes* avez-vous mangées*?* how many apples have you eaten? (*Combien is always followed by **de** before a noun unless 'of the' is meant, in which case the partitive article, *du, de la, des,* is used: agreement is with the noun which follows *de.*) *Voilà combien des lettres qui sont arrivées,* here is how many **of the** letters which have arrived; *combien sont les pommes?* how much are the apples? *je ne sais combien,* I don't know how much/how many; *combien je souffre!* how much I suffer!

commander, to order, command: *le général commande l'armée,* the general commands the army; *commander à qlqn de faire qlqch,* to command sn to do sth; *je lui commande de partir,* I order him to leave; *commander (le dîner),* to order (dinner).

comme, like, as, in the same way as, how: *faites le comme lui,* do it like him (as he does); *elle est comme sa mère,* she is like her mother; *tu sais comme je t'aime,* you know how (much) I love you.

commencer, to begin: *commencer à faire qlqch,* to begin to do sth (or, rarely: *de faire qlqch*). Like **placer**.

comment, how? in what way? *comment a-t-il fait cela?* how did he do that? *comment est son père?* what is his father like? *comment allez-vous?* how are you? Frequently used to express surprise: *Comment! c'est vous?* What! is it you?

commode, convenient: *commode à faire,* easy, convenient to do; *commode pour faire qlqch,* convenient, suitable for doing sth. Adverb: **commodément**, conveniently.

commun, -e, adjective: common. Adverb: *communément*, commonly.

Comparatives: see ADJECTIVES ¶7 and ADVERBS ¶4.

Compound Nouns and Adjectives: see NOUNS ¶11iii and ADJECTIVES ¶5iii.

comprendre, to understand: *je n'y comprends rien*, I don't understand any of it; *se comprendre*, to understand oneself, to understand each other. Like *prendre*.

conclure, to conclude. Pres: *conclue, -es, -e, concluons, -ez, concluent.* Imperf: *concluais*, etc. Fut: *conclurai*, etc. Past hist: *conclus.* Pres subj: *conclue.* Imperf subj: *conclusse, conclût.* Pres part: *concluant.* Past part: *conclu, -e, -s, -es.* Aux: *avoir.*

concourir, to contribute: *à qlqch*, to sth; *concourir à faire qlqch*, to compete for sth. Like *courir*.

Conditional: the conditional tense is **always** formed from the stem of the future of the verb, with the imperfect endings. There being **no** exceptions, conditional tenses are not shown in the irregular verbs: see VERBS ¶18, ¶27. The conditional is used to translate English 'should' and 'would': *je parlerais*, I should speak; *ils viendraient*, they would come, when the suggested action depends on some condition such as 'they would come if they had a car'. (For further examples see *si* i.) The conditional is often used as a **polite form**: *je voudrais*, I should like, instead of *je veux*, I want; *pourriez-vous?* could you? instead of *pouvez*-vous? can you? The conditional does **not** translate 'would' meaning 'was determined to' (use *vouloir*, to wish): nor 'would' when it means 'was accustomed to' or 'used to' (use the imperfect): nor does it translate 'should' meaning 'ought to' (use *devoir*, must). Clauses introduced by *si* (if) coming either before or after a main clause in the conditional are normally in the imperfect: he **would** do it **if** you wished/**if** you wished he **would** do it, *il le **ferait si** vous vouliez/si vous vouliez il le ferait.* The conditional can express an element of uncertainty: I wouldn't have thought it, *je ne le **croirais** pas;* he told me to write when I arrived (= when I should have arrived), *il m'a dit d' écrire quand je serais arrivé.* The **conditional perfect** is formed from the conditional of the auxiliary followed by the past participle of the verb, eg: I should have spoken, *j'aurais parlé;* I should have departed, *je serais parti:* and is used mainly in a main clause following or preceding a supposition or condition expressed in a clause with its verb in the pluperfect or past anterior, eg: if you had asked (= supposition) you should have been able to buy the book, *si vous aviez demandé vous auriez pu acheter le livre;* he would have written the letter as soon as he had received the news (condition on which writing would have depended), *il aurait écrit la lettre dès qu'il eusse reçut les nouvelles.* See also VERBS ¶18, ¶24, ¶25, ¶27.

conduire, to conduct, to lead, to drive (a car, etc): *un permis de conduire*, a driving licence. Pres: *conduis, conduis, conduit, conduisons, conduisez, conduisent.* Imperf: *conduisais, -ais, -ait, -ions, -iez, -aient.* Fut: *conduirai, -as, -a, -ons, -ez, -ont.* Past hist: *conduisis, conduisis, conduisit, conduisîmes, conduisîtes,* conduisirent. Imperat: *conduis, conduisons, conduisez*. Pres subj: *conduise, conduises, conduise, conduisions, conduisiez, conduisent*. Imperf subj: *conduisisse, conduisisses, conduisît, conduisissions, conduisissiez, conduisissent*. Pres part: *conduisant*. Past part: *conduit, conduite, conduits, conduites*. Aux: **avoir**. See also **rouler**

confiance, fem: confidence: *avoir confiance en lui/dans l'avenir*, to have confidence in him/in the future.

confiant, -e, adjective: confident: *en qlqn*, in sn; *dans qlqch*, in sth; *en l'avenir*, in the future.

confire, to pickle, preserve. Like **suffire**.

confit, -e, *en qlqch*, impregnated with, pickled in, steeped in sth.

confondre, to confound: *confondre en*, to blend into; *être confondu de qlqch*, to be dumbfounded/overwhelmed by sth; *être confondu(e) avec*, to be mixed (up) with, mistaken for; *se confondre*, to be confounded, to blend, to mingle.

confus, -e, adjective: *confus de qlqch*, confused by sth. Adverb: **confusément**, confusedly.

congeler, to congeal, solidify. Conjugated like **mener**, with *è* in stem before *e*-mute endings and in future stem, eg: *congèle, congèlerai*. Does **not** double the *-l-*.

congru, -e, adjective: congruous, fitting, proper. Adverb: **congrûment**, fittingly.

conjoindre, to join, unite. Like **joindre**.

Conjugations: see VERBS ¶1, ¶2.

CONJUNCTIONS: see Grammar Section.

Conjunctive Pronouns: see PRONOUNS ¶8 – 14.

conjurer, to entreat: *qlqn de faire qlqch*, sn to do sth.

connaissance, fem: knowledge, consciousness, acquaintance, sn known: **always** feminine whether man or woman.

connaître, to know (a person or a place), to be acquainted/familiar with. (To know a fact: see **savoir**.) Pres: *connais, connais, connaît, connaissons, connaissez, connaissent*. Imperf: *connaissais, -ais, -ait, -ions, -iez, -aient*. Fut: *connaîtrai, -as, -a, -ons, -ez, -ont*. Past hist: *connus, connus, connut* (**no** accent), *connûmes, connûtes, connurent*. Imperat: *connais, connaissons, connaissez*. Pres subj: *connaisse, -es, -e, -ions, -iez, -ent*. Imperf subj: *connusse, connusses, connût, connussions, connussiez, connussent*. Pres part: *connaissant*. Past part: *connu, connue, connus, connues*. Aux: **avoir**.

se connaître, to know oneself: *se connaître à* **or** *en qlqch*, to be a good judge of, to be knowledgeable about, to have an understanding of, sth.

conquérir, to conquer. Like **acquérir**.

consentir, to consent, to agree: to (do) sth, *à (faire) qlqch.* Conjugated like *sentir.*

considérer, to consider, respect, study. Like *céder.*

consister, to consist of/be made of: *consister en qlqch, consister dans*, to consist essentially of/to be essentially; *consister à faire qlqch*, to consist in doing sth.

construire, to construct. Like *conduire.*

se consumer, to be consumed, to wear oneself out: *de qlqch*, with sth; *se consumer à faire qlqch*, to exhaust oneself doing sth.

continuer, to continue: *à(or de) faire qlqch*, to do sth.

contraindre, to constrain (**no** -s- in French). Like *craindre: contraindre qlqn à faire qlqch*, to constrain sn to do sth; *être contraint(e) de faire qlqch*, to be constrained to do sth.

contredire, to contradict. Like *dire:* **except** 2nd plur of present and imperative: *contredisez.*

convaincre, to convince. Like *vaincre.* **Note**: *convainc-t-il?* **Note also**: the *-t-.*

convenable, opportune, suitable, right and proper: for = *à* or *pour: juger convenable de faire qlqch*, to judge it seemly to do sth.

convenir, to suit, to be proper, to be expedient, to agree. Like *venir.* Aux: *avoir*, but *être* sometimes in some senses*: *convenir à qlqn*, to suit sn; *il convient à qlqn de faire qlqch*, it is proper for sn to do sth; *convenir de faire qlqch*, to agree to do sth. *With *être: ils sont convenus de faire qlqch*, they have agreed (= are agreed) to do sth.

convertible en qlqch, convertible into sth.

convertir, convert: *convertir qlqn à*, to convert sn to; *convertir qlqch en qlqch*, to convert sth into sth.

coopérer, to co-operate. Like *céder: coopérer avec qlqn à faire qlqch*, to co-operate with sn to do sth. **No** hyphen: **no** diæresis.

Correspondence: French correspondence uses rather more flamboyant forms than those used in English for beginning and ending formal letters, and to acknowledge their receipt; to **begin** a letter, *'cher'* is **not** always used: start with *Monsieur, Madame, Messieurs, Mesdames, Mademoiselle*, etc. There are many ways to **end** a formal letter: the following is suitable for most occasions: *Veuillez agréer, Messieurs* (use same title as at the beginning) *nos (or mes) salutations distinguées*, please accept, gentlemen, our (or my) respectful greetings. Another useful ending = *Dans l'attente de vous lire, veuillez agréer, Monsieur, nos salutations empressées*, hoping to hear from you soon, please accept our best greetings: slightly less formal, where the relationship is well established = *Veuillez agréer, Monsieur, mes sincères salutations.* Also: *Dans l'attente de vous lire, nous vous prions d'agréer*, etc, hoping to hear from you, please accept, etc. In **personal letters** to sn not actually a close friend or relation the start can be: *Cher Monsieur* (name can be added): and the end can be: *Très cordialement à vous.* For friends and relations the form used doesn't matter. A simple form to say 'Thank you for the . . ./your . . .', is *Merci pour le . . ./votre . . .* To acknowledge receipt of a letter the formal form is *Nous vous accusons réception de votre éstimée* (**or** *honorée*) *du 3 crt* (**or** *courant* – **or** *du 3 écoulé/dernier*) *et nous vous remercions de . . .*= we acknowledge receipt of your esteemed letter of the 3rd inst (**or** 3rd ult) and thank you for . . . **or** *j'ai bien reçu votre lettre du . . .* 'I have well received your letter of the . . .' = thank you for your letter of the . . .: the 3rd of next month = *le trois prochain.* See also **aimable**.

Countries, Towns, etc: prepositions with

i. **to** = *en* before a feminine country, province or continent, **or** one starting with a vowel: he goes to Belgium, *il va en Belgique;* to Israel, *en Israël* (masc, starts with vowel)

ii. **to** = *à* **with the definite article**, before masculine countries, etc, starting with a consonant and all plurals: to Brazil, *au Brésil;* to Canada, *au Canada;* to the United States, *aux États-Unis*

iii. **to** = *à* before towns, cities: to Mexico City, *à Mexico;* to London, *à Londres;* to Dover, *à Douvres*

iv. **from** (or **of**) = *de* before feminine singular countries with **no** article: from/of Ireland, *d'Irlande;* from Cuba, *de Cuba*

v. **from** (or **of**) = *de* + **article** before masculine countries, continents, etc, and all in the plural, and those which have an article as part of the name (masc or fem): from/of Japan, *du Japon;* from the Indies, *des Indes;* from Le Havre, *du Havre;* from the Hague, *de la Haye*

vi. **in** = *en* before feminine (singular) countries, continents, etc, and masculine ones starting with a vowel: in France, *en France;* in England, *en Angleterre;* in Iran, *en Iran* (masc); in Europe, *en Europe* (fem)

vii. **in** = *en* (or *dans*) before a large town or city when considered as an area, not as a single location, or other geographical areas: in Provence, *en Provence* (fem); in Flanders, *en Flandre* (fem); in Paris, *en Paris.* **Note: in** = *à* before a town considered as a location **not** as area within which: in Paris, *à Paris;* in Edinburgh, *à Édimbourg*

viii. **in** = *à* before masculine countries, etc, starting with a consonant: in Mexico (country), *au Mexique;* in Denmark, *au Danemark*

ix. **in** (and **to**) = *aux* before all countries with plural names: in/to the United States, *aux États-Unis* (masc); in/to the Maldives, *aux Maldives* (fem). See also **Geographical Names**.

courir, to run. Pres: *cours, cours, court, courons, courez, courent.* Imperf: *courais, -ais, -ait, -ions, -iez, -aient.* Fut: *courrai, -as, -a, -ons, -ez, -ont.* Past hist: *courus, courus, courut, courûmes, courûtes, coururent.* Imperat: *cours, courons, courez.* Pres subj: *coure, -es, -e, -ions, -iez, -ent.* Imperf subj: *courusse, courusses, courût, courussions, courussiez, courussent.* Pres part:

courant. Past part: *couru, courue, courus, courues*. Aux: *avoir: courir faire qlqch*, to run to do sth.

couvrir, to cover: with sth, *de qlqch*. One of a small group of *-ir* verbs like *ouvrir*.

côté, masc: side: *de tous côtés*, on/from all sides; *de l'autre côté de la rue*, on/at the other side of the street; *à côté*, near by; *d'à côté*, next door; *la maison d'à côté*, the house next door; *à côté de*, near to, beside, at the side of; *du côté de*, in the direction of, on the part of, approximately ('round about'); *de l'autre côté*, on the other hand; *de mon côté*, on my side, as for me; *de chaque côté (de)*, on each side (of).

coûter, to cost. Regular, retains *-û-* throughout.

craindre: to fear, be afraid of. Pres: *crains, crains, craint, craignons, craignez, craignent*. Imperf: *craignais, -ais, -ait, -ions, -iez, -aient*. Fut: *craindrai, -as, -a, -ons, -ez, -ont*. Past hist: *craignis, craignis, craignit, craignîmes, craignîtes, craignirent*. Imperat: *crains, craignons, craignez*. Pres subj: *craigne, -es, -e, -ions, -iez, -ent*. Imperf subj: *craignisse, craignisses, craignît, craignissions, craignissiez, craignissent*. Pres part: *craignant*. Past part: *craint, crainte, craints, craintes*. For examples of usage see **fear** and VERBS ¶33viii.

crédule, adjective: credulous: *à qlqch*, about sth. Adverb: *crédulement*, credulously.

crêpe, **masculine** = black silk, black mourning veil or band: **feminine** = pancake.

crever, to burst. Like *mener*. Aux: *avoir*, **but** *crevé*, **adjective**, is used with *être: le pneu est crevé*, the tyre is/has burst/punctured; *crever de . . .*, to burst with (anger, etc).

critique, **masculine** = a critic: **feminine** = criticism.

crocheter, to pick (a lock), to hoe. Like *mener: il crochète, je crochèterai*, etc.

croire, to believe. Pres: *crois, crois, croit, croyons, croyez, croient*. Imperf: *croyais, -ais, -ait, -ions, -iez, -aient*. Fut: *croirai, -as, -a, -ons, -ez, -ont*. Past hist: *crus, crus, crut, crûmes, crûtes, crurent*. Imperat: *crois, croyons, croyez*. Pres subj: *croie, croies, croie, croyions, croyiez, croient*. Imperf subj: *crusse, crusses, crût, crussions, crussiez, crussent*. Pres part: *croyant*. Past part: *cru, crue, crus, crues*. Aux: *avoir: croire qlqch*, to believe sth; *croire à qlqch (miracles, revenants)*, to believe in (the existence of) sth (miracles, ghosts); *croire en qlqn, en Dieu, en mes amis*, to have faith/confidence in sn, in God, in my friends; *se croire qlqch*, to believe oneself to be sth (= to be sn of importance). **Noun**: *un(e) croyant(e)*, a believer.

croître, to grow. Pres: *croîs, croîs, croît, croissons, croissez, croissent*. Imperf: *croissais, -ais, -ait, -ions, -iez, -aient*. Fut: *croîtrai, -as, -a, -ons, -ez, -ont*. Past hist: *crûs, crûs, crût, crûmes, crûtes, crûrent*. Imperat: *croîs, croissons, croissez*. Pres subj: *croisse, -es, -e, -ions, -iez, -ent*. Imperf subj: *crûsse, crûsses, crût, crûssions, crûssiez, crûssent*. Pres part: *croissant*.* Past part: *crû, crue, crus, crues*. Aux: *avoir*. *****Noun**: *un croissant*, a crescent-shaped breakfast roll (shape of waxing moon).

cueillir, to gather. Pres: *cueille, -es, -e, -ons, -ez, -ent* (like *er* verbs). Imperf: *cueillais*, etc. Fut: *cueillerai, -as, -a, -ons, -ez, -ont* (**note** the *-er-* in Fut stem). Past hist: *cueillis, cueillis, cueillit, cueillîmes, cueillîtes, cueillirent*. Imperat: *cueille, cueillons, cueillez*. Pres subj: *cueille, -es, -e, -ions, -iez, -ent*. Imperf subj: *cueillisse, cueillisses, cueillît, cueillissions, cueillissiez, cueillissent:* accent may be omitted **except** in third person singular. Pres part: *cueillant*. Past part: *ceuilli, -e, -is, -es*.

cuire, to cook, to bake. Like *conduire*.

curieux, curieuse, adjective: unusual, curious = strange, inquisitive: *de qlqch*, about sth. Adverb: *curieusement*, curiously, minutely.

D

dame, une/la dame, is the feminine form of *un/le monsieur*. As a title (meaning 'Mrs' or 'Madam') with or without a name, *madame* is used. See *Madame*.

dangereux, dangereuse, adjective: dangerous: *pour qlqn*, for sn; *ce fleuve est dangereux à traverser*, this river is dangerous to cross. Adverb: *dangereusement*, dangerously.

dans, in: *dans* normally governs a defined or qualified noun: *dans la rue*, in the street; *dans ma boîte*, in my box; *dans son enfance*, in his childhood; *dans quelques expressions*, in some expressions; *je demeure dans cette rue*, I live in this street (**not** *à* or *sur*): *dans* **before a period of time usually means 'after':** *il revient dans une heure*, he'll be back in (after) an hour. **Note:** *dans Paris, Rome*, etc, expresses the idea of 'within the boundaries of' rather than 'at'. See *en*, **in**, and **Countries**.

Dates*:* in dates, 'on' and 'of' are **not** translated, and 'the first' of a month is *le premier* (using the ordinal number), eg: *le premier juin*, **on** the first **of** June: but for **all other dates** the cardinal number is used, eg: *le trois février*, (on) the third of February; *le vingt et un mai*, (on) the 21st of May (**not** *'le vingt premier'*). To ask the date there are many phrases, eg: *quel jour sommes-nous?* what day are we? *le combien est-ce?* 'the how much is it?' and *le combien sommes-nous?* 'the how much are we?'. See **Days**, **Months**, *an*, *année*.

davantage, adverb: more, to a greater degree, further, longer (in time): *il n'en sait pas davantage*, he doesn't know any more (about it); *nous n'y resterons pas davantage*, we won't stay there any longer; *il l'aime davantage que mon frère*, he likes him more than (he likes) my brother.

Day: *jour, journée*

    i. *le jour* is the usual translation for 'the day', and is used when thinking of a day as a single unit of time: *jour après jour*, day after day; 'Good day!' (greeting), *bonjour!* to bring up to date, *mettre à jour* **or** *mettre au jour;* on that day, *ce jour-là* ('on' **not** translated); the day before, *la veille;* the day after/the next day, *le lendemain*

    ii.   *la journée* is used when a day is considered as a period from sunrise to sunset, during which sth happened or as an extended period of time: in the course of the day, *dans la journée;* his studies fill his days, *ses études remplissent ses journées;* to have a good day, *avoir une bonne journée;* paid by the day, *payé par la journée;* a day worker, *un homme/une femme de journée*

    iii. **days of the week** are masculine nouns, spelt **without** capital letters (from Sunday): *dimanche, lundi, mardi, mercredi, jeudi, vendredi, samedi*

    iv. **used as adverbs,** with no article = today, *aujourd'hui;* yesterday, *hier;* tomorrow, *demain;* the day before yesterday, *avant-hier;* the day after tomorrow, *après-demain*

    v. **'on'** is **not** translated in the following cases: on Monday (on that one day) = *lundi;* on Tuesdays (ie: regularly) = *le mardi* (in singular); on the next Wednesday = *le mercredi prochain*

    vi. **other phrases**: every Friday = *tous les vendredis;* next Wednesday = *mercredi prochain;* every other day = *tous les deux jours;* the following morning/afternoon/evening = *le lendemain matin/après-midi/soir;* a week today = *d'aujourd'hui en huit*;* today/tomorrow fortnight = *d'aujourd'hui/ de demain en quinze*;* a week ago = *il y a huit* jours;* a week ago yesterday = *il y a eu hier huit* jours* (*in counting length of periods French count the first day of the period plus the first day of the following period: thus **a week is eight days**); once a day = *une fois par jour;* twice a week = *deux fois par semaine;* from Monday to Friday = *du lundi au vendredi;* the weekend = *le week-end* (noun only): *a weekend' is Saturday to Monday

    vii. **'it'** used with days = *ce: c'est aujourd'hui jeudi,* it is Thursday today; *quel jour est-ce?* what day is it? (**Note**: 'it' with **time** = *il.)*

de, preposition

    i. *de* = 'of', to show possession: *le livre de Jean,* John's book: see *'s, s'*

    ii. *de* = of, from, out of, about, for (and has a variety of other uses): *il parle de son fils,* he speaks of/about his son; *elle vient de Paris,* she comes from Paris; *ils sortent de l'eau,* they come out of the water; *de temps en temps/de temps à autre,* from time to time; *de ce jour-là,* from that day; *je vous remercie de votre lettre,* I thank you for your letter. When combined with the definite article = 'of the' (in combination *de + le = du, de l'* and *de la* remain unchanged, *de + les = des*): *une page du livre,* a page of the book; *une feuille de l'arbre,* a leaf of the tree; *le toit de la maison,* the roof of the house; *les sièges des chaises,* the seats of the chairs

    iii. *du, de l', de la* and *des,* **also** mean 'some', 'any': *il mange du pain,* he eats some bread; *des pages des livres,* some pages of the books; *avez-vous de l'encre?* have you any ink?

    iv. *de* combines with the relative pronoun *lequel* as with the definite article: *de + lequel = duquel, de + lesquels* and *de + lesquelles* form *desquels, desquelles* (see PRONOUNS ¶43). In combination with *qui, de* can become ***dont*** = of whom, of which (see PRONOUNS ¶44). After a word of measure or after a negative *de* or *d'* is used alone: *nous avons beaucoup de pain,* we have a lot of bread (but see ***bien***); *nous n'avons pas de pain,* we do not have any bread/we have no bread

v. *de* is also used before comparative adjectives following *personne* **and** *rien: je ne connais personne/rien de plus utile, de meilleur,* I know no one/nothing more useful, better: and similarly before an adjective after *quelqu'un* **or** *quelque chose: c'est quelqu'un/quelque chose d'important,* it is sn/sth important

vi. *de* is used in stating measurements: *un arbre de dix mètres de haut/de hauteur,* a ten metre tree/a tree ten metres high: **and** to translate 'by' in comparing measurement/age, etc: *plus long de dix mètres,* longer by ten metres; *plus âgé de cinq ans,* older by five years: **and** after numerical nouns: *un million de,* a million; *une centaine de,* a hundred or so; *une vingtaine de,* some twenty; *une douzaine de,* a dozen/some twelve, etc. See also **Dimensions**

vii. *de* translates 'than' after *plus* and *moins: plus/moins de six,* more/less than six

viii. *de* is often used before a noun without an article where in English a noun is used as an adjective (French nouns **cannot** normally act as adjectives), eg: *une maison de campagne,* a country house; *une montre d'or,* a gold watch (see also *en:* preposition)

ix. *de* is used before the infinitive following many verbs, eg: *cesser de faire,* to stop doing (cease to do): **and** *de* may translate 'by', '**for**' or 'with', as well as '**of**' in connection with some verbs (including their participles) and some adjectives: these uses are shown in the entries of individual verbs and adjectives (eg: *crever de rage,* to burst with fury; *ambitieux de,* ambitious for)

x. *de* translates 'by' referring to the author of a book, etc, eg: *'Notre Dame de Paris' de Victor Hugo.*

***dé-* verbs,** the conjugation of irregular verbs with the **prefix** *dé-* is usually the same as that of the verb to which the prefix is attached. Verbs which present problems are given below.

***débattre*,** to debate, discuss, dispute: *se **débattre**,* to struggle; *contre qlqch,* against sth. Conjugated like ***battre*.**

***débrouiller*,** to disentangle, set to rights, extricate: *se **débrouiller**,* to manage (under difficulties), to extricate oneself (from difficulties). Regular *-er* verb.

***débuter*,** to begin: with sth, *par qlqch.*

déceler*,** to reveal, disclose. Conjugated like ***mener (**distinguish from** *desceller,* to unseal).

***déchoir*,** to decay: defective verb. Pres: *déchois, déchois, déchoit, déchoyons, déchoyez, déchoient.* No imperfect. Fut: *déchoirai, -as, -a, -ons, -ez, -ont.* Past hist: *déchus, déchus, déchut, déchûmes, déchûtes, déchurent.* Imperat:

déchois, déchoyons, déchoyez. Pres subj: *déchoie, déchoies, déchoie, déchoyions, déchoyiez, déchoient.* Imperf subj: *déchusse, déchusses, déchût, déchussions, déchussiez, déchussent.* No present participle. Past part: *déchu, déchue.* Aux: *avoir* if action is expressed, *être* if state or condition is described.

décider, to decide: *de faire qlqch*, to do sth; *décider qlqn à faire qlqch*, to induce sn to do sth; *se décider*, to make up one's mind; *à faire qlqch*, to do sth.

dédire, to contradict. Conjugated like *dire* except 2nd plur of present and imperative: *vous dédisez*, you contradict; *dédisez!* contradict! *se dédire de qlqch*, to recant, retract sth.

défendre, to forbid: *à qlqn de faire qlqch*, sn to do sth; *défendre que vous fassiez qlqch*, forbid that you do sth (with subjunctive); *défendre qlqn/qlqch contre qlqn/qlqch*, to defend sn/sth against sn/sth; *se défendre*, to protect oneself; *se défendre qlqch*, to forbid/deny sth to oneself.

Definite Article: see ARTICLES ¶2.

dehors, outside, out of it/them: *de dehors*, from outside: *mettre dehors*, to turn out (of the house, etc). **Noun**: *le dehors*, the outside, the outward appearance. See *hors, au-dehors*.

déléguer, to delegate. Conjugated like *céder*, the *-gu-* counting as one consonant and retained throughout. Pres: *je délègue, nous déléguons, vous déléguez, ils délèguent.* Fut: *déléguerai*, etc. Pres part: *déléguant.* Past part: *délégué.* Related nouns have *-ga-* (**without** *-u-*): *délégateur, délégatrice, délégation:* **and** as noun and adjective: *délégant.*

demand: to ask in a peremptory manner: *exiger* (like *manger*), *requérir* (like *acquérir*). In great demand, *très demandé, très recherché.* See next entry.

demander, to ask (**not** usually so peremptory as English 'demand'): *demander qlqch*, to ask for sth; *demander qlqch à qlqn*, to ask sn for sth; *demander à qlqn de faire qlqch*, to ask sn to do sth (see **ask**); *se demander*, to ask oneself, to wonder (whether/if).

demi, half
    i.   as **masculine noun, only** used with figures: *deux et demi*, two and a half; *quatre demis valent deux*, four halves make two. In football: *un demi* = a half (half-back)
    ii. as **adjective**: (fem: *demie)*: when used before a noun with hyphen is invariable: *une demi-heure*, a half hour: **but** *demi* agrees when coming after a named noun: *une bouteille et demie, une heure et demie*, a bottle and a half, an hour an a half
    iii. *à demi*, **adverbial phrase** as in: *la ville était à demi détruite*, the town was half destroyed (*demi* = a large part: **no** agreement). **Note**: for 'half' in other senses see *moitié*.

Demonstrative Pronouns: see PRONOUNS ¶19 – 37.

se dépêcher, to hurry up (to do sth, *de faire qlqch*).

déplaire, to displease *(à qlqn)*. Like *plaire*.

dépendant, -e, adjective: *dependent de*, upon.

dépendre de, to depend on (sn/sth): *il dépend de vous*, it depends on you. Like *vendre*.

depuis, since, for, from: *j'habite Paris depuis deux ans*, I **have lived** in Paris for two years (**note**: present tense in French for perfect in English); *j'habitais Paris depuis trois ans quand je l'ai rencontrée*, **I had been** living in Paris for three years when I met her (**note**: imperfect tense in French for pluperfect in English); *depuis l'année dernière*, since last year; *j'y habite depuis longtemps*, **I have lived** there for a long time; *depuis sa naissance jusqu'à sa mort*, from his birth to his death; *depuis lors*, from that time; *depuis que*, from the time that; *depuis qu'il est arrivé*, from the time that he arrived (tense as in English).

dernier, dernière, adjective: last: used **before the noun** with article = the last, eg: *le dernier livre que j'ai lu*, the last book (of the many) that I have read; *la dernière année de la guerre*, the last year of the war; *le dernier à faire qlqch*, the last to do sth. **After the noun** = last: *l'année dernière*, last year. See **last** iii.

derrière, behind, after: *derrière la maison*, behind the house; *ma femme est restée derrière*, my wife stayed behind; *il se trouve par derrière*, it is (= it's position is) behind/at the back. **Noun**: the back, the rear: *le derrière du bateau*, the afterpart of the boat.

dès, from the moment of/that (= from that time and onwards), since: *dès son mariage il habite Paris*, from the time of his marriage he has lived in Paris; *dès la fin de la guerre*, since the end of the war; *j'ai travaillé dès six heures du matin*, I have worked since six this morning. As **conjunction** = as soon as: *dès qu'il était arrivé il l'a montré*, as soon as he had arrived he showed it. (**Note**: *mariage*: one 'r' in French.)

descendre, to take down, to lower, to descend sth, to descend, to come down. Conjugated like *vendre*
   i. with auxiliary *avoir* when describing an action that has taken place: *il a descendu le tableau*, he has lowered/taken down the picture; *il a descendu l'escalier*, he came down the stairs
   ii. the auxiliary is *être* when the verb describes a state or condition resulting from descending: *il est descendu*, he has come downstairs, come down, alighted; *il est descendu du duc de Blois*, he is descended from the Duke of Blois.

désirer, to desire: *désirer qlqch*, wish for sth.

désobéir, to disobey: *à qlqn/qlqch*, disobey sn/sth. See *obéir*.

désormais, henceforth, from then: *notre vie désormais devint un véritable vagabondage*, our life, henceforth, became a veritable vagabondage (became completely nomadic).

dessous, **adverb** and **preposition**: under, below, beneath: *elle sortit de dessous la table*, she came out from under the table; *cherchez-le dessous la table*, look for it under the table; *le livre n'était pas sur la table, il était dessous*, the book wasn't on the table, it was underneath; *je l'ai mis au-dessous*, I put it underneath/lower down; *au-dessous de la fenêtre il y a un siège*, beneath the window there is a seat; *en dessous*, beneath; *un vêtement porté en dessous*, a garment worn underneath; *là-dessous*, underneath, thereunder. **Noun**: *le dessous*, the under side (of sth). See **under**.

dessus, **adverb** and **preposition**: on, over, above: *au-dessus*, above, higher up; *au-dessus il y a un balcon, et au-dessus du balcon il y a une banne*, above there is a balcony, and over the balcony is an awning; *en dessus*, upon, on the upper side; *bras dessus dessous*, arm in arm; *sens dessus dessous*, higgledy-piggledy, in confusion, upside down; *par-dessus*, above, besides, over, over and above; *il saute par-dessus le mur*, he jumps over the wall; *par-dessus l'élan de la guerre planait la pensée de la mort*, over and above the enthusiasm for the war hung the thought of death. **Note**: *un pardessus* (one word), an overcoat. **Note also**: *dessus*, **noun** (masc), the under/lower part (of sth).

destiner, to destine, doom: *destiné à qlqch*, doomed to sth.

détester, hate: *détester faire qlqch* **or** *de faire qlqch*, hate doing sth.

devant, **adverb** and **preposition**: before, in front: usually for position (rarely for time): *devant la maison*, before the house; *devant ses yeux*, before his eyes. **Note**: *devant*, **noun** (masc): the front part: *une roue de devant*, a front wheel.

devenir, to become: *qu'est-il est devenu?* **or** *qu'est-ce qu'il est devenu?* what has become of him? *que deviendra-t-il?* what will he become? Like *venir*. Aux: *être*.

devoir, **verb**: must, have to, to owe. Pres: *dois, dois, doit, devons, devez, doivent*. Imperf: *devais, devais, devait, devions, deviez, devaient*. Fut: *devrai, devras, devra, devrons, devrez, devront*. Past hist: *dus, dus, dut, dûmes, dûtes, durent*. Imperat: *dois, devons, devez*. Pres subj: *doive, doives, doive, devions, deviez, doivent*. Imperf subj: *dusse, dusses, dût, dussions, dussiez, dussent*. Pres part: *devant*. Past part: *dû, due, dus, dues* (**note** accent in masc sing only). Aux: *avoir: je dois le faire*, I must do it, I have to do it; *je devrais le faire*, I should (ought) to do it; *il aurait dû le faire*, he ought to have done it; *devoir qlqch à qlqn*, to owe sth to sn. **Note**: *devoir*, **noun** (masc), duty, exercise, school work to be done, homework.

différent, adjective: different (from/to = *de*). Adverb: *différemment*, differently.

différer, to differ (from = *de*).

difficile à faire, difficult to do: *il est difficile à* (**or** *pour*) *Jean de le faire*, it is difficult for John to do it; *il m'est difficile/il lui est difficile de faire qlqch*, it is difficult for me/for him to do sth; *il est difficile à résoudre le problème*, it is difficult to solve the problem; *être difficile sur qlqch*, to be difficult about sth.

diffus,-e, adjective: diffuse, wordy. Adverb, *diffusément*, diffusely, verbosely.

Dimensions are expressed

    i. with **adjectives**, which agree with the noun: *épais, épaisse,* thick; *haut*, haute,* high; *large*,* wide; *long*, longue,* long (*in masculine form these are **also** nouns); *profond, profonde,* deep, eg: **length**: *ces jardins sont longs de cent mètres,* these gardens are 100m long; *des cordes longues de cent mètres,* ropes 100m long: **width**: *la chaussée est large de vingt mètres,* the roadway is 20m wide; *des sentiers larges de 3m,* 3m wide paths: **height**: *la tour est haute de 50m,* the tower is 50m high

    ii. with **nouns**, which **do not alter**: *l'épaisseur* (fem), the thickness; *le haut, la hauteur,* the height; *le long, la longueur,* the length; *le large, la largeur,* the width; *la profondeur,* the depth, eg: **length**: *ce jardin a cent mètres de long* **or** *de longeur,* this garden is 100 metres long: **width**: *la chaussée a vingt mètres de large* **or** *de largeur,* the roadway has a width of 20 metres (= is 20m wide): **height**: *la tour a cinquante mètres de haut* **or** *de hauteur,* the tower has a height of 50m (= is 50m high); *le haut de l'arbre est . . .,* the height of the tree is . . .; *la longueur de la route était . . .,* the length of the route was . . . The other dimensional adjectives and nouns given above can be similarly used, **but** *épais* and *profond* are adjectives only

    iii. with *de,* of: used before a measurement as in English: *une corde de dix mètres,* a rope of 10 metres; *un livre de 200 pages,* a book of 200 pages

    iv. with *sur,* by: used in giving measurements of area = *une chambre de cinq mètres sur quatre,* a room five metres by four. **Note**: 'by', when referring to the amount by which sth is enlarged, reduced, etc = *de: on a réduit la largeur de la rue de deux mètres,* they have reduced the width of the road by two metres. See also **Distance**.

dire, to say, tell. Pres: *dis, dis, dit, disons, dites* (**no** accent), *disent.* Imperf: *disais, -ais, disait, disions, disiez, disaient.* Fut: *dirai, diras, dira, dirons, direz, diront.* Past hist: *dis, dis, dit, dîmes, dîtes, dirent.* Imperat: *dis, disons, dites.* Pres subj: *dise, -es, -e, -ions, -iez, -ent.* Imperf subj: *disse, disses, dît, dissions, -iez, dissent.* Pres part: *disant.* Past part: *dit, dite, dits, dites.* Aux: *avoir: dire qlqch à qlqn,* to say sth to sn; *dire à qlqn de faire qlqch,* to tell sn to do sth; *il dit l'avoir trouvé,* he says he has found it (**no** *de*); *c'est à dire,* that is to say; *pour ainsi dire,* so to speak; *vouloir dire,* to mean (= what a word, sign, etc 'means'), wish to say. **Note**: with the exception of *redire* all compounds of *dire* have *-disez* in 2nd plur present and imperative, eg: *vous prédisez,* you predict.

Direct Object Pronouns: when used as pronoun objects of a verb *le, la, l'* and *les* are **always** direct objects: *me, te, se, nous* and *vous,* when used as objects before a verb can be **both** direct or indirect. There **cannot** be a direct object pronoun if a direct object noun follows the verb. In compound tenses, the past participle of a verb conjugated with *avoir* agrees with a direct object pronoun preceding the verb: see **Indirect Object** and VERBS ¶44.

disconvenir, to deny: usually in the negative: *je ne disconviens pas que cela (ne) soit vrai*, I don't deny that that is true; *je n'en disconviens pas*, I admit it; *disconvenir d'avoir fait qlqch*, to deny having done sth; *disconvenir à qlqn/qlqch*, not to suit sn/sth; *disconvenir de qlqch*, to contradict sth. Like *venir*.

Disjunctive Pronouns: see PRONOUNS ¶15 – 17.

disparaître, to disappear. Like *connaître*. Aux: *être:* for state: *avoir:* for an action.

disputer, to dispute, contest, quarrel: *disputer de qlqch*, to quarrel about sth; *disputer qlqch à qlqn*, to dispute with sn about sth; *disputer un prix*, contest a prize; *se disputer*, to quarrel.

Distance: from = *de:* to = *à:* at ten kilometres from Paris, *à dix kilomètres de Paris;* how far is it from . . . to . . .? *combien y a-t-il de . . . à . . .?* to walk, to run, to do, ten kilometres, *marcher, courir, faire dix km:* by = *de*, eg: to advance by/withdraw by ten km, *avancer de/reculer de dix kilomètres*. See also **Dimensions** above.

distinct, -e, adjective: distinct: *de qlqch*, from sth.

divers, -e, adjective: different, various, divers, sundry.

dix, ten. Before a plural noun starting with a consonant or *h*-aspirate the final *-x* is not sounded: *di(x) livres*. In all other cases it should be sounded (like 'deess'), including before all months: *le dix février:* and when counting. In practice this rule is not always adhered to.

do: most often = *faire*. **Note**: in questions it is **not** translated: do you speak? *parlez-vous?* to have to do with sth, *avoir affaire de qlqch* or *avoir à voir à qlqch* or *dans qlqch;* to have nothing to do with sth, *n'être pour rien dans qlqch;* what is he going to do with . . . ? *que va-t-il faire de . . . ?* to have nothing to do with it, *n'y être pour rien;* that won't do, *cela ne va pas*. See *faire*.

donc, then, therefore, so, consequently: *donc* is a conjunction, but is frequently placed in the body of a sentence, usually after the verb: *je le ferai, donc, si vous voulez*, I shall do it, then, if you wish (could be put at the beginning **or** at the end of the sentence): *donc* is used to give emphasis: *je suis donc destiné à mourir*, I am, then, doomed to die; *que sa femme est donc jolie!* how very pretty his wife is! *donnez-lui donc l'argent*, just give him the money, then.

dont, of whom, of which: extensively explained in PRONOUNS ¶44.

dormir, to sleep. Pres: *dors, dors, dort, dormons, dormez, dorment*. Imperf: *dormais, -ais, -ait, -ions, -iez, -aient*. Fut: *dormirai, -as, -a, -ons, -ez, -ont*. Past hist: *dormis, dormis, dormit, dormîmes, dormîtes, dormirent*. Imperat: *dors, dormons, dormez*. Pres subj: *dorme, -es, -e, -ions, -iez, -ent*. Imperf subj: *dormisse, dormisses, dormît, dormissions, -issiez, -issent*. Pres part: *dormant*. Past part: *dormi* (invariable). Aux: *avoir*.

douter, to doubt: *douter de qlqch*, to doubt sth, be doubtful about sth; *se douter de qlqch*, to suspect sth; *je m'en doute*, I doubt it (I have my doubts about it); *ne se douter de rien*, to suspect nothing.

dur, -e, adjective: hard, difficult: *dur à faire*, hard to do.

during: preposition: ***pendant, durant:*** during the war, *pendant la guerre;* during the whole period of, throughout, ***durant;*** during (for the whole period of) an hour, *durant une heure:* in some expressions follows the noun, eg: during (throughout) his life, *sa vie durant* (**no** agreement).

E

each: **adjective**: *chaque* (masc and fem: **always** sing): each girl, *chaque fille:* **pronoun**: each one, *chacun, chacune*, eg: each one of the girls, *chacune des filles*. The **reflexive pronoun** is often used to express the reciprocal idea of 'each other', eg: to love each other, *s'aimer l'un(e) l'autre;* to fight each other *se battre*. See **Reciprocal Verbs** and **every**.

Easter: see **Feasts and Festivals**.

s'ébahir, to be amazed: *de voir qlqch*, to see sth. See VERBS ¶33vii.

écarteler, to (hang, draw and) quarter: also used for 'to quarter' in heraldry. Like *mener*.

échanger, to exchange: *qlqch pour* **or** *contre qlqch*, sth for sth.

échapper, escape: *de qlqch*, from sth; *échapper à qlqn/qlqch*, to avoid sn/sth; *échapper au danger*, to escape (the) danger; *l'échapper belle*, to have a narrow escape; *le mot m'échappe*, the word escapes me; *laisser échapper de la main*, to let slip, drop (from one's hand).

échoir, to expire, to be due, befall, happen. Impersonal verb, rare except in the following persons and tenses. Pres: *il échoit, ils échoient*. No imperfect. Fut: *il écherra, ils écherront* **or** *il échoira, ils échoiront*. Past hist: *il échut, ils échurent*. Imperf subj: *qu'il échût*. Pres part: *échéant*. Past part: *échu, échue*. Aux: *être:* **but** '*mon billet a échu le 3 mai*' may be used for, 'my account has fallen due on 3 May' when the actual date is stated. **Note**: *le cas échéant* = in that case, that being the case.

économe, **adjective**: economical, sparing: *une femme économe*, an economical woman; *être économe de*, to be sparing with. **Noun**: *un économe*, an economist, treasurer, bursar.

économique, inexpensive, cheap, economical in price or in use.

écouter, to listen to, harken to: transitive verb followed by direct object: *écouter qlqn/qlqch* (no preposition), to listen to sn/sth; *écoutez-moi*, listen to me (*moi* here is the after-verb direct object form of *me*); *écoutez-le/la/les*, listen to him/her/them; for *écouter* when followed by infinitive with object pronouns see PRONOUNS ¶12.

écrire, to write. Pres: *écris, écris, écrit, écrivons, écrivez, écrivent.* Imperf: *écrivais, -ais, -ait, -ions, -iez, -aient.* Fut: *écrirai, -as, -a, -ons, -ez, -ont.* Past hist: *écrivis, écrivis, écrivit, écrivîmes, écrivîtes, écrivirent.* Imperat: *écris, écrivons, écrivez.* Pres subj: *écrive, écrives, écrive, écrivions, écriviez, écrivent.* Imperf subj: *écrivisse, écrivisses, écrivît, écrivissions, écrivissiez, écrivissent.* Pres part: *écrivant.* Past part: *écrit, écrite, écrits, écrites.* Aux: **avoir**: *écrire avec un stylo,* to write with a pen; *écrit(e) de sa propre main,* written with his own hand.

-éer, **verbs** so ending: see example *agréer.*

égal, égale, égaux, égales, **adjective**: equal: *à qlqn/qlqch,* to sn/sth; *cela m'est égal,* it's all the same to me, I don't mind. **Noun**: *un/une égal,* masc/fem: an equal: plur: *les égaux, les égales* (**note**: feminine form used in plural only).

égaler, to equal: verb is singular in, *trois plus trois égale six,* three plus three equals six.

either: *l'un(e) ou l'autre:* either . . . or, *ou . . . ou:* I shall take either the pen or the pencil, *je prendrai (ou) le stylo ou le crayon* (the first *ou* is often omitted in everyday language); nor (me) either, *ni (moi) non plus.*

élever, to raise, rear: *s'élever,* to get up, to rise: takes *-è-* before *e*-mute endings and in future stem, eg: *élève, élèvent, élèverai,* etc.

Elision: the cutting off of a letter at the end of a word

    i.   two-letter words ending in *-e* are elided before a word starting with a vowel or *h*-mute, and before *y* (= there). These words are: *je, me, te, se, ne, de, le* (when meaning 'the', 'him' or 'it'), eg: *j'ai, je t'aime, l'homme, j'y vais,* etc: *ce,* pronoun, is similarly elided when meaning 'he', 'she', 'it', 'they', etc (eg: *c'est,* it is: **but** when *ce* is the adjective 'this' or that', qualifying a noun, it becomes *cet* before a vowel or *h*-mute: *cet homme*): *ce* elided before an *a* takes a cedilla, *ç'a: ç'a a été,* it has been (see PRONOUNS ¶23ff)

    ii. when used for 'the', 'her' and 'it', the *a* of *la* is elided before a vowel or *h*-mute: *la maison – je l'ai vue,* the house – I have seen it

    iii. the *i* of *si,* is elided before *il, ils* (**not** before *elle* or *on*), but **only** when meaning 'if/whether' – it is **not** elided when *si* means 'so'

    iv. the final *e* of *que* (but **not** the *i* of *qui*), whatever its meaning, is elided before a vowel or *h*-mute: *le livre qu'il a acheté,* the book which he has bought: the same applies to *jusque, puisque* and *parce que: jusqu'ils arrivent,* until they arrive; *puisqu'ils sont ici,* since/seeing that they are here; *parce qu'elle le veut,* because she wishes it: elision occurs in *quelque* before *un* or *une: quelqu'un(e),* sn: *presque* is elided **only** in *la presqu'île,* the peninsular: in **speech**, elision occurs in the **sound** of both *quelque* and *presque* when they come before a vowel, eg: '*presque impossible'* **sounds** 'preskimpossible'

    v. *entre* is elided when prefixed to a very few words of which it forms an integral part, eg: *s'entr'aimer,* to love each other

vi. *le* **and** *de* **are not elided** before *onze*, eg: *le onze mai*, the eleventh of May; *un enfant de onze ans*, a child of eleven (years): although *d'onze* occurs in: *la messe/le train d'onze heures*, etc, the eleven o'clock Mass/train, etc: before *onzième*, eleventh, both *le* and *l'* are used: *l'onzième* and *le onzième*: *le* **is not elided** before *un* when meaning 'the figure one' (*le un*): **nor** before *oui*

vii. *le* **is not elided** before the initial *y-* of a number of non-French words, the *y-* being counted as a consonant, eg: *le yacht* (should be pronounced *iak*) and *le yak, le yankee, le Yémen, le yen, le yeoman, le yiddish, le yoghourt, le yogi*, etc

viii. neither ***cela*** nor its abbreviated form *ça* are elided, eg: *cela a été* or, as usually pronounced when spoken, *ça a été*, that has been. **Neither** *ça* nor *là* are elided in the phrase *çà et là*, here and there

ix. when *je, ce, le* and *la* **follow** the verb there is **no** elision, eg: *dois-je écrire?* must I write? *donnez-le aux enfants*, give it to the children (this does **not** affect *me* and *te* because when these follow the verb they become *moi* and *toi:* see PRONOUNS ¶9).

elle

i. 'she' **or** 'it': when the **subject of a verb** if referring to a feminine noun (animal or thing): *elle parle*, she speaks; *la table – elle est grande*, the table – it is big: **and** *elle* also means 'she' or 'it' (fem) when the complement of *être: c'est elle*, it is she/it is it (fem)

ii. 'her' **after prepositions**, eg: *avec elle*, with her; *il va à elle*, he goes to her (**but** after verbs which govern *à* before an indirect object 'to her' = *lui*, placed before the verb: *il lui parle*, he speaks to her; *il lui obéit*, he obeys her: see ***obéir***). See PRONOUNS ¶1ff.

emmener, to lead: *qlqn faire qlqch*, sn to do sth; *qlqn à la maison*, sn to the house. Conjugated like ***mener***. For reflexive pronoun dropped after *emmener* see PRONOUNS ¶14.

émouvoir, to move/touch/stir (sn's emotions): conjugated like ***mouvoir*** except in its past participle: *ému, émue, émus, émues*, **without** the circumflex in masc sing.

empêcher, to prevent: *qlqn de faire qlqch*, sn from doing sth; *je ne peux (pas) l'empêcher de faire qlqch*, I can't prevent him from doing sth (his doing sth).

employer, to employ, use: *qlqn/qlqch (à faire qlqch)*, sn/sth (to do sth); *s'employer à faire qlqch*, to busy oneself doing sth. The *y* changes to *i* before *e*-mute endings, and in future stem. Pres: *emploie, emploies, emploie, employons, employez, emploient*. Imperf: *employais, employais, employait, employions, employiez, employaient*. Fut: *emploierai*, etc. Past hist: *employai, employas, employa, employâmes, employâtes, employèrent*. Imperat: *emploie, employons, employez*. Pres subj: *emploie, emploies, emploie, employions, employiez, emploient*. Imperf subj: *employasse, employasses, employât, employassions, employassiez, employassent*. Pres part: *employant*. Past part: *employé(e)(s)*. **Other verbs in *-oyer* and *-uyer*** are conjugated in the same way, **but** not necessarily those in *-ayer* (see *payer* for these). See also *envoyer*, to send, which has an irregular future stem.

empreindre, to impress. Like *craindre*.

s'empresser, *s'empresser à faire qlqch*, to be eager to do sth; *s'empresser de faire qlqch*, to hasten to do sth, to busy oneself with sth.

emprunter, to borrow: *qlqch à* (sometimes *de*) *qlqn*, sth from sn.

en, **preposition**: in, during, to, while, (made) of, like/as: *en* is used for 'in' mainly when there is no definite article*: *en France*, in France; *en hiver*, in winter; *en été*, in summer; *en automne*, in autumn (**but** *au printemps*, in spring); *en janvier*, in January, etc; *en mil neuf cent quatre-vingt-dix*, in 1990; *en tout cas*, in any case; *en prison*, in prison; *en vacances*, on holiday; *en retard*, late; *en marche*, going (= working, of a machine); *en marchant*, while marching; *en parlant*, whilst speaking (a usual construction, with the present participle, used as verb noun or gerund, see VERBS ¶43iii); *de jour en jour*, from day to day; *un buste en marbre*, a bust of marble; *des vêtements en laine*, clothes of wool (**but** *de* is also used, especially if it is a figure of speech: *un cœur de granit*, a heart of granite, see *de* vi); *habillé en soldat*, dressed as/like a soldier; *en face de*, opposite = 'in face of'. **en* is used before the definite article in a number of set phrases, including: *en l'absence de*, in the absence of; *en l'air*, in the air; *en l'espace*, in space; *en l'an 1802*, in the year 1802. Verbs which govern *en*, eg: *consister en qlqch*, to consist **of** sth, will be found listed separately.

en, **pronoun/adverb** = of him/her/it/them, some, any, from it/there

    i.   *en* may be the **indirect object** of a verb (see PRONOUNS ¶3, ¶4iv): *j'en parle*, I speak of it (of him/her/them); *j'en ai parlé*, I have spoken of it (of him/her/them); *j'en ai mangé* tout*, I have eaten all of it (*the past participle does **not** agree with *en* when it refers to sth feminine or plural, because it is not the direct object of the verb; **but** nor does *tout*)

    ii.   *en* is used to replace a noun which, as indirect object of a verb, is governed by *de*, meaning 'of' **or** 'from', eg: *je parle de votre bonté*, I speak **of** your kindness, changes to: *j'en parle*, I speak **of** it; *je viens de la ville*, becomes: *j'en viens*, I come **from it** (the town)

    iii. combined with other pronoun-objects before a verb – *en* is always last, eg: *il lui en a parlé*, he has spoken to him of it; *il y en a beaucoup*, there is a lot of it. In the **interrogative** *en* retains its position: *lui en a-t-il parlé?* has he spoken to him of it? In the **imperative** *en* comes last after the verb: *chargez-vous-en*, take care of it (= take it upon yourself)

    iv. it is **not** possible to have a direct object pronoun (*le, la, les*, him/it, her/it, them) **and** *en* as objects of the same verb, but *en* can be used together with *lui, leur*, to him/her/it, to them, and with *y* (= there).

enceindre, to surround. Like *craindre*.

enchanter, to enchant: *enchanté de faire votre connaissance*, delighted to make your acquaintance.

enclore, to enclose. Like *clore*.

encore, still, yet, again, furthermore: after *encore* pronoun subjects (including *ce*), are usually put after the verb: *et encore est-il vrai que,* and further, it is true that (see **Inversion** iii.); *encore du* café,* more coffee (*partitive article used).

encourager, to encourage. Like *manger* with *-e-* inserted after *-g-* before '*a*' and '*o*' endings, eg: *encourageons, encourageais: encourager qlqn à faire qlqch,* to encourage sn to do sth.

-ener, **verbs** so ending are conjugated like *mener*.

enfant, child: usually masculine: feminine if specifically a girl (**no -e**).

enfreindre, to infringe. Like *craindre*.

enjoindre, to enjoin, to bid, to command: *enjoindre à qlqn de faire qlqch,* bid sn to do sth. Like *joindre*.

enlever, to lift, take away: *enlever qlqch à qlqn,* to take sth from sn. Like *élever,* eg: *enlève, enlèvent, enlèverai,* etc. See also *mener*.

ennuyer, to annoy, bore, tire, tease: *s'ennuyer,* to be bored, tired, weary; *s'ennuyer à* (sometimes *de*) *faire qlqch,* to be tired of doing/bored with doing/sth. Like *employer*.

énorme, adjective: enormous. Adverb: *énormément,* enormously.

enough: *assez:* he has worked enough, *il a assez travaillé;* we were pleased enough with it, *nous en étions assez contents;* you have done well enough (quite well), *vous avez fait assez bien;* have you enough room? *avez-vous assez de place?* thank you, but I've had enough, *merci, mais j' (en) ai eu assez.*

enseigner, to teach: *qlqch à qlqn,* to teach sn sth (teach sth to sn).

entendre, to hear, to listen to, to consent: *entendre qlqn faire qlqch,* to hear sn doing sth; *je l'ai entendu dire,* I have heard it said; *entendre mal,* to hear badly, to misunderstand; *s'entendre,* to agree; *s'entendre à qlqch,* to understand/be well versed in sth; *entendu!* agreed! *bien entendu,* well understood; *cela s'entend,* that's understood, of course. Like *vendre.* For usage when followed by infinitive with pronoun objects see PRONOUNS ¶12.

enthousiaste de, enthusiastic about. **Noun**: masc/fem: *un/une enthousiaste,* an enthusiast.

entre, between, among: *entre les maisons,* between the houses; *entre les arbres,* among the trees; *entre amis,* between/among friends; *entre deux et trois heures,* between two and three o'clock; *entre tous,* among all/above all others; *entre autres choses,* among other things; *l'un d'entre eux,* one of them; *ils se battent entre eux,* they fight among themselves.

entrer, to enter: '*in*' usually translated by *dans* but **note**: to enter a school, college, hospital, etc: *entrer à,* eg: *il est entré au collège, à l'hôpital,* he has entered college, hospital. Aux: *être*.

entretenir, to maintain, to keep in good order, to entertain, to talk with, to speak with: *entretenir qlqn de qlqch,* to talk to sn about sth; *s'entretenir avec qlqn de qlqch,* to talk/converse with sn about sth. Like *tenir.*

envelopper, to envelope, surround: *qlqn/qlqch de* (occasionally *dans*) *qlqch,* to envelope sn/sth with/in sth.

envier, to begrudge: *qlqch à qlqn,* sth to sn (begrudge sn sth).

envoyer, to send. With *renvoyer* and *aller,* one of the only really irregular *-er* verbs (irregular future stem). Pres: *envoie, envoies, envoie, envoyons, envoyez, envoient.* Imperf: *envoyais, -ais, -ait, -ions, -iez, -aient.* Fut: *enverrai, -as, -a, -ons, -ez, -ont.* Past hist: *envoyai, envoyas, envoya, envoyâmes, envoyâtes, envoyèrent.* Imperat: *envoie, envoyons, envoyez.* Conditional: *enverrais, -ais, -ait, -ions, -iez, -aient.* Pres subj: *envoie, envoies, envoie, envoyions, envoyiez, envoient.* Imperf subj: *envoyasse, envoyasses, envoyât, envoyassions, envoyassiez, envoyassent.* Pres part: *envoyant.* Past part: *envoyé, envoyée, envoyés, envoyées.* Aux: *avoir: envoyer qlqch à qlqn,* to send sth to sn; *envoyer qlqn (pour) faire qlqch,* to send sn to do sth; *envoyer chercher qlqch,* to send for sth/to look for sth. When followed by infinitive with pronoun objects, and for omission of following reflexive pronoun, see PRONOUNS ¶12, ¶14.

-er, **verbs**: for verbs so ending see VERBS ¶1.

ès, in the: *en + les:* now used **only** in degree titles: *maître ès arts,* Master of Arts (MA).

espérer, to hope: *espérer qlqch,* to hope **for** sth; *espérer qlqch de qlqn,* to hope for sth of sn; *espérer faire qlqch,* to hope to do sth (**but** sometimes in spoken language: *espérer de faire qlqch* is used); *espérer en qlqn/qlqch,* to trust in sn/sth (= put one's hope in); *j'espère qu'il viendra,* I hope he will come. Like *céder:* takes *è* before *e*-mute endings, **but** retains *é* in the future stem, and elsewhere, eg: *j'espère, ils espèrent,* **but** *j'espérerai, espérant, espéré.* See VERBS ¶33iv for use with subjunctive in negative and interrogative.

esquimau, esquimaude, Eskimo: **adj.** And with capital 'E' = **noun.**

essayer, to try, test: *de faire qlqch,* to do sth; *s'essayer à qlqch,* to try one's hand at sth. Like *payer,* keeping *y* or optionally changing it to *i* before *e*-mute endings and in future stem.

essentiel, essentielle, adjective: proper, essential (to = *à*): *la raison est essentielle à l'homme,* reason is proper to (of the essence of) man: **note:** different spelling in French and English.

essuyer, to wipe, to dry. Like *employer.*

et, and: used as in English with a few minor differences: in literary French 'both . . . and' is translated by *et . . . et,* eg: *et le père et le fils,* both the father and the son: **but** the first *et* is omitted in more casual French. In a series, the last mentioned person or thing when preceded by *et* is not also preceded by a comma, eg: *les livres étaient grands, lourds et chers,* the books were big, heavy and expensive: *et* may precede a relative clause which follows an adjective or adjectival clause, which it further qualifies: *un homme digne, et qu'on pouvait prendre pour un prêtre,* a dignified man whom one might take for a priest (= 'a man dignified and one whom . . .'); *il est sauvage et qui habite la forêt,* he is wild and (one) who lives in the forest. **In numbers** *et* appears **only** in: 21, 31, 41, 51, 61 and 71 (*soixante et onze*), **but** not in 81 or 91. **No hyphens** are used in numbers before or after *et,* eg: thirty-one, *trente et un: et* is **not** used in any other numbers (see NUMBERS).

s'étonner, to be astonished, surprised: *de qlqch,* at sth; *de faire qlqch,* to do sth; *d'avoir fait qlqch,* at having done sth. With subjunctive see VERBS ¶33.

être, to be: **auxiliary verb** for all reflexive verbs and for verbs of change of position or condition, eg: *venir,* to come; *devenir,* to become. (Most of the verbs having *être* as auxiliary will be found listed separately.) Pres: *suis, es, est, sommes, êtes, sont.* Imperf: *étais, étais, était, étions, étiez, étaient.* Fut: *serai, seras, sera, serons, serez, seront.* Past hist: *fus, fus, fut, fûmes, fûtes, furent.* Imperat: *sois, soyons, soyez.* Pres subj: *sois, sois, soit, soyons, soyez, soient.* Imperf subj: *fusse, fusse, fût, fussions, fussiez, fussent.* Pres part: *étant* (invariable). Past part: *été* (invariable). **Auxiliary** = *avoir,* eg: *j'ai été,* I have been; *elle avait été,* she had been; *être à qlqn,* to belong to sn, eg: *ce livre est à moi,* this book is mine/belongs to me; *c'est à vous à faire qlqch,* it's for you (your duty) to do sth: for *c'est, ce sont,* see PRONOUNS ¶23 – 31. Adjectives which follow the verb *être* as its complement, and qualify its subject, agree with the subject in gender and number: *la maison est grande,* the house is big.

eux, elles, them. See PRONOUNS ¶15 – 17. See also *elle.*

even: adverb: *même:* I shall go even if/even though it rains (= even though it should rain), *j'irai, quand même il pleuvrait;* even now, *à l'instant, en ce moment;* even as he speaks, *(tout) comme il parle;* even so (= nevertheless), *tout de même.* (See *même* for the many different meanings and uses of this word.)

ever: have you ever done sth? *avez-vous jamais fait qlqch?* for ever/ever after, *pour toujours, à jamais;* I shall not ever do it (= I shall never do it), *je ne le ferai jamais.*

every

i. **adjective: every** = **each,** *chaque:* each boy, *chaque garçon;* each tree, *chaque arbre;* each girl, *chaque fille:* **every** = **all the, tous les, toutes les:** every boy, *tous les garçons;* every tree, *tous les arbres;* every girl, *toutes les filles* (**or** all the boys, all the trees, all the girls); every day, *tous les jours;* every other day, *tous les deux jours*

ii. **pronoun: every** (single) one, *chacun, chacune,* eg: there were ten men – every one of them wore a hat, *il y avait dix hommes – chacun d'eux portait* (singular verb) *un chapeau.*

everyone: *tout le monde* (verb in singular): everyone was on the beach, *tout le monde était sur la plage;* everyone came to see the king, *tous sont venus voir le roi* (= a less usual construction: verb in plural).

everything: *tout:* I know everything (= all), *je sais tout*; I have given you everything, *je vous ai donné tout.* (See *tout.*)

exceller, to excel: *à faire qlqch,* at/in doing sth.

except: preposition
  i.   except/except for = *excepté,* eg: there was nothing to see except (for) the snow, *il n'y avait rien à voir excepté la neige*
  ii. except = apart from = *hors,* eg: apart from us there is no one here, *hors nous il n'y a personne ici.* **Note**: *hors* when meaning 'except' is used before a noun, pronoun or number: they have all gone, except two or three, *ils sont tous partis, hors deux ou trois:* **but** it can be used with *de* before an infinitive, eg: there was nothing to do except to eat it, *il n'y avait rien à faire hors de le manger.* For other uses see *hors.* See also **each** and *sauf.*

exciter, to excite, incite, rouse: *qlqn à faire . . . ,* sn to do . . .

excuser, to excuse: *excuser qlqch à qlqn,* to excuse sn for sth; *excuser qlqn d'avoir fait qlqch,* to excuse sn for having done sth; *de faire qlqch,* from doing sth; *excuser qlqn auprès de qlqn,* make excuses to sn for sth; *s'excuser,* to ask pardon, make one's excuses; *s'excuser d'avoir fait qlqch,* to excuse oneself for having done sth; *être excusable d'avoir fait qlqch,* to be excusable for having done sth.

exempt, -e, adjective: *de qlqch,* exempt from sth.

s'exercer, de faire qlqch, to train oneself to do sth.

exhorter, to exhort: *qlqn à faire qlqch,* sn to do sth.

experimenté à (or *dans*) *qlqch,* experienced in sth.

exprès*, expresse, adjective: precise, distinct. Adverb: *expressément,* plainly, expressly. **Also** as adverb: *exprès*,* on purpose (*-*s* sounds only in the adjective).

express, **noun** or invariable **adjective**: *un (train) express,* an express train.

exquis, -e, adjective: exquisite. Adverb: *exquisément,* exquisitely.

extorquer, to extort: *qlqch à qlqn,* sth from sn.

-eyer, **verbs** retain the *-y-* throughout with **no** accent before the *-y-,* eg: *susseyer,* to lisp: *il susseye.* Such verbs are few in number and not often used.

F

fâcher, to anger: *être fâché contre qlqn,* to be angry with sn; *de qlqch,* about sth; *se fâcher,* to get angry (*contre qlqn,* with sn; *de qlqch,* about sth); *se fâcher avec qlqn,* to fall out with sn; *il me fâche de le dire,* I'm sorry to say it.

faillir, to fail: rare except in infinitive and in fut: *faillirai*, etc. Condit: *faillirais*, etc. Past hist: *faillis, faillîmes*, etc. Compound tenses: *j'ai failli*, etc. Pres part: *faillant: faillir faire qlqch*, to just miss/escape from doing sth (nearly do sth); *il a failli tomber*, he nearly fell; *le cœur lui a failli*, his heart failed him (he lacked the courage, etc); to fail at sth, *faillir à qlqch:* **faire faillite**, to go bankrupt.

faim, fem: hunger: *j'ai faim*, I am hungry; *avoir grand-faim*, to be very hungry.

faire, to do, to make. Pres: *fais, fais, fait, faisons, faites, font.* Imperf: *faisais, -ais, -ait, -ions, -iez, -aient.* Fut: *ferai, feras, fera, ferons, ferez, feront.* Past hist: *fis, fis, fit, fîmes, fîtes, firent.* Imperat: *fais, faisons, faites.* Pres subj: *fasse, fasses, fasse, fassions, fassiez, fassent.* Imperf subj: *fisse, fisses, fît, fissions, fissiez, fissent.* Pres part: *faisant.* Past part: *fait, -e, -s, -es.* Aux: **avoir***: faire qlqch*, to do/make sth; *ce qui est à faire*, that which is to be done; *un domestique/une bonne à tout faire*, a general servant capable of doing everything; *je lui ai fait faire son devoir*, I made him do his duty/homework/ task (= 'I to him made . . .'); *il la* fit bâtir par son ami* (**or** *à son ami*), he had it built (note **infinitive** = to build) by his friend (if in a compound tense, eg: *l'a fait bâtir*, the past participle *fait* does **not** agree with *l':* fem = 'it', because he did not 'make the house' but 'made to build'); *elle les fît (se**) laver*, she made them wash (themselves); *il lui* fait se** diriger vers l'église*, he makes him go towards the church (*the pronoun object is placed **before** faire, not before the infinitive of which it may appear to be the object: it is usually in the accusative case: but the dative is sometimes better. **The reflexive pronoun may be omitted unless necessary to avoid misunderstanding). For *faire* followed by an infinitive with its own object pronouns: see PRONOUNS ¶12.

falloir, to be necessary: impersonal verb (subject *il*). Pres: *il faut.* Imperf: *il fallait.* Fut: *il faudra.* Past hist: *il fallut.* Pres subj: *il faille.* Imperf subj: *il fallût.* No present participle. Past part: *fallu* (invariable). Aux: third person sing of the relevant tense of **avoir***: il faut manger pour vivre*, it is necessary to eat (in order) to live. **Also** used to translate 'must', eg: *il faut que je le fasse*, I must do it = it is necessary that I do it (subjunctive in the dependent clause). **Also** = to need: *il lui faut un stylo plus grand*, he needs a bigger pen (= 'it to him is necessary a bigger pen'); *il lui faut de l'argent*, he needs some money (= 'it to us is necessary some money'). **Also** = have to: *c'est un livre qu'il me faut lire*, it's a book I have to read. **Note**: *comme il faut*, as it should be, as is right and proper; *il le faut* **or** *il faut*, it must be (done); *il fallait voir!* you should have seen it! *pourquoi faut-il le faire?* why must it be done? **s'en falloir**, to be wanting, to fall short; *il s'en faut (de beaucoup)!* (very) far from it! *il s'en faut (de beaucoup) qu'il (ne*) puisse le faire*, he is (very) far from being able to do it (it falls (far) short of his being able to do it); *peu s'en faut*, not far from it; *il s'en est peu fallu qu'il (ne*) l'ait tué*, he/it nearly killed him (*ne, pleonastic, is optional); *il s'en est peu fallu qu'il **ne** l'ait **pas** vu*, he nearly didn't see him (in the negative *ne . . . pas* is used normally. **Note** the subjunctive in the dependent clauses); *Jean n'est pas si intelligent que son frère, il s'en faut* *beaucoup,* John is not so intelligent as his brother, far from it (by a long chalk); *Jean n'a pas tant de vaches que son frère, il s'en faut de** beaucoup,* John has not so many cows as his brother, far from it (John has not nearly so many . . .) (**without *de* when comparing a quality, with *de* when a quantity is compared).

fatiguer, to tire: *être fatigué de (faire) qlqch,* to be tired of (doing) sth; *fatiguer qlqn par qlqch,* to tire sn with sth; *se fatiguer,* to get tired; *se fatiguer de faire qlqch,* to tire of doing sth; *se fatiguer à faire qlqch,* to tire oneself (out) doing sth. Conjugated regularly.

faux, **adjective**: fem = *fausse,* false. **Nouns**: **masc** = forgery: **fem** = scythe.

fear: verb: to fear: to be afraid of sth, *avoir peur de qlqch;* to be afraid to do sth, *avoir peur de faire qlqch;* he fears/is frightened to go up, *il a peur de monter;* never fear! *n'ayez pas peur!* to fear that/be afraid that, *avoir peur que + ne +* subjunctive, eg: I fear that/I am afraid that he will (= may) do it, *j'ai peur qu'il ne le fasse* (the *ne* has the sense of 'lest': I fear lest he may do it). In the **negative** *ne . . . pas* is used normally: I do **not** fear that he will die, *je n'ai pas peur qu'il meure* (subjunctive). Alternatively, use *craindre,* to fear: he fears dogs, *il craint les chiens;* to fear to do sth, *craindre de faire qlqch;* there is nothing to fear, *il n'y a rien à craindre;* I fear he may do it, *je crains qu'il ne le fasse* (with *ne* + subjunctive: see VERBS ¶33viii). In the **interrogative** *ne* is usually (but not always) omitted, eg: do you fear that he will (= may) do it? *craignez-vous qu'il (ne) le fasse?* In a **negative interrogative**: do you not fear that he may do it? *ne craignez-vous pas qu'il (ne) le fasse?* In a **double negative**, *ne . . . pas* is necessary for the second negative, eg: do you not fear that he may **not** do it? *ne craignez-vous pas qu'il ne le fasse pas?* **Nouns**: fear = *la peur, la crainte* (usually interchangeable): a great fear, *une peur bleue;* for fear of, *de peur de;* from fear, *par peur;* to die of fear, *mourir de peur* **or** *de crainte;* for fear lest he come (for fear that he may come – the *ne* is sometimes omitted), *de crainte qu'il (ne) vienne;* for fear of the enemy, *de crainte de l'ennemi* (**also**: *dans la crainte de* and *par crainte de*). See *craindre.*

Feasts and Festivals, etc, are preceded by the definite article: New Year's Day, *le jour de l'an, le nouvel an;* Lent, *le carême;* Ash Wednesday, *le mercredi de cendres;* Good Friday, *le vendredi saint.* **Note**: capitals used for: Whitsun, *la Pentecôte;* All Saints' Day, *la Toussaint, le jour de la Toussaint;* St John's Day, *la (fête de) Saint-Jean;* advent, *l'Avent* (masc). **Christmas**, usually **without article**, and is then **masculine**: Christmas, *Noël;* Happy Christmas! *joyeux Noël!* Christmas Day, *le jour de Noël;* the feast of Christmas, *la fête de Noël:* **if with article** is **feminine**: at Christmas, *à Noël* or *à la Noël;* Christmas Eve, *la veille de Noël.* **Easter** is without article: *Pâques* (sometimes spelt without the final *s*), treated as **masculine singular**, eg: when Easter had arrived, *quand Pâques était arrivé.* **Note**: *Pâques* meaning 'Easter duties' (the partaking of Easter Communion) is **feminine plural**: to make a good Easter Communion, *faire de bonnes Pâques.* It is **also** feminine plural when wishing 'a Happy Easter', *joyeuses Pâques*. **The Jewish festival**, the time of the Passover (Paschal time), *le temps de la Pâque*.

feindre, to feign: *feindre la mort*, to feign death; *feindre de tomber*, to pretend to fall. Like *craindre*.

féliciter, to congratulate: *qlqn de* (or *sur*) *qlqch*, sn for (or on) sth.

Feminines: see ADJECTIVES ¶2, ¶3, and NOUNS ¶1ff.

feu

    i.   **noun** (masc): fire: plur = *les feux: un coup de feu*, a shot (with a firearm = *une arme à feu*); *les feux d'artifice*, fireworks

    ii.   **adjective** (fem = *feue*): late (ie: recently deceased). Often used before the article or possessive adjective, and is then invariable: *feu le roi*, the late king; *feu la reine*, the late queen; *feu ma tante*, my late aunt: **but** can be used after the article or possessive adjective: *le feu roi, ma feue tante* (in which case it agrees). Plural: *feus, feues* (rare).

fidèle, **adjective**: faithful: to = *à*. **Noun**: *un/une fidèle*, believer, true friend.

fier, fière, adjective: proud of = *de*. Adverb: *fièrement*, proudly, thoroughly.

se fier, to trust: *se fier à qlqn*, to trust (put one's trust in) sn; *se fier à qlqn du soin de qlqch*, to entrust sn with the care of sth.

se figurer, to imagine: *se figurer le savoir*, to imagine ('kid oneself') that one knows it.

finir, to finish: *finir de faire qlqch*, to finish doing sth. See VERBS ¶13ff.

fils, (masc): son. Pronounced feess.

se flatter, to flatter oneself, to claim to be sth, *se flatter d'être qlqch*.

fois, fem: time as in: *six fois*, six times; *deux fois dix*, 2 x 10.

for

    i.   on behalf of, for the benefit of, for the purpose of, for the destination of = *pour*: for me, *pour moi*; for the poor, *pour les pauvres*; for one's country, *pour la patrie*; he has left for Paris/school, *il est parti pour Paris/l'école*

    ii.   for how long up to now = *depuis*: I have been waiting already for two hours, *j'attends déjà depuis deux heures*

    iii.   for how long in the past = *pendant*: I studied French for two years, *j'ai étudié le français pendant deux ans*

    iv.   for a proposed/planned period of time = *pour*: I am here for a month, *je suis ici pour un mois*

    v.   in order to do sth = *pour*: I am here in order to study the language, *je suis ici pour étudier la langue*

    vi.   from/as result of = *de*: to weep for joy, *pleurer de joie*

    vii.   on account of/because of = *blâmer/pardonner/punir/remercier de*, blame/forgive/punish/thank for: I thank you for (on account of) your letter, *je vous remercie de votre lettre* (*pour* is **also** used)

viii. because = ***car:*** he cries for it hurts, *il pleure car il fait mal*

ix. **'for'** not translated: (a) that is (im)possible for him, *cela lui est (im)possible* (b) I have paid for it, *je l'ai payé.*

forcer, to force: *forcer qlqn à faire qlqch*, to force sn to do sth; *être forcé de faire qlqch*, be forced to do sth. Like ***placer*** with *ç* before endings starting with *a* or *o.*

***fort, -e*, adjective**: strong, firm, robust, able, loud: *du café fort*, some strong coffee; *une voix forte*, a strong (loud) voice; *bien fort*, very strong; *être fort à, en, sur qlqch*, to be strong (good) at, in, on sth, eg: *il est fort aux sports*, he is good at sports (games); *c'est fort ça!* **or** *c'est un peu fort!* that's a bit strong/thick! *se faire fort* de faire qlqch*, to claim to be able to do sth, to boast that one can do sth; *se porter fort* pour*, to claim to be up to/strong enough for (*in these two constructions if the subject is feminine *fort* should be invariable, **but** *elle se fait forte de, elle se porte forte de . . .* is permitted). **Noun**: *un fort, une forte*, a strong man, a strong woman. As **adverb**

i. very: *il est fort fatigué*, he is very tired; *fort bien*, very well

ii. vigorously, hard, strongly, loud(ly): *chanter fort*, to sing loudly; *bien plus fort*, much louder/more strongly, much harder.

fou, adjective: foolish, mad, silly: masc plur = *fous:* masc sing before a vowel or *h*-mute = *fol:* fem sing = *folle:* fem plur = *folles.*

fourmiller, to swarm: *de qlqch*, with sth.

fournir, to furnish, supply: *qlqch à qlqn*, sth to sn; *qlqn de qlqch*, sn with sth; *se fournir de qlqch*, to furnish oneself with sth.

frémir or ***frissoner,*** to shudder, tremble, thrill: *de peur*, with fear.

frire, to fry: (transitive or intransitive) defective verb: **only** found in following persons and tenses. Pres: *fris, fris, frit* (no plural). No imperfect. Fut: *frirai, -as, -a, -ons, -ez, -ont*. No past historic. Imperat: *fris*. No present participle. Past part: *frit, frite*. Aux: ***avoir***, from which all compound tenses can be formed. *For missing parts use *faire frire*. *Pres: *nous faisons frire qlqch*, we fry sth.

se frotter, to rub: *contre qlqch*, against sth; *se frotter à qlqn/qlqch*, to associate with sn, 'rub shoulders with sn', to come against sn/sth.

from

i. usually ***de***, which elides with the definite article: *de + le = du, de + les = des*, **but** *de l'*, and *de la* are **not** elided: from the garden, *du jardin;* from the children, *des enfants;* from the man, *de l'homme;* from the town, *de la ville*

ii. from the moment of = ***dès:*** from the moment of his arrival, *dès son arrivée*

iii. from = since (= from that time onwards) = ***depuis/à partir de:*** since that day, *depuis/à partir de ce jour-là*

iv. from = out of = *dans:* to drink from a glass, *boire dans un verre;* to take from a drawer/box, *prendre dans un tiroir/une boîte*

v. far from = *loin de*

vi. from Mr Brown's = *de chez monsieur Brun;* from the grocer's, *de chez l'épicier*

vii. from the way he behaved/his manner = *d'après sa manière*

viii. from = on behalf of = *de la part de:* tell it to him from me (on my behalf), *dites-le-lui de ma part.*

fuir, to flee, fly = escape, shun, avoid: *fuir qlqn*, to flee from sn; *fuir qlqch*, to shun/avoid sth. Pres: *fuis, fuis, fuit, fuyons, fuyez, fuient.* Imperf: *fuyais, fuyais, fuyait, fuyions, fuyiez, fuyaient.* Fut: *fuirai, fuiras, fuira, fuirons, fuirez, fuiront.* Past hist: *fuis, fuis, fuit, fuîmes, fuîtes, fuirent.* Imperat: *fuis, fuyons, fuyez.* Pres subj: *fuie, fuies, fuie, fuyions, fuyiez, fuient.* Imperf subj: *fuisse, fuisses, fuît, fuissions, fuissiez, fuissent.* Pres part: *fuyant.* Past part: *fui, fuie, fuis, fuies.* Aux: *avoir.*

fun: *gaieté* (fem): *plaisanterie* (fem): *amusement* (masc): for fun, *pour rire;* to have (lots of) fun, *s'amuser (bien);* we had lots of fun, *nous nous sommes bien amusés* (**note** position of *bien*); to make fun of sn/sth, *se moquer de qlqn/qlqch.*

furieux, furieuse, adjective: furious, angry: *contre* (sometimes *après*) *qlqn*, with sn; *de qlqch*, about sth. Adverb: *furieusement*, furiously.

future: the time to come: *l'avenir* (masc). In the future, henceforth, *à l'avenir;* sn with a future (showing promise), *qlqn qui a de l'avenir;* in the near future, *dans un avenir prochain;* his future wife, *sa future;* her future husband, *son futur.*

Future Tense = *le futur;* 'in the future tense' = *au futur.* The stem of **all** future tenses ends in *-r-*, and endings are **always** *-r/ai, -r/as, -r/a, -r/ons, -r/ez, -r/ont.* For use of the future tense and further details see VERBS ¶15, ¶16. The **immediate future** can be expressed, as in English, by using *aller*, to go: I am going to do it now, *je vais le faire maintenant.* The future **stem** is **also** used with the conditional tense, **but** with the **imperfect** endings: see VERBS ¶18.

G

gagner, to gain, win: *gagner à faire qlqch*, to gain/win by doing sth; *gagner qlqch à qlqn*, to win sth from sn; *gagner qlqn de vitesse*, to outrun sn; *gagner sur qlqn*, to prevail upon sn; *gagner qlqn à . . .*, to win sn over to . . .

garde, guard (see NOUNS ¶10). Used in compounds does **not** take *-s* in plural, eg: *un garde-chasse*, a game-keeper. Plural: *des garde-chasses* or *-chasse.*

se garder de qlqch, to beware of sth.

Gender: see NOUNS in Grammar Section. Nouns that change meaning with gender ¶14.

gêner, to inconvenience, trouble, disturb, get in way of: *j'espère que je ne vous gêne pas,* I hope I don't trouble you; *se gêner pour faire qlqch,* to put oneself out to do sth; *ne pas se gêner pour faire qlqch,* not to scruple to do sth.

gens, plur: people: adjectives before or after are masc, eg: *tous les gens heureux:* **but** if **immediately preceded** by an adj **not** ending in *e*-mute in sing, all adjs are fem: *toutes les vieilles gens heureuses* (sing: *vieux*).

gentil, gentille, adjective: nice, kind, pretty: *pour* **or** *avec qlqn,* with, towards sn; *vous êtes très gentil,* you are very kind; *c'est (bien) gentil à vous de le faire,* it is (very) kind of you to do it. Adverb: **gentiment**, nicely, gently, in a well-behaved way (of children). (English adverb: kindly = *avec bonté, volontiers, avec bienveillance.)*

Geographical Names are spelt with a capital initial letter as in English, including a person of a certain nationality, eg: an Englishman, *un Anglais:* **but** not for an adjective of nationality, eg: an English lady, *une dame anglaise:* **nor** for a national language, eg: he speaks English, he learns French: *il parle (l')anglais, il apprend le français.* The **definite article** is usually used with names of countries, continents, geographical areas: *l'Europe,* fem; *la France,* etc. **All continents are feminine,** as are most countries, **but** there are numerous exceptions. **Important countries which are masculine are**: *l'Afghanistan, le Brésil, le Canada, le Chili, le Danemark, les États-Unis, l'Israël, le Japon, le Liban, le Mexique, le Paraguay, l'Uruguay* and *le Zoulouland.* The gender of other geographical names varies considerably: **masculine** are: *Athènes, Berlin, Cambridge, Dublin, Édimbourg* (sic), *Londres, Lyon* (without final *-s*), *Madrid, Moscou, New-York, Oxford, Paris, Pèkin, Strasbourg, Zurich* (the ch sounds 'k'): **feminine** are: *Alicante, Bâle, Bruxelles, Calcutta, Cologne, Copenhague, Dieppe, Genève, Lille, Nice, Rome, Sydney, Vienne.* A few French towns are used with the article and their gender is then obvious: *le Havre, la Rochelle* **and** some other towns are usually given the article, eg: *le Caire* (Cairo). Mountains, rivers and provinces, like countries, are usually used with the article: *les Alpes, le Rhin, le Rhône, la Loire, la Seine, la Tamise* (Thames), *la Normandie.* For prepositions to or from Countries, etc, see **Countries**.

gésir, to lie (be prostrate). Used **only** in the following persons and tenses. Pres: *il gît, nous gisons, vous gisez, ils gisent.* Imperf: *gisais, -ais, -ait, -ions, -iez, -aient.* Pres part: *gisant* (**or** *gissant*). **Note**: on gravestones: 'here lies', *ci-gît.*

get: for 'get' used in such English phrases as 'get on', 'get going', 'get off', 'don't get frightened', etc, some alternative in better English must be found before translating, eg: 'advance', 'begin', 'go away', 'do not fear', etc. There is **no** French equivalent for 'get' as used in loose English.

gît, gisant, ci-gît, see **gésir** above.

go

    i.   depart: see ***aller, partir***

    ii. 'work' (as for a watch, etc): see ***marcher***

    iii. go out: see *sortir*

    iv. go in: see *entrer*

    v. go down: see *descendre*

    vi. go up: see *monter*

    vii. go away: see *aller, s'en aller: aller* can be used, like 'go' in English, to express the immediate future: I am going to do it now, *je vais le faire maintenant.*

got: as in 'I have got to do sth': use 'must' or 'have to': see *falloir* or *devoir.*

goulu, -e, adjective: gluttonous, greedy. Adverb: **goulûment**, gluttonously, greedily.

goûter, to taste, try (the taste of), relish (the taste of): *goûter à qlqch*, to sample (taste of) sth. **Noun**: *le goûter*, afternoon snack ('tea').

grace, fem: favour, grace: *grace à qlqn/qlqch*, thanks to sn, sth.

grand, -e, adjective: usually placed before the noun

    i. **large, big** (as compared with other things): *l'éléphant est un grand animal*, the elephant is a big animal; *Paris est une grande ville*, Paris is a large town

    ii. **great** (= renowned, famous, accomplished, etc): *un grand poète*, a great poet

    iii. **tall**: *un grand homme brun*, a tall dark man: **but** 'tall' alone is often placed after the noun: *un homme grand*, a tall man

    iv. **note** also: *une grande personne*, a grown-up (adult); *un grand froid*, a severe frost; *au grand air*, in the open air (**also** *en plein air*)

    v. **wide**, but better to use *large*

    vi. *grand* normally follows a noun if that noun is further qualified: *un garçon grand pour son âge*, a boy tall for his age

    vii. *grand-* as **prefix**: **note** the use of *grand-* in the following feminines: *grand-mère*, grandmother; *grand-tante*, great aunt; *pas grand-chose*, not much; *grand-messe*, Solemn (High) Mass; *grand-route*, main road; *grand-faim*, great hunger; *grand-soif*, great thirst; *grand-peur*, great fear: **and** a few other similar phrases in which *grand-* is used as prefix, and in which, **if the noun is feminine**, it **remains unchanged. In the masculine plural**, *grand-* takes *-s: les grands-pères*, etc, **but** not usually in the feminine: *les grand-mères*, although this rule is **not** always adhered to, and 'Grand Duchess', as a title, is *la grande-duchesse*. The prefix *grand-* before a feminine noun was formerly written *grand'*, and is sometimes so spelt. See also **big**.

grand-chose, indefinite pronoun: used with *ne . . . pas:* has a negative sense: nothing much, no great matter: *ce n'est pas grand-chose*, it's not much, nothing much, of no importance: **without** a verb it is used with *pas* by itself: *—Qu'est-ce que vous avez là? —Pas grand-chose!* 'What have you got there?' 'Not much!'.

grave, adjective: heavy, serious, solemn. **Adverbs**

    i. *gravement*, gravely, solemnly

    ii. *grièvement*, grievously, seriously, sadly.

grave, accent: see **Accents**.

great: see *grand* above.

gré , noun (masc): will, good will, wish, inclination: *à son gré*, to one's (his) liking; *bon gré* , *mal gré* , willy-nilly; *de bon gré*, willingly.

grec, *grecque*, **adjective** and **noun**: Greek: with capital for a Greek (person), eg: *un Grec*, *une Grecque* (retains the *-c-*): **but** *le grec*, (the) Greek (language); *le grec ancien ou modern*, ancient or modern Greek.

grêler, to hail (hailstones). Impersonal verb, conjugated regularly in 3rd person singular only, retaining *ê* throughout: *il grêle, grêlait, grêlera*. No imperative. Imperf subj: *il grêlât*. Pres part: *grêlant*. Past part: *grêlé*.

grêlon, masc: hailstone: *grésil*, masc: powdered hailstone, sleet, calx.

grimper, to climb: *grimper une montagne, l'escalier*, to climb a mountain, climb the stairs; *grimper sur un arbre, sur un mur*, climb (up into/on to) a tree, a wall; *grimper à qlqch*, to climb up sth (with special effort, 'shin' up), eg: *à une corde*, up a rope; *à un mât*, up a mast; *à une falaise*, up a cliff.

se gripper contre qlqn, take a dislike to sn.

gronder, to grumble: *sur/au sujet de qlqch*, about sth; *contre qlqn*, at sn; **to scold**: *qlqn d'avoir fait qlqch*, sn for having done sth.

gros, *grosse*, big, large, bulky, corpulent: *gros de*, fraught with.

guéer, to ford, to rinse. Like *agréer*: **but** preferably use *passer à gué* (masc) for 'to ford' and *rincer* (like *placer*) for 'to rinse'.

guère
- i. with *ne* = hardly, not much, not very: *il n'a guère d'argent*, he has hardly any money; *il n'a guère trois ans plus que moi*, he is scarcely three years older than I am; *elle n'a guère moins de vingt ans*, she is scarcely less than twenty years old; *il ne l'aime guère plus que l'autre*, he hardly likes him/her/it better than the other; *l'élève n'est guère diligent*, the pupil is not very diligent
- ii. *guère* = hardly anything: *ce nom ne me dit guère*, this name means hardly anything to me; *celui qui ne voit guère n'a guère à dire*, he who sees hardly anything has hardly anything to say. Occasionally where there is no verb *guère* means 'hardly' without *ne*: *j'ai peut-être dix francs, mais guère plus*, I have perhaps ten francs, but hardly more.

guérir
- i. to get well
- ii. to cure: *qlqn/qlqch*, sn, sth (from illness or from some other defect); *se guérir*, to get well.

guest: the visitor: *l'hôte, l'hôtesse* (these two words also mean 'host' and 'hostess'): **a guest at a feast, party** = *un* or *une convive*, **or** *un invité, une invitée*.

guide, **masc** = a guide (person), guide-book: **fem** = a driving rein.

guillemets: see **Punctuation**.

H

h-aspirate, *h*-mute: h is **never** sounded at the beginning of a French word, but the *h*-aspirate is treated as a consonant so that there is **no** elision before it, eg: *la haie,* the hedge; *de haut en bas,* from top to bottom: **and** there is no liaison with the final consonant of the preceding word, eg: *le(s) héros,* the heroes: in the case of the *h*-**mute** the word is treated as if it started with a vowel – that is, there **is** elision: *l'herbe,* the grass: **and** in speech there is liaison with the final consonant of the preceding word, thus, *les héroïnes* (the heroines) sounds: '*lay zéroïnes*'. There is **no** rule governing which words start with *h*-mute and which with *h*-aspirate; dictionaries normally show the *h*-aspirate with some mark before the initial, thus: ***h*** at the beginning of a French word indicates *h*-aspirate. The majority of words starting *ha*- are *h*-aspirate (**but** with very many exceptions): **all** the words starting *hy*- are *h*-mute: among other words, *h*-mute is somewhat commoner than *h*-aspirate. See also **Elision** and **Liaison**.

habiter, to live in, inhabit: *j'habite une grande maison,* I live in a big house; *j'habite rue de la Gare,* I live in Station Road; *j'habite la France,* I live in France (**or** use *demeurer*).

habituer, to accustom: *qlqn à faire qlqch,* sn to do sth; *s'habituer à qlqn/qlqch,* to get used to sn/sth.

had

     i.   **had to** = must: translated by the imperfect or perfect of *devoir*, eg: he had to do it, *il devait le faire*

    ii.   **had** is used as auxiliary in both the pluperfect and the past anterior (the English pluperfect translates both): I had spoken, *j'avais parlé, j'eus parlé.* For the difference between these two tenses see VERBS ¶24, ¶25.

haïr, to hate: keeps the diæresis (¨) (called *tréma* in French) over the *i* throughout, **except** in the singular of present and imperative: and thus there is **no circumflex** in past historic or imperfect subjunctive: the *h*- is aspirate, so there is **no** elision of *je*, and **no** liaison after *nous, vous* or *ils*. Pres: *je hais* (pronounced *hé*), *hais, hait, nou(s) haïssons, vou(s) haïssez, il(s) haïssent.* Imperf: *je haïssais, -ais, -ait, -ions, -iez, -aient.* Fut: *haïrai, -as, -a, -ons, -ez, -ont.* Past hist: *haïs, haïs, haït, haïmes, haïtes, haïrent.* Imperat: *hais, haïssons, haïssez.* Pres subj: *haïsse, -es, -e, haïssions, -iez, -ent.* Imperf subj: *haïsse, haïsses, haït, haïssions, haïssiez, haïssent.* Pres part: *haïssant.* Past part: *haï, haïe.*

haleter, to pant, gasp for breath. Like *mener*. The *h* is aspirate: *je halète* (with **no** liaison between subject and verb).

half

    i.   *moitié* (a) **noun** (fem): for half the time he was asleep, *pendant la moitié du temps il était endormi;* half the population, *la moitié de la population;* he has told me only half the story, *il ne m'a dit que la moitié de l'histoire;* three is the half of six, *trois est la moitié de six;* you can have it at half price, *vous pouvez l'avoir à moitié prix* (b) **adverb:** *à moitié:* this apple is half bad, *cette pomme est à moitié pourrie;* he was half dead, *il était à moitié mort* (**but** *il était demi mort* is also used)

    ii.   *demi* (a) **noun** (masc): a mathematical half: two halves make a whole, *deux demis valent un entier: un demi* is also used for a 'half back' in football (b) **adjective:** *demi, demie:* two and a half times bigger, *deux et demie fois plus grand* (**note** agreement in gender with *fois,* fem); it is half past midday/midnight, *il est midi/minuit et demi;* half past two, *deux heures et demie* (agreement with *heure,* fem = 'and one half hour'); half an hour, *une demi-heure*;* a half bottle, *une demi-bouteille** (*when coming before a noun *demi* is joined to the noun by a hyphen and is invariable); the half hour has sounded, *la demie est sonnée;* this clock sounds (chimes) the half hours, *cette pendule sonne les demies* (*demie* agrees with *heures,* understood). Although *demi* means an actual physical or numerical half in size or number it is occasionally used more loosely, as in *demi-nu,* half naked (c) **adverb:** *à demi* (with **no** agreement): *la ville était à demi détruite,* the town was half destroyed; *il fait tout à demi,* he does everything by halves.

hardly: see *guère*

has just, had just, have just, done sth: I had just arrived, *je venais d'arriver;* he had just spoken, *il venait de parler,* etc, = **the imperfect of *venir* followed by *de* and the infinitive. I have just,** he **has just,** etc, **are similarly formed with the present of *venir*:** he has just arrived, *il vient d'arriver.*

hasarder, to risk: *de faire qlqch,* doing sth; *se hasarder à faire qlqch,* to risk doing sth, to take a chance at doing sth, to risk/to try doing sth.

he = *il:* when subject of verb: he speaks, *il parle;* does he speak? *parle-t-il?* **he** = *lui,* when complement or separated from verb: it is he, *c'est lui;* he or she, which one? *lui ou elle, lequel?* he did it, he did, *il l'a fait, lui.* **Note**: he who (speaks), *celui qui (parle).* See *il* and PRONOUNS ¶3, ¶4, ¶15 – 17, ¶19, ¶20.

her: as direct object of verb = *la:* we hit her, *nous la frappons;* 'it's her' (= it is she), *c'est elle;* I speak to her, *je lui parle.* See *elle* and **she**. After a preposition 'her' = *elle:* I come without her, *je viens sans elle.* See PRONOUNS ¶3 – 7, ¶15 – 17. *lui* = 'her' after a verb governing the preposition *à:* I give it her (= to her), *je le lui donne;* I obey her (see *obéir*), *je lui obéis.* (The preposition *à* is contained in *lui* = *à* + *elle.*) *à elle* can be used after the verb instead of *lui* before the verb if it is necessary to distinguish between 'him' and 'her', eg: I gave it to her, not to him, *je l'ai donné à elle, pas à lui.* For 'her' as possessive adjective (as in 'her book') see *son, sa, ses,* in ADJECTIVES ¶10 and PRONOUNS ¶15, ¶16 and ¶38.

hésiter, to hesitate: *à faire qlqch* (less common: *de faire qlqch*), to do sth.

heure, fem: hour. For use in telling time see **Time** and also **half** ii.

heureux, *heureuse*, adjective: happy: *de faire qlqch*, to do sth; *de qlqch*, with sth; *c'est fort heureux pour vous*, it's very lucky for you.

him: when **direct object** of a verb = *le:* he hits him, *il le frappe*. 'To him' as **indirect object** of verb = *lui:* they speak to him, *ils lui parlent;* give it to him, *donnez-le-lui*. **After a preposition** 'him' = *lui:* they arrive with him, *ils arrivent avec lui:* 'him' and 'to him' are both translated by *lui* before the verb when object of a French verb governing *à*, eg: I obey him (see *obéir*), *je lui obéis;* I give it to him, *je le lui donne*. See PRONOUNS ¶3ff and compare with **her** above. (**Note**: when used with a verb *lui* means 'to him', 'to her' and 'to it': **but** 'to it' meaning 'coming to it', 'going to it', and also 'thinking about it', etc = *y*, eg: we go to it = we go there, *nous y allons*. See *y*, *en* pronoun and **it** viii)

his: see *son*, *sa*, *ses*, ADJECTIVES ¶10, *sien* and PRONOUNS ¶38.

honnête, honest: *envers/avec*, towards/with sn.

honorer, to honour: *honorer qlqn/qlqch de sa présence*, to honour sn/sth with one's presence.

horrible à voir, horrible, dreadful, shocking to see.

hors, out, out of, without, beyond: *hors la loi*, outside the law; *hors ligne*, exceptional, very superior; *hors vous*, except for you; *hors de chez nous*, outside our home, outside where we live; *hors de danger*, out of danger; *hors d'haleine*, out of breath; *hors de combat*, no longer in the battle; *hors de soi*, out of oneself (eg: with fear, excitement, etc); *être hors (de) pair*, unequalled (above one's peers).

hostile, hostile: *à/envers qlqn*, towards sn.

hour: *heure* = fem. For telling time see **Time of Day** and **half** ii.

how

    i.   *comment* = in what way: how are you? *comment allez-vous?* I wouldn't know how to do it, *je ne saurais comment le faire*

    ii. *comme* (a) as/like: do it as I do (how I do, like me), *faites-le comme moi* (b) to what extent: *vous voyez bien comme il est gros*, just see how fat he is.

how many/much: *combien de:* how many apples have you bought? *combien de pommes* avez-vous achetées?** (*Note agreement.) how many books are in his room? *combien de livres se trouvent dans sa chambre?* how much money have you? *combien d'argent avez-vous?* Note: *combien* is followed by *de (d')* unless the meaning is 'of the': *combien de l'argent avez-vous retrouvé?* how much of the money have you found (recovered)?

huit, eight: the *h* is aspirate: before a noun starting with a vowel or *h*-mute the final *-t* is sounded, eg: *huit hommes:* **but** not before a consonant, eg: *hui(t) pommes:*

the -*t* is also sounded in dates, eg: *le hui̱t février:* and when used as a number of a king, etc, eg: *Henri hui̱t.*

hurler, to howl: *de douleur,* with pain: **but** 'together with' = *avec: hurler avec les autres,* to howl with the others.

Hyphens: although some laxity in the use of hyphens may be encountered their value is obvious, especially where they link conjunctive pronouns to the verb in questions and commands, and in compound nouns like *grand-père.*

I
I

i. **conjunctive pronoun** = *je*, with **no** capital letter except at start of a sentence. Used **only** as the subject of a verb: *je* elides before a vowel or *h*-mute, eg: I have, *j'ai;* I dwell, *j'habite: je* does **not** elide before *h*-aspirate, eg: I hate, *je hais:* nor after a verb: have I had? *ai-je eu?*

ii. **disjunctive pronoun** (when not subject or separate from verb): I = *moi:* it is I, *c'est moi;* no, not I, *non, pas moi;* who? I? *qui? moi?* there! I'll do it! *voilà! moi, je le ferai;* you and I, *vous et moi.* See PRONOUNS ¶3 – 5, ¶15, ¶16.

if (also, 'whether') see *si* i.

if only: provided that, *pourvu que:* subordinating conjunction followed by the subjunctive, eg: provided he comes! *pourvu qu'il vienne!* you may take my car provided you leave me my bike, *vous pouvez prendre ma voiture pourvu que vous me laissiez mon vélo;* if only I had the money! *pour peu que j'avais l'argent!*

il, personal pronoun = he, it (masc)

i. *il* usually translates both 'he' and 'it' (if masculine), and 'they' (masc) in its plural form *ils* – **except** when replaced by *ce* as explained in PRONOUNS ¶23, ¶24, ¶27, ¶33, ¶34

ii. *il* translates 'it' as the subject of *être* followed by an adjective if 'it' refers to something following that adjective, eg: *il est **facile** de voir la mer d'ici,* it is easy to see the sea from here; *il est **vrai** qu'il est riche,* it is true that he is rich; *il est **utile** à travailler,* it is useful to work. (For 'it' translated by *ce,* as subject of *être* followed by an adjective qualifying someone or something already referred to, see PRONOUNS ¶24 and ¶33.)

iii. *il* = it, before impersonal verbs, eg: *il faut,* it is necessary *(falloir); il advint,* it happened *(advenir):* and in verbs about the weather, *il pleut,* etc, it is raining, etc: see also **Impersonal Verbs**, below.

iv. *il* **must** be used for 'it' for telling or asking the **time**: *il est deux heures,* it is two o'clock; *il est midi,* it is midday; *quelle heure est-il?* what is the time? (= what hour is it?): but **not** for dates (see **Day** – end of entry and **Dates**)

v. *il* translates 'it', referring to a masculine noun, when it is the subject of a verb other than *être: j'attends le train; il doit arriver à trois heures,* I am waiting for the train; it's supposed to arrive at three o'clock; *j'ai lu ce livre; il a 500 pages,* I have read this book; it has 500 pages; *j'ai un nouveau stylo: il écrit bien,* I have a new pen: it writes well. See also *il y a* and **it,** below.

il y a, there is (literally 'it there has'). The *il* is invariable. The verb, *a,* is **always** 3rd person singular, **but** may alter in tense: *il y aura* = there will be; *il y avait* = there was/used to be; *il y aurait* = there would be. In the **negative**: *il n'y a pas,* there is not. In the **interrogative**: *y a-t-il?* is there? In literary French and poetry *il y a* is sometimes replaced by *il est.* See also **Impersonal Verbs** below and *y.*

Imperative: see VERBS ¶19.

Impersonal Verbs and phrases: impersonal verbs, and verbs used impersonally, normally have *il* as their subject (*ce* is rare): these include all verbs referring to the weather: *il pleut,* it is raining; *il tonne,* it thunders, etc: see **Weather.** The verb *faire* is used impersonally in such phrases as: *il fait chaud,* it is hot; *il fait froid,* it is cold, etc: also usually referring to the weather. Some impersonal verbs can be used figuratively with another subject, eg: *les dieux tonnent,* the gods thunder. Some impersonal verbs can be given an object: *il pleut/grêle de grosses pierres,* it rains/hails big stones. A number of non-impersonal verbs can be used impersonally, eg: *chaque jour il part un train pour Paris,* each day there leaves a train for Paris. The phrase *il y a* (= there is/are) is an example of *avoir* used impersonally in this way (see *il y a* above). The verb *falloir* is a very frequently used impersonal verb: *il me faut le faire,* **it** is necessary for me to do it (I have to do it). There are a number of **impersonal phrases** which have no subject, eg: *advienne que pourra,* come what may; *n'importe,* it doesn't matter; *peu s'en faut,* all but, very nearly, eg: *–Il est mort? –Peu s'en faut!* 'Is he dead?' 'All but!' *mieux vaut/vaudrait,* it is/it would be better (see *valoir*); *suffit!* **or** *cela suffit!* = enough of that! that's enough! See *importer* below.

impitoyable, pitiless: *à* **or** *vers,* towards.

implacable, implacable: *à (l'égard de) qlqn,* towards sn.

importer

    i. to matter, to be of consequence: regular impersonal verb – used in third person singular **only**: *il importe,* it is important; *n'importe quoi,* no matter what; *qu'importe?* what does it matter? *peu importe,* it matters little; *il lui importe de faire qlqch,* it is important for him to do sth/important that he should do sth; *il importe de faire qlqch,* it is necessary to do sth

    ii. to import. Regular -*er* verb in **all** persons and tenses.

importun, -e, adjective: importunate, intrusive, troublesome: *à,* towards. Adverb: *importunément,* importunately.

impuni, -e, adjective: unpunished. Adverb: *impunément,* with impunity.

in: preposition: see *à* iii, *dans* and *en,* preposition. For 'in' a country see **Countries.**

incliner, to incline: *être incliné à faire qlqch*, to be inclined/disposed to do sth; *incliner qlqn à faire qlqch*, to influence sn to do sth; *incliner à qlqch*, to incline towards sth.

incommode, adjective: inconvenient. Adverb: ***incommodément***, inconveniently.

incommoder, to inconvenience: *cela ne m'incommodera pas (de faire)*, that will not inconvenience me (to do).

incongru, -e, adjective: incongruous. Adverb: ***incongrûment***, incongruously.

inconnu, -e, **adjective**: unknown: *de tout le monde*, by everyone; *inconnu à moi*, unknown to me; *une quantité inconnue*, an unknown quantity (in mathematics). **Noun**: *un(e) inconnu(e)*, a stranger.

Indefinite Adjectives: see ADJECTIVES ¶13.

Indefinite Article: see ARTICLES ¶4.

Indefinite Pronouns: see PRONOUNS ¶50.

s'indigner, to be indignant: *contre qlqn*, with sn.

Indirect Objects: **an indirect object is one that is governed by a preposition**, eg: he writes with a pencil, *il écrit avec un crayon*. A verb can have **both** direct and indirect objects: he writes the letter with a pencil, *il écrit la lettre avec un crayon;* he writes the letter to his friend, *il écrit la lettre à son ami*. Both direct and indirect objects may be pronouns, and the pronoun may precede the verb. When used as objects of a verb, the pronouns *le, la, l'* and *les* (= him/it, her/it, them – *l'* may be either gender) are **always** direct objects: but *me, te, se, nous* and *vous*, may be both direct and indirect objects: **when indirect they are always dative** (ie: governed by 'to'): he speaks to me, to us, etc, *il me parle, il nous parle*, etc. The third person indirect dative object pronoun in the singular is *lui* for both genders: he speaks to him/her, *il lui parle:* in the plural the dative third person pronoun is *leur:* he speaks to them, *il leur parle* (either gender). If the indirect object pronoun is governed by any other preposition it will follow the verb: he comes without me/you/him/her/them, *il arrive sans moi/toi/lui/elle/eux/elles*. See PRONOUNS ¶13. The indirect pronoun for 'of it', 'of them', 'some' is *en:* see *en*, pronoun: he eats some (of it/them), *il en mange;* he knows the name of it (its name), *il en sait le nom*. The indirect object pronoun/adverb for 'there', 'in that place', 'to there', 'in it' (locative) is *y* (see *y*): he goes there, *il y va*. It is **not** possible to have **both** *en* and a direct object pronoun in the same sentence, **but** otherwise several pronouns may be used: see PRONOUNS ¶3ff. The past participle of a verb conjugated with *avoir* does **not** agree with *en*. See 'it' ii, as **Indirect Object**, below.

indu, -e, adjective: undue, improper. Adverb: ***indûment***, unduly, unlawfully.

s'infatuer, to be infatuated: *de/pour qlqn/qlqch*, by sn/sth.

Infinitive: see VERBS ¶35 – 41: with conjunctive pronoun objects, see PRONOUNS ¶12, ¶13.

influer, to influence, have an influence: *sur qlqn/qlqch*, on sn/sth.

informer, to inform: *qlqn de qlqch*, sn about sth; *s'informer de qlqch*, to find out/inquire about sth.

s'ingénier, to contrive, set one's wits: *à* or *pour faire qlqch*, to do sth.

injurieux, injurieuse, adjective: unjust, injurious, offensive: *à qlqn*, towards sn.

inquiéter, to worry, to alarm: *qlqn*, sn; *s'inquiéter*, to worry; *de* (or *au sujet de*) *qlqch*, about sth. Like *céder*.

insister, to insist: *sur qlqch*, on sth; *à* (or *pour*) *faire qlqch*, on doing sth; *insister auprès de qlqn*, to take up strongly with/put sth strongly to sn.

inspirer, to inspire: *qlqn de faire qlqch*, sn to do sth; *être inspiré de faire qlqch*, to be inspired to do sth.

instruire, to instruct, to teach, to inform: *instruire qlqn dans* (or *en*) *qlqch*, to instruct sn in sth, to teach sth to sn; *instruire qlqn de*, to acquaint sn with/inform sn about; *être (bien) instruit(e) de qlqch*, to be (well) versed in sth.

intercéder, to intercede: *pour qlqn*, for sn; *auprès de qlqn*, with sn. Like *céder*.

interdire, to forbid. Like *dire* except 2nd person plural of present and imperative: *interdisez: interdire qlqch à qlqn*, to forbid sn sth/sth to sn; *à qlqn de faire qlqch*, sn to do sth; *il est interdit de faire qlqch*, it is forbidden to do sth; *on lui a interdit le vin*, he has been forbidden wine; *c'est interdit*, it is forbidden.

intéresser, to interest: *qlqn à qlqch*, sn in sth; *être intéressé à faire qlqch*, to be interested in doing sth; *s'intéresser à qlqn/qlqch*, to take an interest in sn/sth.

Interrogative: a question can be asked by simply raising the voice at the end of a sentence retaining the construction of a normal statement, eg: *il vient*, is he coming, *il vient?* (voice raised at end). **Questions can also be formed by using one of the following interrogative constructions**:
  i. by putting '*est-ce que*' (= is it that?) at the beginning of the otherwise unaltered statement: is he coming? *est-ce qu'il vient?* (= 'is it that he comes?')
  ii. **by inversion**: that is, by putting a **pronoun subject** after the verb with a hyphen: is he coming, *vient-il?* (= 'comes he?'): if the subject is a noun, the noun remains before the verb and a pronoun is added after the verb: does the man come?/is the man coming? *l'homme, vient-il?* In compound tenses the pronoun follows the auxiliary: has he spoken? *a-t-il parlé?* has the man arrived? *l'homme, est-il arrivé?* Other pronouns attached to the verb remain in their normal position, eg: normal statement: M. Brun has spoken to him about it, *Monsieur Brun lui en a parlé*: interrogative form: has M. Brun spoken to him about it? *Monsieur Brun, lui en a-t-il parlé?* **Note** the insertion of *-t-* when *il, elle* or *on* are attached to a verb ending in a vowel, and also in *(con)vainc-t-il?* In a negative question – *ne . . . pas* keep their usual positions: hasn't Joan spoken of it? *Jeanne, n'en a-t-elle pas parlé?*

iii. **by using the interrogative adjective** *quel?* as an adjective it agrees in gender and number with the noun it qualifies: which man/woman/men/women? *quel homme? quelle femme? quels hommes? quelles femmes?* how old is Peter? *quel âge Pierre a-t-il?* (**note** inversion after noun)

iv. **by using an interrogative adverb**, eg: when do you leave? *quand partez-vous?* See ADVERBS ¶5

v. **by using an interrogative pronoun**, usually with inversion of subject and verb, eg: what is he saying? *que dit-il?* which do you want? *lequel voulez-vous?* There is, however, **no inversion** after *qui?* = who? when used alone, eg: who is coming? *qui vient?* who is this man? *qui est cet homme?* **But** there is inversion after *qui* in: *qui est-ce?* eg: who is coming? *qui est-ce qui vient?* And inversion occurs after *qui* if it is governed by a preposition: of whom are you speaking? *de qui parlez-vous?* with whom do you work? *avec qui travaillez-vous?* And after *que?* = what? what do you say? *que dites-vous?* what has happened? *qu'est-ce qui est arrivé?* (= what is it which has happened?) And after *quoi?* = what? what are you thinking about? *à quoi pensez-vous?* (See *penser.*) what is this for? *à quoi sert ceci?* what are you talking about? *de quoi parlez-vous?* See also: *qui est-ce qui?* and PRONOUNS ¶45 – 49.

interrompre, to interrupt: *s'interrompre de faire*, to break off from doing. Like *rompre.*

Inversion: inversion (the subject following the noun) occurs:

i. in **questions**: see **Interrogative** above and ADVERBS ¶5

ii. **it also** occurs in phrases following direct speech, such as: *dit-il,* he says/said; *demande-t-elle,* she asks; *répond Jean,* John answers (the **noun**, whether a name or not, is put after the verb in such cases), eg: –*Venez avec moi, dit-elle,* 'Come with me', she said (**or** said she). In a compound tense: –*Venez avec moi, a-t-elle dit,* 'Come with me,' she said. –*Il faut le faire, s'est dit Pierre,* 'It must be done,' Peter said to himself. –*Je viens, je viens, a crié la jeune fille,* 'I'm coming, I'm coming,' the girl shouted. This inversion does **not** occur if no word of the reported speech precedes the 'he said' phrase, eg: *Il a répondu, Non, monsieur,* He answered, 'No, sir.'

iii. it is **also** usual in good French after the adverbs: *à peine,* hardly; *au moins/du moins,* at least; *encore,* furthermore, still more (**but** not when *encore* means 'again'); *en vain,* vainly; *peut-être,* perhaps; *toujours,* nevertheless, still (**but** not when it means 'always/forever'), eg: *à peine a-t-il parlé quand . . . ,* hardly had he spoken when . . . ; *j'ai très peu d'argent, mais toujours veux-je l'acheter; peut-être mon père va-t-il m'aider,* I have very little money, but I still want to buy it (but nevertheless I want to . . .); perhaps my father will help me ('goes he to help me')

iv. it is **also** used after *aussi* **or** *aussi bien* meaning 'besides' as in: *je ne* *veux pas y aller, aussi bien fait-il trop chaud,* I don't want to go there, besides it's too hot

v.   and inversion is used for effect especially in exclamations and poetry.

Inverted commas are not usually used in French. Before quoted speech it is usual to put a *tiret* (a long dash), but otherwise not to mark the end or recommencement of words quoted by the same speaker, the next dash marking the beginning of the next speaker's words, eg: *–Non, dit-it, donnez-le-lui,* 'No,' he said, 'give it to him.' *–Le voilà, a-t-elle répondu,* 'There it is,' she replied. For quotations from texts *guillemets* are usually used: << . . .>>: although inverted commas are used by some printers.

inviter, to invite: *qlqn à (faire) qlqch,* sn to (do) sth.

-ir, **verbs** so ending: see VERBS ¶1ii.

s'irriter, to get annoyed: *contre qlqn,* with sn; *de qlqch,* with sth.

it: '**it**' **as the subject of a verb** is translated by: *il, elle* or by *ce*

i.   **it** = *il* or *elle*: when 'it' is the subject of a verb other than *être,* and refers to a noun of known gender: *le livre est lourd; il a 500 pages,* the book is heavy; it has 500 pages; *j'ai acheté une montre; elle marche bien,* I have bought a watch; it works well

ii.   **it** = *il* when the **subject of an impersonal verb**: *il faut lui parler,* it is necessary to speak to him: see **Impersonal Verbs** above

iii.   **it** = *il* when used in 'it is' before an adjective followed by *que* or *de: il est **vrai que** je ne l'aime pas,* it is true that I don't like him; *il est **difficile de** faire mon devoir ici,* it is difficult to do my homework here

iv.   **it** = *il* when speaking of **time** or **weather**: *il est trois heures,* it is three o'clock; *il fait beau,* it is fine (but *ce* is at times used for 'the time then was': *c'était minuit, c'était l'heure,* it was (then) midnight, it was the hour (ie: the time for sth to happen)): see **Time**, **Weather** and *il,* above

v.   **it** = *ce* as the subject of *être* if the complement is **not** an adjective (**but** may contain an adjective): *c'est moi,* it is I; *ce sont eux qui l'ont fait,* it is they who have done it; *c'est mon père qui décidera,* it is my father who will decide: *ce* is **also** used to translate 'it' as subject of *être,* even if followed by an adjective if 'it' refers back to something previously mentioned: *c'était une bonne idée,* it was a good idea; *c'est vrai,* it's true

vi.   **it** = may be translated by *ce* as the subject of the following verbs when they are followed by *être: devoir,* must; *pouvoir,* can; and, less frequently, *aller,* to go; *devenir,* to become; *paraître,* to appear; *sembler,* to seem, eg: *ce doit être vrai,* it must be true; *ce pourrait être difficile,* it could be difficult; *ce va être amusant,* it is going to be amusing. **Note** that 'it' = *ce* in such cases because *ce* usually refers back to something already spoken about. **For further information about the use of** *ce* **as subject of** *être* **see PRONOUNS ¶23ff, ¶32, ¶34**

vii.   '**it**' and '**them**': as the **object of a verb**: when a **direct object**, '**it**' is translated by *le, la* or *l'* placed before the verb, eg: I eat it (sth masculine), *je le mange:* or if feminine, *je la mange.* In a compound tense the past participle agrees with this preceding 'it', eg: if 'it' is masculine: I have eaten it, *je l'ai mangé:* **or** if 'it' is feminine, *je l'ai mangée.* In questions, only the subject pronoun follows the verb, and *le, la,* or *l'* remains before the verb: have you eaten it? *l'avez-vous mangé(e)?* In the imperative 'it' follows the verb, eg: eat it! *mangez-le! mangez-la!* If there are other, indirect, pronoun objects, *le* and *la* take precedence over **all but** reflexive pronouns: I give it to him, *je le lui donne;* I have put it (fem) there, *je l'y ai mise;* **but**, he gives it to himself, *il se le donne: le* **and** *la* **cannot** both be objects of the same verb, *les* = them, must be used: and in a compound tense the past participle will be masculine plural unless *les* is exclusively feminine: *je les ai donnés:* if the writer wishes to emphasise mixed genders, a phrase can be added, eg: I have given **them**, *je les ai donnés:* **adding** *l'une et l'autre* (**or** *les unes et les autres*) – the (feminine) one(s) and the other (masculine) one(s)

viii. **it as indirect object**: the pronoun/adverbs *y* and *en* are used: *y* for 'at it', 'in it', 'on it', 'to it', 'about it'. For examples of use and meanings see *y* and *en* ('of it'or 'some', 'from it'). ***Note**: (a) the past participle never agrees with *y* or *en,* whatever they may refer to (b) if there are several pronoun objects, *y* followed by *en,* come last, eg: I have given them some = to them of it, *je leur en ai donné;* give him some, *donnez-lui-en;* he has seen some of it there, *il y en a vu* (c) *le* or *la* **cannot** be used with *en* (you cannot, for example, 'eat some' **and** 'eat it')

ix. **it: omission of**: 'it' is not always expressed in French where it would be in English. For example: 'outside **it**' = *dehors;* 'inside **it**' = *dedans;* 'under **it**' = *dessous;* 'in front of **it**' = *devant;* 'behind **it**' = *derrière;* 'beside **it**/next to **it**' = *à côté;* 'in the middle of **it**' = *au milieu,* eg: 'Is the dog on the table?' 'No, it is under **it**', –*Est-ce que le chien est sur la table? –Non, il est dessous;* a house with a tree in front of **it**, *une maison avec un arbre devant.*

its = **possessive** of **it** = *son, sa, ses,* agreeing in gender and number with the thing possessed: *sa page,* its page (of a book); *ses fenêtres,* its windows. See ADJECTIVES ¶10. (Do **not** confuse 'its' possessive = 'of it' with 'it's' = 'it is'.)

J

jamais, adverb: ever: *si jamais je le fais,* if ever I do it. Usually used with *ne* before the verb for '**never**': *il ne pleut jamais,* it never rains. In a compound tense *jamais* comes after the auxiliary: *il ne l'ai jamais lu,* he has never read it, **or** in the interrogative: *n'avez-vous jamais visité le Louvre?* have you never visited the Louvre? *jamais* may be used at the beginning of the sentence for greater effect, eg: *jamais on ne vaincra l'ennemi,* never will we beat the enemy (there is **no** inversion after *jamais*). When there is no finite verb *jamais* may be used to mean 'never' without *ne: ce qu'il dit est toujours exacte, jamais exagéré,* what he says is always correct, never exaggerated. *jamais* is used in exclamations without *ne: jamais!* = never! **Note**: *à jamais, pour jamais, à tout jamais*, all = forever.

je, **conjunctive pronoun = I**: used only as **subject of a verb** (it is I = *c'est moi;* not I = *pas moi*): *je* is spelt **without** a capital unless at beginning of a sentence: it elides before a vowel or *h*-mute: *j'ai*, I have; *j'en parle*, I speak of it; *j'habite*, I dwell/inhabit: **but** not before *h*-aspirate: *je haïs*, I hate: *je* does **not** elide when coming after the verb, eg: *puis-je avoir?* can I have? See **I**.

jeter, to throw: **example of verbs ending in -*eter*:** the rule is that the -*t*- is doubled before *e*-mute endings and also in the future stem. Pres: *jette, jettes, jette, jetons, jetez, jettent*. Imperf: *jétais, -ais, -ait, -ions, -iez, -aient*. Fut: *jetterai, -as, -a, -ons, -ez, -ont*. Past Hist: *jetai, jetas, jeta, jetâmes, jetâtes, jetèrent*. Imperat: *jette, jetons, jetez*. Pres subj: *jette, jettes, jette, jetions, jetiez, jettent*. Imperf subj: *jetasse, jetasses, jetât, jetassions, jetassiez, jetassent*. Pres part: *jetant*. Past part: *jeté, jetée, jetés, jetées*. Aux: ***avoir***.

joindre, to join. Like ***craindre***. Pres: *joins, -s, joint, joignons, -ez, -ent*. Imperf: *joignais*, etc. Fut: *joindrai*, etc. Past hist: *joignis*, etc. Pres subj: *joigne, -es, -e, -ions, -iez, -ent*. Imperf subj: *joignisse, joignît*, etc. Pres part: *joignant*. Past part: *joint*.

jouer, to play: *jouer du piano/du violon*, etc, to play the piano, violin, etc; *jouer au football*, to play football; *aux cartes*, at cards (or any sport or game); *jouer à la Bourse*, to play the Stock Exchange; *jouer un rôle*, to play a part/role; *jouer dans un film*, to act in a film; *jouer qlqn*, to cheat/deceive someone; *jouer une valse*, to play a waltz; *jouer la surprise*, to pretend surprise; *se jouer de qlqn/qlqch*, to make fun of sn/sth; *jouer beaucoup*, to gamble a large sum.

jouir, to enjoy: *jouir de qlqch*, enjoy something. Regular, conjugated like ***finir***.

jour, masc: ***journée***, fem: day: see **Day** for difference between these two words.

jusque, preposition: till, until, as far as, up to (in time or position): elides before a vowel: *jusqu'à trois heures*, until three o'clock; *jusqu'à Paris*, as far as Paris; *jusqu'ici*, as far as here; *jusque-là*, up to there/as far as there. Strictly should be followed by *à*, **but** sometimes in less formal speech by other prepositions, or by a noun or adverb. Occasionally (mainly in poetry) spelt with final -*s* before a vowel.

jusqu'à ce que, subordinating conjunction: until (with subjunctive): *jusqu'à ce qu'il fût arrivé*, until he had arrived. See VERBS ¶33i.

just: **adjective** and **adverb**: see *juste* below.

juste

    i.   **adjective**: just, fair: a just man, *un homme juste;* a just woman, *une femme juste*

    ii.   **adverb**: exactly, precisely: *chanter juste*, to sing in tune; *frapper juste*, to hit the nail on the head; *tout juste/tout au juste*, exactly, only just; *comme de juste*, as is right and proper/as is reasonable.

K

keep on doing something: *continuer à faire qlqch.*

kind (kind-hearted): adjective: see *gentil.*

kind: noun = species, *genre* (**masc**): mankind, *le genre humain.* **kind** = type, sort, *espèce, sorte* (**fem**): a good kind of apple, *une bonne espèce de pomme;* all kinds of apples, *toutes sortes de pommes.*

know: see *savoir* for to know a fact. See *connaître* for to know someone, know a place, be acquainted with.

L

la

    i.   **definite article** = the: see ARTICLES ¶2

    ii. **conjunctive pronoun** = her, it: see **her** and **it** and PRONOUNS ¶4i, ¶6, ¶13.

laisser, to allow, to permit, to leave (including to leave by a will), to abandon: *laisser tomber,* to let fall; *laisser qlqch à qlqn,* to leave sth to sn; *laisser une fortune,* to leave a fortune; *laisser qlqn faire qlqch,* let sn do sth; *cela laisse beaucoup à désirer,* that leaves much to be desired; *cela laisse à penser,* that needs thinking about: when followed by an infinitive with its own object pronouns see PRONOUNS ¶12: **and** for omission of reflexive pronoun of following infinitive see PRONOUNS ¶14. (To let a house, rent out = *louer.*)

lancer, to throw, to launch. Like *placer.*

languages: names of languages are masc and spelt without a capital, eg: *le français:* to learn French, *apprendre le français;* to speak French, *parler (le) français* (usually **without** *le*).

large, **adjective**: wide, ample: *un sentier large de trois mètres,* a path three metres wide; *une chemise large,* a shirt of ample proportions; *une conscience large,* a broad (not too particular) conscience. **Noun** = width: see **Dimensions**: *gagner le large,* to reach the open sea.

large

    i.   **big**: *gros, grosse*

    ii. **tall, high**: *grand, -e*

    iii. **extensive**: *étendu, -e*

    iv. **ample**: *large*

    v. **at large** (free): *en liberté.*

las, lasse, adjective: weary.

last

    i.   **verb**: to last, to endure, *durer:* the war lasted (for) ten years, *la guerre a duré dix ans;* to last out, *surpasser en durée*

    ii. **adjective**: *dernier, dernière:* the last page (of book), *la dernière page;*

the last week (of a period), *la dernière semaine;* last week (the week just past), *la semaine dernière;* last Tuesday, *mardi dernier;* the last born, *le dernier-né, la dernière-née*

iii.   **adverb**: last (in time, in succession): he arrived last, *il arriva le dernier;* at last! *enfin!* the last but one, *l'avant-dernier.* **Lastly, finally**: *finalement* (*one *-l-*): finally, lastly, ultimately, *en dernier lieu;* last in place, *au dernier rang.* ***Note**: *dernièrement,* adverb = lately, of late, recently: **not** lastly or finally.

late: late in the day, etc = *tard:* it is late, *il est tard;* it is getting late/it grows late, *il se fait tard.* Late = recently deceased: see *feu.*

latter: *celui-ci, celle-ci.* See PRONOUNS ¶20.

le, la, les

i.   **definite article** = the: see ARTICLES ¶2

ii.   **conjunctive pronouns** = him, her, it, them: see PRONOUNS ¶2 – 13.

le mien, le sien, le nôtre, le vôtre, etc: see PRONOUNS ¶38.

least: *le moins:* with an adverb *le* is invariable: she works the least, *elle travail le moins* (see ADVERBS ¶5); with an adjective *le* agrees: *elle est la moins belle (des femmes dans le film),* she is the least beautiful (of the women in the film): see ADJECTIVES ¶7. See also **less**: at least, *au/du moins;* at the very least, *tout au moins;* the least (that) I can do, *le moins que je peux faire.*

lequel, relative and interrogative pronoun = who, whom, which: see PRONOUNS ¶43, ¶49.

less

i.   **adjective** = smaller: *plus petit(e)* **or** *moins grand(e).* **Less**, smaller in dimensions, quantity or degree = *moindre:* the smaller (lower) price, *le moindre prix;* at a slower speed, *à une moindre vitesse:* **note**: *moindre* is mainly a literary form: *plus petit* being used more in everyday speech

ii.   **adverb**: *moins* (with *de* before a noun or number): he has less friends, *il a moins d'amis;* he is less than ten years old, *il a moins de dix ans;* he is less rich, *il est moins riche.*

lest: *de peur que, de crainte que:* see **fear**.

leur = **to them**: see PRONOUNS ¶3, ¶4. **Their**: see ADJECTIVES ¶10.

Liaison: the carrying over, in speech, of the sound of the final consonant of a word to sound as if it were the beginning of the next word if that word starts with a vowel or *h*-mute. Usage varies, but the following rules cover the most important cases

i.   if there is a pause in **speech, no liaison** occurs

ii.   there is **no liaison** after *et* but there is after *est*

iii.   **liaison** only occurs in the case of those final consonants of **nouns** which are normally sounded, eg: liaison does **not** occur after *forêt* because the final *-t* is not normally sounded: *la forê(t) est:* **but** there is liaison after *cheval* because the final *-l* is normally sounded: *le cheval_saute,* therefore, *le cheval_est (cheva-les)*

iv. **liaison occurs** between a **pronoun** ending in a consonant and the following verb: and between subject and object pronouns before verbs and wherever *-t-* is inserted: *il_est (i-les), on_a (o-na) vu, il_y a (i-ly a), vous_en (vou-sen) mangez, nous_en_avons (nou-s'enavons), a-t-il (a-til) parlé?*

v. **liaison occurs** between a verb in the 3rd person ending in *-t* and a following object, adjective, complement, infinitive **or** preposition: *elle fait_un (fai-tun) gâteau, il paraît_ennuyé (paraî-tennuyé), il doit_arriver (doi-tarriver), il vient_avec (vien-tavec) nous*

vi. **liaison occurs** between *les, un, des* and a following noun or adjective starting with a vowel or *h*-mute, and between an adjective ending in a consonant and a following vowel or *h*-mute: *un_encrier (u-nencrier), un_ancien_ami (u-nancie'nami), des_hommes (de-s'hommes), les_eaux (le-seaux)*

vii. **liaison occurs** between the following prepositions and the words they govern: *après_une (aprè-sune) heure, avant_eux (avan-teux), dans_une (dan-sune) chambre, devant_une (devan-tune) maison, en_Angleterre (e-n Angleterre), sans_âme (san-sâme), sous_un_arbre (sou-sun'arbre)*

viii. **liaison occurs** after *dont: dont_il (don-til) parle,* and after *quand:* **note** that the final *-d* is pronounced *-t* in liaison: *quan(d)-til vient*

ix. **liaison occurs** after *pas* (used as a negative), and in a number of everyday phrases such as: *elle n'est pas_ici (pa-sici), de temps_en (ton-sen) temps, tout_à (tou-ta) fait, en_hiver (o-n'iver), de haut_en (doh-ton) bas, de mieux_en (mieu-zon) mieux, mot_à (mo-ta) mot, vis_à (vi-sa) vis:* and in other groups of words which form together a single idea: *un mois_après (moi-zaprès), très_aimé (trè-zaimé), bien_aimé (bie-naimé), les Champs-Élysées (lay chon-zelysées), les_États-Unis (lay_zéta-zunis)*

x. there is **no liaison** of the *-s* termination of 2nd person singular in verbs: *tu porte(s) un chapeau:* nor of the plural *-s* in the first part of composite words: *des arc(s)-en ciel (day_zark-en-ciel),* rainbows.

libre, adjective: free: *de qlqch,* of, from sth; *de faire qlqch,* to do sth; *entrée libre,* entrance free; *vers libres,* free verse.

like: like me, *comme moi;* do like him, *faites comme lui;* he looks like his brother, *il ressemble à son frère* (see **comme**); I like apples, *j'aime les pommes;* I would like to do it (very much), *j'aimerais (bien) le faire* **or** *je voudrais (bien) le faire;* I like reading, *j'aime lire* **or** *j'aime à lire.* See **aimer.**

lire, to read. Pres: *lis, lis, lit, lisons, lisez, lisent.* Imperf: *lisais,* etc. Fut: *lirai, -as, -a, -ons, -ez, -ont.* Past hist: *lus, lus, lut, lûmes, lûtes, lurent.* Pres subj: *lise, -es, -e, lisions, -iez, lisent.* Imperf subj: *lusse, lusses, lût, lussions, lussiez, lussent.* Pres part: *lisant.* Past part: *lu, lue, lus, lues.* Aux: **avoir.**

little

i. **adjective** = small: *petit, petite.* Usually comes before the noun it qualifies. The **comparative**, smaller, less = *plus petit(e), moindre:* he is smaller (littler, in size), *il est plus petit:* but he is less (in importance or significance) than, *il est moindre que:* see **less**. The **superlative**, smallest, least = *le/la plus petit(e), les plus petit(e)s, le/la/les moindre(s):* he is the smallest (littlest) of the children, *il est le plus petit des enfants;* I have not the least idea, *je n'ai pas la moindre idée;* the least of things, *la moindre des choses* ('*la*' because meaning is 'the least thing of things': *chose* is fem)

ii. **adverb**: little = not much: he speaks little, *il parle peu*

iii. **noun**: the little he has is not enough, *le peu qu'il a n'est pas assez;* he has little bread, *il a peu de pain;* there is a little **of the** bread left, and also a little cheese, *il reste un peu du pain, et aussi un peu de fromage.*

live

i. exist, be alive = *vivre*

ii. dwell (at/in) = *demeurer*

iii. live at/inhabit = *habiter.*

The Eskimos live in igloos and live in Greenland, *les Esquimaux* (**or** *Eskimos*) *vivent dans des igloos et habitent le Groenland;* one says that one lives **in** a street but **on** an avenue, **on** a boulevard and **on** a square, *on dit qu'on demeure dans une rue mais sur une avenue, sur un boulevard et sur une place;* I live in Station Road, *j'habite la rue de la Gare;* farmers live in the country, *les fermiers habitent la campagne* **or** *vivent à la campagne.* **Note** the verbs *habiter, demeurer* and *vivre* overlap each other when meaning 'have one's existence at/in somewhere'.

livre, **masculine** = book: **feminine** = pound (weight or money).

louer

i. to praise: *qlqn de qlqch,* sn for sth; *pour avoir fait qlqch,* for having done sth

ii. to let: *qlqch à qlqn,* sth to sn: **or** to rent: *louer une maison,* to rent a house (as landlord or as tenant).

lorsque, subordinating conjunction = when: *je le verrai lorsqu'il viendra,* I shall see him when he comes (*lorsque* elides: *quand* could have been used); *je le ferai lorsque cela sera nécessaire,* I shall do it when it is (French say 'will be') necessary. But *où* (or *que*), **not** *lorsque* or *quand,* **must** be used for a clause following a stated or implied time, eg: *le jour où* (or *que*) *cela arrivera, sera . . .*, the **day when** that happens will be . . . See **when**.

lui

i. **indirect object with verb, conjunctive pronoun** = 'to him', 'to her', 'to it': see PRONOUNS ¶3, ¶4i.

ii. **after a preposition, disjunctive pronoun** = 'him' (but **not** 'her', nor 'it' – unless a personified animal): see PRONOUNS ¶15 – 17.

luire, to shine. Pres: *luis, luis, luit, luisons, luisez, luisent.* Imperf: *luisais,* etc. Fut: *luirai,* etc. Past hist: *luisis, -is, -it, luisîmes, luisîtes, luisirent* **or** *luis, luîmes, luirent,* etc. Pres subj: *luise, -es, -e, luisions, -isiez, luisent.* Imperf subj: *luisisse, luisisses, luisît, luisissions, luisissiez, luisissent.* Pres part: *luisant.* Past part: *lui* (invariable). Aux: ***avoir***.

M

madame, 'madam' or 'Mrs': plural = ***mesdames***. If addressed in direct speech, Madame is spelt with a capital: *–Oui, Madame, oui, Madame Brun,* 'Yes, Madam, yes Mrs Brun': **but** when writing about someone with name attached a small *m* is used: *elle s'appelle madame Brun,* her name is Mrs Brun, abbreviated to *Mme. Brun.* **Note**: 'a lady' = *une dame*.

mademoiselle, Miss. Use of capital and small initial letter as for ***madame***, above. Abbreviated to *Mlle.* Plural = ***mesdemoiselles***.

main, fem: hand: *à la main,* in my/his/her/their hand: singular unless in both hands.

maint, mainte, adjective: many, many a: *mainte fois* (fem sing), many a time **or** *maintes fois* (fem plur), many times; *en mainte occasion,* on many an occasion **or** *en maintes occasions,* on many occasions; *à mainte(s) reprise(s),* repeatedly ('at many re-doings').

maintenir, to maintain. Conjugated like ***tenir***.

mal, adverb: badly. **Comparative**: *plus mal,* worse **or** *pis,* in certain expressions, eg: *aller de mal en pis,* to go from bad to worse; *de pis en pis (de pee-zon pee),* worse and worse; *tant pis!* so much the worse! **Superlative**: *le plus mal* **or** *le pis,* the worst; *au pis,* at worst; *au pis aller,* at the worst (that could happen). **Noun**: *un mal: faire mal,* to hurt; *faire du mal à qlqn,* to do evil, to hurt, to injure (sn); *le mal de mer,* sea-sickness; *le mal de dents,* toothache; *avoir mal aux dents,* to have toothache.

malade, **adjective**: ill, unwell, sick: *de qlqch,* with sth; *malade à mourir,* mortally ill. **Noun**: *un(e) malade,* an invalid.

malfaire, to do evil: used **only** in present infinitive, eg: *il est incliné à malfaire,* he is inclined to do evil/disposed to do evil.

malheureux, -euse, **adjective**: unhappy, unlucky. **Noun**: an unfortunate, poor, wretched person, a despicable person.

mander, to send for sn: *mander à qlqn de faire qlqch,* instruct sn to do sth.

manger, to eat: **sample for verbs ending in -ger.** Conjugated like a regular *-er* verb **except** *-e-* is inserted before endings starting with *-o* or *-a.* Pres: *mange, manges, mange, mangeons, mangez, mangent.* Imperf: *mangeais, mangeais, mangeait, mangions, mangiez, mangeaient.* Fut: *mangerai, -as, -a, -ons, -ez, -ont.* Past hist: *mangeai, mangeas, mangea, mangeâmes, mangeâtes, mangèrent.* Imperat: *mange, mangeons, mangez.* Pres subj: *mange, manges,* *mange, mangions, mangiez, mangent.* Imperf subj: *mangeasse, mangeasses, mangeât, mangeassions, mangeassiez, mangeassent.* Pres part: *mangeant.* Past part: *mangé, mangée, mangés, mangées.* Aux *avoir.*

manière, fem: manner: *de cette manière,* in this way.

manche, masculine = handle: **feminine** = sleeve: *la Manche* = the English Channel.

manquer, to miss: *manquer le train,* to miss the train; *manquer un ami,* to miss a (departed) friend; *il y a une roue qui manque,* there is a wheel missing: **to lack**: *je manque d'argent,* I lack money: **to fail in**: *vous manquer à votre devoir,* you are failing in your duty; *vous avez manqué à le faire,* you have failed to do it/just missed doing it; *il a manqué de se tuer,* he just missed killing/almost killed himself: **lack/not have**: *il lui manque un bras,* he has an arm missing ('there lacks to him an arm'); *il me manque dix francs,* I am five francs short ('there lacks to me five francs').

many, much

i. ***beaucoup,*** before a noun takes *de* without article: he has many pencils, *il a beaucoup de crayons:* **but** with *de* + article if 'of the' is intended: he has many **of the** red pencils, *il a beaucoup des crayons rouges;* with much care, *avec beaucoup de soin;* I love you very much, *je t'aime beaucoup;* thank you very much, *merci beaucoup;* this wine is much better, *ce vin est beaucoup meilleur.* **Note**: it is not possible to put *très* or another adverb (other than *pas*) with *beaucoup: beaucoup* can, as in the last example, qualify a comparative adjective, eg: the house is much bigger, *la maison est (de) beaucoup plus grande* (the inserted *de* is optional); he is by far (= much) wiser than his brother, *il est (de) beaucoup plus sage que son frère;* not many/much, *pas beaucoup.* **Noun** (masc) = 'a lot' (of people/things), 'many': many (a lot of people) have said the same thing, *beaucoup ont dit la même chose;* he has seen a lot (of places/things), *il a vu beaucoup;* he has done a lot for me, *il a fait beaucoup pour moi;* he knows a lot about it, *il en sait beaucoup*

ii. ***bien*** can be used as an alternative to mean 'many', 'a lot of': he has many books, *il a bien des livres;* he has a lot of money, *il a bien de l'argent* (**note** that *bien* is followed by *du, de la, de l'* or *des*); thanks a lot, *merci bien.* (For 'as many, as much' see ***autant:*** for 'how many, how much' see ***combien:*** for 'so many, so much' see ***tant:*** for 'too many, too much' see ***too.*** See also ***beaucoup*** and ***bien*** for further examples of these two words.)

marcher, to march, to walk. **Also** 'to work' speaking of machinery, etc, eg: *ma montre marche bien,* my watch works/goes well. Aux *avoir.*

mars, March (month): the final *-s* **is** sounded: should be spelt **without** a capital.

maudire, to curse. Pres: *maudis, maudis, maudit, maudissons, maudissez, maudissent.* Imperf: *maudissais, -ais, -ait, -ions, -iez, -aient.* Fut: *maudirai, -as, -a, -ons,*

-ez, -ont. Past hist: *maudis, maudis, maudit, maudîmes, maudîtes, maudirent.* Imperat: *maudis, maudissons, maudissez.* Pres Subj: *maudisse, maudisses, maudisse, maudissions, maudissiez, maudissent.* Imperf subj: *maudisse, maudisses, maudît, maudissions, maudissiez, maudissent.* Pres part: *maudissant.* Past part: *maudit, -e, -s, -es.* Aux: ***avoir.***

marteler, to hammer, strain, worry. Like **mener**.

may (can), **might (could)**: he may/can do it = to be able, ***pouvoir***, eg: he can do it/has permission to do it, *il peut le faire;* may I go out? *puis-je sortir?* would that I might see her again (may I see her again), *puissé-je la revoir* (using the 1st person sing of present subjunctive of *pouvoir*: **note** the *-é* in the inverted subjunctive); (See also ***pouvoir***.) May God bless you! *(que) Dieu vous benisse!* For 'someone may/might perhaps do something' and 'to fear lest/that something may/might happen' see '**Use of subjunctive**': VERBS ¶33 and also see **fear**.

me (English pronoun) = French *me* for both 'me' and 'to me' when before the verb: he sees me, *il me voit;* he speaks to me, *il me parle.* When coming after the verb or separate from it 'me' = ***moi***: look at me, *regardez-moi;* give it to me, *donnez-le-moi;* come with me, *venez avec moi;* it's me! *c'est moi!* **But** before *y* and *en, moi* is eldied to *m':* give me some, *donnez-m'en.* See PRONOUNS ¶3, ¶4, ¶14, ¶16.

Measurements: see **Dimensions**.

méchant, -e, **adjective**: naughty, wicked, perverse: usually **after noun**: *un enfant méchant,* a naughty child; *un chien méchant,* a vicious dog. When **before noun** = worthless, troublesome, unpleasant: *un méchant poète,* a bad (poor quality) poet. As **noun**: *un méchant* = an ill-disposed, evil, wicked person: *faire le méchant,* to bully. As **adverb**: ***méchamment***, wickedly, naughtily, waywardly.

méconnaître, not to recognise, to disown, to misunderstand. Like ***connaître***.

mécontent, -e, dissatisfied: *de qlqch,* with sth. **Noun**: *un(e) mécontent(e),* a discontented person, a malcontent.

médecin, a doctor, physician: lady doctor, *une femme médecin.* Address as *Monsieur le Docteur, Madame le Docteur.*

médecine, fem: the science of medicine (**not** a medicine: **nor** a lady doctor).

médicament, masc: a medicine.

médire, to slander: *de qlqn* = speak ill of sn. Like ***dire* except** 2nd sing present and imperative: *médisez.* Past participle: *médit* : has **no** feminine form.

méfaire, to do evil. Like *faire*.

se méfier, to suspect, to beware, to mistrust, to be mistrustful: *de qlqn, de qlqch,* of sn, of sth.

mêler, to mix. Retains the *ê* throughout: conjugated like a regular *-er* verb: *se mêler à qlqch*, to take part in sth, to join in sth; *se mêler dans qlqch*, to merge/blend in with sth, eg: *il s'est mêlé dans la foule*, he merged/blended into/with the crowd; *se mêler de (faire) qlqch*, to interfere in sth.

même

    i.   **adjective** (a) **same**: *la même année*, the same year; *les mêmes jours*, the same days; *ils ne sont pas les mêmes*, they are not the same; *la même chose*, the same thing (b) **self** (joined to pronoun with hyphen): *moi-même*, myself; *vous-même*, yourself (one person); *vous-mêmes*, yourselves (more than one person); *il l'a fait lui-même*, he has done it himself; *ils l'ont fait eux-mêmes*, they have done it themselves (c) '**the very**': *les bêtes mêmes lui obéissent*, the very animals (the animals themselves) obey him

    ii.   **adverb**: **even** (with **no** agreement): *les bêtes même* or *même les bêtes lui obéissent*, the animals even/even the animals obey him; *ses amis même/même ses amis le croient*, even his friends/his friends even believe it; *tout de même/quand même*, all the same, nevertheless, even so: *de même*, in the same way, likewise

    iii.   **pronoun**: **the same person/thing**: *le même, la même, les mêmes*, eg: *elle n'est plus la même*, she is no longer the same; *ils sont toujours les mêmes*, they are always the same; *cela revient au même*, that comes to the same thing; *à même de faire qlqch*, able/free to do sth; *un seul et même*, one and the same; *refaire au même*, to give as good as one gets

    iv.   **conjunction**: *de même que*, in the same way as.

mémoire, **masculine** = memorandum: **feminine** = memory.

menacer, to menace, to threaten. Like *placer* (*ç* before '*a*' and '*o*' endings): *menacer qlqn de qlqch*, to threaten sn with sth; *de faire qlqch*, to do sth.

ménager, to manage, take care of, to husband. Like *manger* with *-e-* inserted after the *-g-* before '*a*' or '*o*', eg: *ménageant, nous ménageons: ménager qlqn*, to show consideration for sn; *ménager qlqch à qlqn*, to prepare sth for sn; *ménager son revenu*, to manage one's income; *ménager de qlqch*, to take care of, be careful with, sth.

mener, to lead. **Sample for verbs ending in *e* + consonant + *er*,** which take *-è-* in the final syllable of the stem before an *e*-mute ending and in the future stem. Pres: *mène, mènes, mène, menons, menez, mènent*. Imperf: *menais, menais, menait, menions, meniez, menaient*. Fut: *mènerai, -as, -a, -ons, -ez, -ont*. Past hist: *menai, menas, mena, menâmes, menâtes, menèrent*. Imperat: *mène, menons, menez*. Pres subj: *mène, mènes, mène, menions, meniez, mènent*. Imperf subj: *menasse, menasses, menât, menassions, menassiez, menassent*. Pres part: *menant*. Past part: *mené, menée, menés, menées*. Aux: *avoir*.
Followed

    i.   by infinitive with object pronouns: see PRONOUNS ¶12

    ii.   by infinitive with reflexive pronoun: see PRONOUNS ¶14.

mentir, to (tell) a lie. Pres: *mens, mens, ment, mentons, mentez, mentent.* Imperf: *mentais, -ais, -ait, -ions, -iez, -aient.* Fut: *mentira, -as, -a, -ons, -ez, -ont.* Past hist: *mentis, mentis, mentit, mentîmes, mentîtes, mentirent.* Imperat: *mens, mentons, mentez.* Pres subj: *mente, mentes, mente, mentions, mentiez, mentent.* Imperf subj: *mentisse, mentisses, mentît, mentissions, mentissiez, mentissent.* Pres part: *mentant.* Past part: *menti* (**no** feminine form).

se méprendre, to make a mistake: *sur* **or** *quant à qlqch*, about sth. Like **prendre**.

merci, **masculine** = thanks (*merci beaucoup:* 'many thanks') (see **thank**): **feminine** = mercy.

messeoir, to be unseemly, to ill become. Defective verb*. Pres: *il messied, ils messiéent.* Imperf: *il messeyait, ils messaient.* Fut: *il messiéra, ils messiéront.* Pres subj: *messeye.* Pres part: *messeyant* **or** *messéant.* Past part: *messis, messise: cela messied à ton âge,* that ill becomes/does not befit your age. (*Note: is sometimes used in other persons.)

mettre, to put. Pres: *mets, mets, met, mettons, mettez, mettent.* Imperf: *mettais, -ais, -ait, -ions, -iez, -aient.* Fut: *mettrai, -as, -a, -ons, -ez, -ont.* Past hist: *mis, mis, mit, mîmes, mîtes, mirent.* Imperat: *mets, mettons, mettez.* Pres subj: *mette, mettes, mette, mettions, mettiez, mettent.* Imperf subj: *misse, misses, mît, missions, missiez, missent.* Pres part: *mettant.* Past part: *mis, mise, mis, mises.* Aux: *avoir*.

mi-, prefix: = mid-: invariable.

mien, le mien, la mienne: see **mine** below.

might: see **may**.

mil, thousand: used in year numbers: see NUMBERS ¶1, the last few lines.

mile: *un mille* (**note** gender): takes *-s* in plural: *deux milles,* two miles. See *mille*.

mille, noun (masc)
    i.   **mile.** See **mile**, above.
    ii. **thousand**: invariable: *il a des mille de livres,* he has thousands of books.

mille, **numerical adjective**: thousand: invariable: *mille soldats,* a thousand soldiers; *deux mille soldats,* 2,000 soldiers ('a' **not** translated); *trois mille un,* three thousand and one ('and' **not** translated). In **dates** AD 'thousand' = *mil* when followed by another number: *en mil neuf cent dix,* in 1910. **But** the year 1,000 is *l'an mille,* and years BC keep *mille* throughout: *l'an mille neuf cent dix avant JC* (*avant Jésus-Christ* – the second *-s* is **not** sounded). See also NUMBERS, end of ¶1.

mine: possessive pronoun = *le mien, la mienne:* it is mine*, *c'est le mien, la mienne* (agreeing with gender of thing possessed): plural: *les miens/miennes* (*note: it is mine, it belongs to me, can also be: *c'est à moi,* using the disjunctive pronoun): a friend of mine, *un de mes amis;* a doctor friend of mine = a doctor of my friends, *un médecin de mes amis;* it is your opinion, but it's not mine, *c'est votre opinion, mais ce n'est pas la mienne.* See PRONOUNS ¶15 – 17 and ¶38.

modèle, model in all senses: **noun** (masc): *un modèle,* a model: *un modèle d'un avion,* a model aeroplane; *un mannequin présente les nouveaux modèles,* a mannequin presents the new models (of dresses). **Adjective**: *un élève modèle,* a model pupil.

modeler, to model, to mould. Like *mener*.

moi, me, to me. See PRONOUNS ¶15 – 17, and **me**, above.

moins, less

    i.   **comparative** of *peu:* little (adverb): see **less**

    ii. **conjunction**: *à moins que,* see **unless** and CONJUNCTIONS ¶5

    iii. for use with *ne* and subjunctive: see *ne*.

money: *argent* (masc): loose cash, small change, *la monnaie;* bank note, *un billet;* foreign currency, *les devises étrangères* (fem).

monsieur, plur = *messieurs:* noun and title: *un monsieur,* a (gentle)man (with small *m*). Writing direct **speech**, if a person is addressed, *Monsieur* is spelt with capital, eg: *–Oui, Monsieur, s'il vous plaît, Monsieur Brun, a-t-il dit,* 'Yes, sir, if you please, Mr Brun', he said: **but** *monsieur* is spelt with small *m* if used as 'Mr' together with a name when writing about sn: *j'ai vu monsieur Brun hier,* I saw Mr Brun yesterday. Abbreviated to *M.* = Mr. See *madame*.

monter, to mount, to climb, go up: *il est* monter à sa chambre,* he has gone up to his room; *monter sur un arbre,* to climb up a tree; *monter en avion, en auto,* to board a plane, get into a car; *monter à cheval,* to mount a horse; *monter à mille mètres,* to rise up to/have the height of a thousand metres; *monter à dix francs,* to amount to ten francs; *se monter de,* to supply oneself with, set oneself up with. *Aux: *être,* **unless there is a direct object**: *il a monté l'escalier,* he has mounted (gone up) the stairs; *il a monté le prix,* he has raised the price.

Months of the year: should be spelt with a small initial letter, a rule **not** always kept: *janvier, février, mars* (the final *-s* **is** sounded), *avril, mai, juin, juillet, août* (the final *-t* should **not** be sounded, **but** sometimes is), *septembre, octobre, novembre, décembre:* a month, *un mois;* in May, in June, etc, *en mai, en juin,* etc; in the month of May, in the month of August, *au mois de mai, au mois d'août;* a day in March, *un jour de mars;* by the month, *au mois;* a month today, *d'aujourd'hui en un mois;* a month ago, *il y a un mois;* monthly, *par mois;* every month, *tous les mois;* a monthly visit, *une visite mensuelle.* For 'inst', 'ult' etc, see **Correspondence**.

Moods: indicative, imperative, subjunctive: see VERBS ¶3.

se moquer de qlqn/qlqch, to laugh at/make fun of sn/sth.

mordre, to bite. Like *perdre*.

more: *plus, plus de:* I have more books than you, *j'ai plus de livres que vous;* there are more than ten, *il y a plus de dix;* a little more, *un peu plus;* much more, *beaucoup plus/bien plus;* he spoke more about it, *il en a parlé davantage;* I don't know any more (about it), *je n'en sais davantage* (*davantage* comes at end of phrase or sentence: see **davantage**); one more, *encore un(e);* more and more, *de plus en plus;* not any more = no longer, *ne . . . plus,* eg: I shall speak no more, *je ne parlerai plus;* I have no more (of it), *je n'en ai plus;* nor do I/not me either, *ni moi non plus;* the more I read the more I learn, *plus je lis, plus j'apprends;* no more work! *plus de travail!* See also **encore**.

morigéner *qlqn,* to reprimand sn: *d'avoir fait qlqch,* for having done sth. Conjugated like **céder**.

mort, noun: **masc** = *le mort,* the dead body/person, corpse (of either gender): **feminine** = *la mort,* death. **Adjective:** *mort, -e,* dead. See **mourir**.

most: *le plus (de):* what we like most, *ce que nous aimons le plus;* at the most, *(tout) au plus;* the most money, *le plus d'argent;* the most (part) of, *la plupart de* + definite article; most people, *la plupart des gens;* most of the time/ordinarily, *la plupart du temps;* most of the country is arid, *la plupart du pays est aride;* most men work, *la plupart des hommes travaillent* (the verb agrees with the noun which follows *la plupart*).

Motion: **verbs of:** it is usual to give as a rule that verbs of motion are conjugated with *être*. This rule is misleading: *marcher,* to walk and *courir,* to run, may both be thought of as 'verbs of motion', **but** both take *avoir* as auxiliary. A better rule is that verbs which as a result of their action imply a necessary 'change of position or condition' take *être*. To walk and to run describe motions, but no certainty of ending up elsewhere. **But** *aller,* to go and *venir,* to come, imply essentially a change of position **and** *devenir,* to become, implies a necessary change of condition, eg: she has become fatter, *elle est devenue plus grosse.*

mou, adjective (masc): soft: masc plur = *mous:* masc sing before vowel or *h*-mute = *mol:* fem sing = *molle:* fem plur = *molles.*

moudre, to grind. Pres: *mouds, mouds, moud, moulons, moulez, moulent.* Imperf: *moulais, -ais, -ait, -ions, -iez, -aient.* Fut: *moudrai, -as, -a, -ons, -ez, -ont.* Past hist: *moulus, moulus, moulut, moulûmes, moulûtes, moulurent.* Imperat: *mouds, moulons, moulez.* Pres subj: *moule, -es, -e, -ions, -iez, -ent.* Imperf subj: *moulusse, -es, moulût, -ussions, -ussiez, -ussent.* Pres part: *moulant.* Past part: *moulu, -e, -s, -es.* Aux: *avoir.*

mourir, to die. Pres: *meurs, meurs, meurt, mourons, mourez, meurent.* Imperf: *mourais, -ais, -ait, -ions, -iez, -aient.* Fut: *mourrai, mourras, mourra, mourrons, mourrez, mourront.* Past hist: *mourus, mourus, mourut, mourûmes, mourûtes, moururent.* Imperat: *meurs, mourons, mourez.* Pres subj: *meure, meures, meure, mourions, mouriez, meurent.* Imperf subj: *mourusse, mourusses, mourût, mourussions, mourussiez, mourussent.* Pres part: *mourant.* Past part: *mort, morte, morts, mortes.* Aux: *être: se mourir,* to be dying, to be on the point of death, to disappear, to be going out of fashion/use/existence; *mourir de qlqch,* to die of sth; *mourir de rire,* to die of laughing. **Adjective**: *mourant, -e,* dying. **Noun**: *un mourant, une mourante,* a dying person. See *mort,* masc and fem, above.

mouvoir, to move = to displace (sth). Pres: *meus, meus, meut, mouvons, mouvez, meuvent.* Imperf: *mouvais, -ais, -ait, -ions, -iez, -aient.* Fut: *mouvrai, -as, -a, -ons, -ez, -ont.* Past hist: *mus, mus, mut, mûmes, mûtes, murent.* Imperat: *meus, mouvons, mouvez.* Pres subj: *meuve, meuves, meuve, mouvions, mouviez, meuvent.* Imperf subj: *musse, musses, mût, mussions, mussiez, mussent.* Pres part: *mouvant.* Past part: *mû, mue, mus, mues* (accent on masc sing only). Aux: *avoir: se mouvoir,* to be in motion, to move (oneself). Aux for reflexive form: *être.* See **move**, below.

move: verb
    i.   to move oneself about, stir: *se mouvoir, se remuer, bouger, s'agiter*
    ii. to move from one place to another: *aller, partir*
    iii. to move forward: *s'avancer*
    iv. to move house, to go off, get away: *déménager*
    v. to stir, excite (sn, sth): *agiter*
    vi. to move sn's emotions: *toucher, émouvoir* (conjugated like *mouvoir,* above, **except** that the past participle has no circumflex on the *-u*)
    vii. to displace sth: *remuer, faire mouvoir qlqch, mettre qlqch en mouvement*
    viii. to move a motion for debate, etc: *proposer.*

moyen, masc: means: *au moyen de . . . ,* by means of (sing in French).

much: see **many**, above.

must: see *devoir, falloir.*

munir, to supply: *qlqch,* sth; *munir qlqn de qlqch,* to supply sn with sth; *se munir de,* to provide oneself with.

my: possessive adjective: *mon, ma, mes:* see ADJECTIVES ¶10.

N

naître, to be born. Pres: *nais, nais, naît, naissons, naissez, naissent.* Imperf: *naissais, -ais, -ait, -ions, -iez, -aient.* Fut: *naîtrai, -as, -a, -ons, -ez, -ont.* Past hist: *naquis, naquis, naquit, naquîmes, naquîtes, naquirent.* Imperat: *nais, naissons, naissez.* Pres subj: *naisse, naisses, naisse, naissions, naissiez, naissent.* Imperf subj: *naquisse, naquisses, naquît, naquissions, naquissiez, naquissent.* Pres part: *naissant.* Past part: *né, née, nés, nées.* Aux: *être.*

Names
    i. **of persons**. The **plural of** ordinary family names is shown by the article: the name itself does **not** take *-s:* the Aragons, *les Aragon;* the house of the Fontenoys, *la maison des Fontenoy.* **But** historical or

illustrious family names, types of persons based on names, and nationalities all take a plural -*s: les Bourbons, les Windsors, les Cicérons* (Ciceronians = great orators), *les Incas.* **When written,** names of persons and places are spelt with capitals as in English: the definite article before names of French nobility usually has a capital, **but** not the *de,* eg: *madame de La Fayette,* but usage is **not** consistent: titles however have a small initial, as do *monsieur*, madame*, mademoiselle** used before the name of the person: *monsieur Bonhomme, le roi d'Angleterre, saint Pierre* (*the abbreviations *M, Mme* and *Mlle* **always** have capitals). When writing **direct speech,** a capital is usually used for the title of sn who is addressed, with or without the name: *–Oui, Madame; –Très bien, Mademoiselle Legrand; –Mais, non Monsieur le Comte/Président,* etc

ii. **names of places** also have capitals, **but** not the definite article: *le Havre, la France:* nor other nouns qualifying the name: *la mer Méditerranée, la rue du Bac,* etc: points of the compass when used to indicate a district or area have capitals, eg: *le Nord,* the North: **but** when used to indicate a direction they are spelt with a small initial, eg: *vers le sud.* See also **Geographical Names.**

nantir, to provide for: *qlqn de qlqch,* sn with sth; *se nantir de qlqch,* to secure sth for oneself. **Noun:** plur: *les nantis,* the well-healed.

navrer, to distress: *être navré de (faire) qlqch,* to be distressed at/by (doing) sth; *je suis navré,* I am very sorry **or** *j'en suis navré,* I am very sorry about it; *navré que,* distressed that: with subjunctive.

ne, negative adverb, coming between the subject and the verb, usually used with some other word placed after the verb (see **Negative**), to express negative ideas: *ne* can also express the idea of **lest,** without negative force, when it comes before a verb in the subjunctive in a clause linked by *que* ('that') to a preceding verb or noun expressing the idea of fearing or uncertainty, eg: *je crains qu'il ne vienne,* I fear lest he come = I fear that he may come; *de crainte/de peur qu'il ne meure,* for fear lest he die, for fear of his dying (see **fear**): *ne* is similarly used after *à moins que:* **unless:** *à moins que vous ne le vouliez,* unless you wish it (see CONJUNCTIONS ¶5): **and also** in a clause introduced by *que* = 'than' following a clause expressing a comparison: *il est autre que je ne croyais,* he is other than I believed; *il est plus petit que je ne pensais,* he is smaller than I thought. Words of comparison taking this construction include: *autre,* other; *mieux,* better; *moins,* less; *pire,* worse; *plus,* more; *plutôt,* rather/preferably. See **Negative** and **neither, nor.**

near: near the house, *près de la maison;* to draw near sth, *s'approcher de qlqch.*

nearly: nearly touching, *presque touchant;* nearly one o'clock, *près d'une heure.*

nécessaire, adjective: necessary: *à qlqn,* for sn **but,** *pour qlqch,* for sth.

nécessiter, make necessary, compel: *qlqn à faire qlqch,* compel sn to do sth.

Negative: a verb is put into the negative by *ne* being placed immediately after the subject, with *pas* (**or** sometimes *point*) following the verb, eg: *je suis*, I am; *je ne suis pas*, I am not. In the case of a compound tense the auxiliary acts as the verb: *je n'ai pas donné*, I have not given. Pronoun objects which precede the verb come between *ne* and the verb: *je ne le lui ai pas donné*, I have not given it to him: thus *ne* always comes first except for the subject, if there is a subject before the verb: besides *ne . . . pas*, not **and** *ne . . . point*, not (a bit more emphatic): **other negative combinations are**: *ne . . . aucun(e)* + noun, no, not any (see **no**); *ne . . . guère*, hardly; *ne . . . jamais*, never; *ne . . . ni . . . ni . . .*, neither . . . nor . . . (see **neither . . . nor** below); *ne . . . nul(le)* + noun, no, not any (alternative to *ne . . . aucun(e)*); *ne . . . nullement*, in no way; *ne . . . plus*, no more, no longer; *ne . . . personne*, no one, nobody; *ne . . . que*, only; *ne . . . rien*, nothing. See separate entries for **ne, pas, aucun, guère, jamais, nul, personne, plus, que, rien**. In the **negative imperative** *ne* comes first, and the pronoun objects (if any) revert to their position between *ne* and the verb, and *pas, rien*, etc, follow the verb, eg: affirmative: *donnez-le-lui*, give it to him: negative: *ne le lui donnez pas*, don't give it to him. In the **negative infinitive** *ne* together with *guère, jamais, pas, plus point*, or *rien* precede the verb: *ne pas parler*, not to know; *ne rien savoir*, to know nothing; *il m'a dit de ne pas y aller*, he told me not to go there: **but** *aucun, ni, personne, nul* and *personne* follow the verb, eg: *ne trouver personne*, to find no one. See also PRONOUNS ¶2, ¶10. **Note** the expressions: *il n'importe*, it's of no importance; *à Dieu ne plaise!* God forbid!

négliger, to neglect: *de faire qlqch*, to do sth; *négliger rien pour faire qlqch*, to leave no stone unturned in order to do sth. Pres part: *négligeant*. Adj: *négligent*.

neiger, to snow: normally an impersonal verb, conjugated like *manger* (Pres part: *neigeant*, snowing.) **but** can be used figuratively with a noun as subject: *des fleurs neigeant sur la terre*, flowers snow on to the ground. Aux: *avoir*.

neither . . . nor: *ne* (verb) *ni . . . ni . . .*, eg: he has neither (the) pen nor (the) pencil, *il n'a ni (le) stylo ni (le) crayon*; **or** *ni . . . ni . . . ne* (verb), eg: neither the dog nor the cat is playing in the garden, *ni le chien ni le chat ne joue dans le jardin*. Neither of them = *ni l'un(e) ni l'autre*, with *ne* before the verb if there is one: *ils ne prennent ni l'un ni l'autre des (deux) livres*, they take neither of the (two) books.

n'est-ce pas? = is it not so? This useful single expression translates varied forms used in English such as: aren't you? don't they? won't we? isn't he? It is used to ask for confirmation of, or agreement with, a statement made: *il pleut, n'est-ce pas?* it's raining, isn't it? *tu viens, n'est-ce pas?* you're coming, aren't you? *ils l'ont acheté, n'est-ce pas?* they've bought it, haven't they? etc: *-ce* is **always** singular in this construction.

neuf, nine: pronounce the f as 'f' (eg: *le neuf mai*), **except** before *ans* and *heures*, when it sounds like a 'v': *neu(f)_v_ans, neu(f)_v_heures*.

new: adjective

  i.   brand new, newly made: *neuf, neuve*

  ii. another, different one, etc: *nouveau(x), nouvel, nouvelle(s)*. He has a new girl-friend, *il a une nouvelle amie* (she is not '*neuve*', 'brand new')

  iii. newfangled: a new (kind of) racket, *une raquette nouvelle;* a new-born child, *un enfant nouveau-né;* a new-born girl, *une fille nouveau-née* (*nouveau* – invariable); The New World, *Le Nouveau Monde;* New Year, *le nouvel an.* **Noun**: fem: *la nouvelle,* tidings, piece of news, 'the latest': plur: the news, *les nouvelles.*

nier, to deny: *(d')avoir fait qlqch,* having done sth.

no

  i.   as opposite to 'Yes' = *non:* he has said 'no', *il a dit que non*

  ii. 'not any', etc: I have no . . . , *je n'ai pas de . . .,* eg: I have no bread, *je n'ai pas de pain* (**or,** with more emphasis: *je n'ai aucun pain*); I have no hope, *je n'ai nul espoir;* no hope remains, *nul espoir ne reste;* I have not one friend, *je n'ai pas un ami;* it is no good = it is worthless, *il ne vaut rien* (see *valoir*); it is no good = it is no good trying/making the effort, *il ne vaut pas la peine;* it is no good = useless (doing sth), *c'est inutile (il est inutile de faire qlqch).* (See also **Negative**.)

no longer, no more: *ne plus:* I shall no longer do it, *je ne le ferai plus;* I have no more money, *je n'ai plus d'argent;* I have no more of the money I found, *je n'ai plus de l'argent que* j'ai trouvé.* (*The relative pronoun **cannot** be omitted in French.)

no one, nobody: *ne . . . personne:* there was nobody in the house, *il n'y avait personne dans la maison;* no one is here, *personne n'est ici:* used **without** *ne* if there is no verb: 'Who is there?' 'No one!' *–Qui est là? –Personne!*

non = 'No', opposite to 'Yes': *dire non,* to say 'No'. (See **no** above.)

non plus = either/neither, nor – after a negative statement, eg: *vous ne le voulez pas, ni moi non plus,* you don't want it, nor me either (neither do I); *on ne peut pas vivre sans argent, non plus (vivre) sans pain,* one cannot live without money, nor (can one live) without bread. See **no more, no longer** (above) and **nor** (below).

none, not one: I have none, *je n'en ai pas;* he has none of the chairs, *il n'a aucune des chaises.* For greater emphasis: **no**, I have not one (of them)! *non, je n'en ai pas une!* (Fem: referring to *chaises.*) (See *aucun, nul.*)

nor: *ni:* I have neither pen nor pencil, *je n'ai ni stylo ni crayon;* nor me (him, you, etc) either, *ni moi (lui, vous,* etc) *non plus;* neither the one nor the other, *ni l'un(e) ni l'autre.* (See **neither . . . nor**.)

not: with verb = *ne . . . pas:* I do not believe it, *je ne le crois pas;* it may not happen, *cela peut ne pas arriver;* (See *ne* above.) I hope not, *j'espère que non;* true or not, *vrai ou non;* not at all, *(pas) du tout, nullement;* not I (him, you, etc), *pas* moi (*lui, vous,* etc); not here, *pas ici.*

nothing: *ne . . . rien:* he has eaten nothing, *il n'a rien mangé;* nothing annoying has happened, *rien d'ennuyeux n'est arrivé.* **Noun**: masc: *rien* (**without** *ne*): he who risks nothing has nothing, *qui ne risque rien a **rien***; God created the world out of nothing, *Dieu a créé le monde de **rien**.* See also *ne* above and *rien.*

notre, nos, **possessive adjective** = our: *notre fils et notre fille,* our son and our daughter; *nos fils et (nos) filles,* our sons and our daughters (the possessive adjective should be repeated before each if before two singular nouns, **but** may be used once only if before two plural nouns). See ADJECTIVES ¶10.

nôtre, **possessive pronoun** = ours: *le/la nôtre, les nôtres* – **note the circumflex**: *ce livre, c'est le nôtre,* this book, it's ours; *cette maison, c'est la nôtre,* this house, it's ours (the article agrees); *la nôtre est celle qui est près de l'église,* ours is the one near the church; *ces arbres* (masc) *et ces fleurs* (fem), *ce sont les nôtres,* these trees and these flowers are ours. (The plural, the same for both genders, is formed differently from the plural of the possessive adjective above.)

NOUNS: see Grammar Section.

nous, we, us, to us, ourselves: see PRONOUNS ¶3, ¶4I and ¶14 – 17.

nouveau, nouvelle, adjective: new, fresh: see **new**, above.

noyer, to drown (sth): *se noyer,* drown (oneself). Like *employer.*

nu, nue, naked, bare: invariable before parts of body: *nu-pieds,* bare footed, **but** after a noun agrees: *la tête nue,* head bare. Adverb: *nûment,* nakedly, frankly (**note** accent).

nuire, to harm, to hurt, to prejudice, to damage: *nuire à qlqn,* to harm sn; *nuire à qlqch,* to damage sth. Pres: *nuis, nuis, nuit, nuisons, nuisez, nuisent.* Imperf: *nuisais, -ais, -ait, -ions, -iez, -aient.* Fut: *nuirai, -as, -a, -ons, -ez, -ont.* Past hist: *nuisis, nuisis, nuisit, nuisîmes, nuisîtes, nuisirent.* Imperat: *nuis, nuisons, nuisez.* Pres subj: *nuise, nuises, nuise, nuisions, nuisiez, nuisent.* Imperf subj: *nuisisse, nuisisses, nuisît, nuisissions, nuisissiez, nuisissent.* Pres part: *nuisant.* Past part: *nui* (invariable). Aux: *avoir: se nuire,* to injure oneself/each other; *elle s'est nui,* she hurt herself: **no** agreement with *se nuire.*

nul, nulle

    i. **indefinite adjective** = no, nil, void: *le testament est nul,* the will is void (null and void): used with *ne* when before the verb, eg: *nul homme ne peut le faire seul,* no man can do it alone: *nul, nulle,* is sometimes used as an alternative to *aucun(e),* eg: *nous n'avions nul espoir,* we had no hope: as for *aucun,* the noun following *nul,* adjective, is nearly always in the singular, with which it agrees, eg: *nulle part,* nowhere: *ils se* *trouvaient nulle part dans le parc,* they weren't anywhere (were nowhere) in the park

ii. **pronoun** = no one, not any: *nul n'est exempt de faire la tâche,* no one is exempt from doing the task; *nulle, parmi ces filles, n'est plus belle,* none, among these girls, is more beautiful. (See **no** above.)

NUMBERS: see Grammar Section.

O

obéir, to obey: *obéir à qlqn/qlqch,* to obey sn/sth; *il leur obéit,* he obeys them; *il y obéit,* he obeys it (eg: the law); *il est obéi,* he is obeyed; *se faire obéir,* to get oneself obeyed. See VERBS ¶8. **Note**: intransitive verbs cannot normally take a passive form: *obéir, désobéir* and *pardonner* are exceptions.

Object

i. the object of a verb may be **direct (accusative)** or **indirect (genitive or dative)**. **Transitive** verbs take a direct object: **intransitive** verbs take an object governed by a preposition. Some English transitive verbs are intransitive in French, and vice versa. Where the pronoun required after a verb (usually *à* or *de*) differs from that in English usage, or is likely to cause difficulty to English speakers using French, the correct usage will be found in the alphabetical entry of that verb. If a verb (unless it be a very unusual one) is not listed, its usage (whether it takes a direct or indirect object, what prepositions it governs, etc), should be as in English, assuming *à* equivalent to 'to', *de* equivalent to 'of' and 'from'

ii. French **nouns** do not alter in form when used as subject, as direct object, or as indirect object (there is no possessive or *'s*): but **most pronouns** (as do some in English) have such forms, eg: he (**subject**) = *il:* him (**direct object, accusative**) = *le* (**pronoun**): to him (**indirect object, dative**) = *lui*. Where a verb governs the preposition *à*, a pronoun object will be in its dative form. Such verbs, eg: *obéir,* to obey, are, in these pages, shown thus: '*obéir à qlqn/qlqch,* to obey sn/sth', which means it takes *à* before the person or thing obeyed: therefore in 'they (fem) obey him', the French will be: *elles lui obéissent* ('they obey **to** him'), '*lui*' (= *à* + *le*), being here the dative* or indirect object form of *il* (he): 'he obeys it' (eg: the law) will be: *il y obéit* (see *y*) (*All the conjunctive pronouns *(je, tu, il, elle, nous, vous, ils, elles)* have accusative and dative forms, though these do **not** always differ from their subject (nominative) form. See PRONOUNS ¶3.)

iii. if the object of a verb is governed by *de,* the object pronoun will be *en,* eg: *jouir de qlqch,* to enjoy sth; thus 'he enjoys it' (direct object in English), will be: *il en jouit, en* (= *de* + *le)* being the indirect object in French. (See *en.)*

obliger, to oblige, force: *qlqn à faire qlqch*, sn to do sth; *être obligé de faire qlqch*, to be obliged to do sth. Like *manger* with *-ge-* before endings starting with *-a-* or *-o-*, eg: *nous obligeons, j'obligeais, obligeant*.

obscur, -e, adjective: obscure, sombre. Adverb: *obscurément*, obscurely, dimly.

observer, to keep/observe (laws, etc), to notice: *qlqn faire qlqch*, (observe/watch) sn do(ing) sth; *faire observer qlqch à qlqn*, to draw sn's attention to sth.

s'obstiner à faire qlqch, to persist in doing sth.

obtenir, to obtain. Like *tenir*.

obtempérer à qlqch, to obey sth, acquiesce in sth. Like *céder*. Pres: *j'obtempère*. Fut: *j'obtempérerai*.

occuper, to occupy: *occuper ses loisirs à faire qlqch*, to occupy one's leisure by doing sth/with sth; *s'occuper à (faire) qlqch*, to busy oneself with/by (doing) sth; *s'occuper de qlqch*, to take care of, to see to sth.

of: *de:* combines with the definite article: *de + le = du* (*de la* and *de l'* do **not** change), *de + les = des* (*des* means both 'of the', plural, and 'some' plural). For something 'made **of**' some material, 'of' is frequently *en*, eg: *une table en marbre*, a marble table; *des vêtements en laine*, woollen clothes: *en* is similarly used for some verbs which in English govern 'of', eg: *consister en qlqch*, to consist **of** sth: for those that do so see individual entries.

off = from = *de:* to take off, *enlever;* to raise/lift, *ôter;* to go off, *s'en aller;* turn/switch off (electrical apparatus, etc), *fermer;* far off, *loin d'ici;* well off, *aisé(e), assez riche;* 'off' = sour (eg: milk), *tourné(e);* off duty, *libre*.

s'offenser de qlqch, to take offence at sth.

offrir, to offer: *qlqch à qlqn*, sth to sn; *de faire qlqch*, to do sth. Like *ouvrir*. Pres: *offre, -es, -e, -ons, -ez, -ent*. Imperf: *offrais*. Fut: *offrirai*. Past hist: *offris*. Pres subj: *offre*. Imperf subj: *offrisse, offrît*. Pres part: *offrant*. Past part: *offert(e)*.

s'ombrager de qlqch, to shade oneself with sth.

omettre, to omit: *omettre qlqch*, to omit sth; *omettre de faire qlqch*, to omit to do sth. Like *mettre*.

omission of: *pas*, see *pas:* **omission of reflexive pronoun**, see PRONOUNS ¶14: **omission of article**, see ARTICLES ¶9.

on, on to: usually = *sur*, **but** many English phrases containing 'on' need re-phrasing as some of the following examples suggest:

    i.   on = *sur:* to arrive on a bike, *arriver sur un vélo* (see **by** ii); to put on a table, *mettre sur une table;* she writes on love, *elle écrit sur l'amour;* the dog jumps on to the bed, *le chien saute sur le lit*. See also *sur* and *dessus*

    ii. on = *à:* on the telly (television), *à la télé (la télévision);* to walk on the right/left, *marcher à droite/gauche;* on my arrival, *à mon arrivée;* on one's head, *à la tête;* on one's (his/her) finger, *au doigt;* on one's feet, *aux pieds;* to put on a diet of bread and water, *mettre au pain et à l'eau;* on the ground floor, *au rez-de-chaussée;* I haven't a penny on me, *je n'ai pas un sou sur moi;* hung on, *suspendu à;* the picture is on the wall, *la peinture est suspendue au mur*

   iii. on = *de:* on this side of the street, *de ce côté de la rue;* on the other side of the street, *de l'autre côté de la rue*

   iv. 'on' for **days** and **dates** is **not** translated, eg: on Monday, *lundi;* on Mondays, *les lundis.* See **Dates**

   v. on = *par:* on a fine day in June, *par un beau jour de juin*

   vi. **switched on**: *allumé(e):* to turn/switch on, *allumer;* to switch/turn on an engine, *mettre en marche*

   vii. 'on' with **pres part**: on entering, *en entrant* (see VERBS ¶43v)

   viii. **with a coat on**, *en pardessus;* with gloves on, *ganté(e)(s);* with one's shoes on, *chaussé(e)(s),* etc

   ix. **to put on** (clothes, etc) = *mettre;* to have on (clothes, etc) = *porter*

   x. **to go on**: he speaks on (and on), *il parle toujours:* or to keep on doing sth, *continuer à faire qlqch;* he keeps on walking, *il continue à marcher.*

on = 'one' as in 'what does one do now?' see PRONOUNS ¶18.

one

   i. I have one (**number**), *j'en ai un(e):* see NUMBERS

   ii. he is one of those who, *il est un de ceux qui;* she is one of those who, *elle est une de celles qui;* to be at one, *être d'accord;* with one another, *l'un(e) avec l'autre;* one another (each other), *l'un l'autre*

   iii. **impersonal pronoun** 'one' (as in 'one must not do that') = *on:* see PRONOUNS ¶18

   iv. **demonstrative pronoun:** *celui, celle:* it is **the one** (that) I am looking for, *c'est celui que je cherche;* of the two houses, I am going to buy **the one** near the beach, *des deux maisons je vais acheter **celle** près de la plage:* see PRONOUNS ¶19, ¶20

   v. **interrogative pronoun:** which one? *lequel? laquelle?* eg: which **one** do you prefer, this one or that one? see PRONOUNS ¶45.

only

   i. **adjective:** *seul, seule,* unique: an only child, *un seul enfant;* an only son, *un fils unique;* only I (I alone), *moi seul;* only her, *elle seule;* only us, *nous seul(e)s:* (see also *seul*)

   ii. **adverb:** (a) *seulement* = only/not more than: there are only two, *il y a seulement deux;* he is only ten years old, *il a seulement dix ans;* he arrived only yesterday, *il est arrivé seulement hier;* not only me, but you too, *non moi seulement mais vous aussi* (see also end of (b) below) (b) *ne . . . que* = only: **cannot be used to refer to the subject**: *ne* follows the subject, preceding any pronoun objects and the verb: *que* comes after the verb or, in a compound tense, after the auxiliary, **but** not necessarily directly after: it should come immediately before the word it is intended to modify. In English we frequently put 'only' in the wrong place, eg: we often say: 'he only writes books to earn a living' which actually means 'he writes books and nothing else' when the intended meaning is 'he writes books only to earn a living', *il n'écrit des livres que pour gagner sa vie:* the *'que'* qualifying *'gagner sa vie'*, **not** *'il écrit'.* I have written only one (single) letter to him, *je ne lui ai écrit qu'une (seule) lettre;* a fool is normally praised only by another fool, *un sot n'est loué d'ordinaire que par un autre sot* ('only' qualifies 'by another fool'): **but:** *'un sot n'est que loué d'ordinaire . . .,'* would mean: 'a fool is normally only praised' – ie: not blamed, punished etc. **Note:** *seulement* could replace *d'ordinaire* in which case 'normally' becomes 'only' (c) *ne . . . que* can be used with *pas* in a negative, and this, with other words, may come between the verb (or auxiliary) and *que*, eg: he doesn't do it quickly enough only out of spite (= for no reason but for spite), *il ne le fait **pas** assez vite **que** par malice.* With an infinitive *que* precedes the word it qualifies: *ne voir que la mer,* to see only the sea (d) *ne faire que* is used with an infinitive to express 'only': *je ne fait que vieillir,* I only grow old (= I do nothing but grow old); *elle n'a fait que pleurer,* she only wept (= she did nothing but weep).

onze, le onze, l'onzième: see **Elision** v.

opportun, -e, adjective: opportune. Adverb: *opportunément,* timely.

oser, to dare: *oser qlqch,* to dare sth; *oser faire qlqch,* to dare do sth; *il n'ose faire,* he does not dare to do: usually *pas* is omitted in a negative followed by an infinitive: see *pas,* **omission of.**

ôter, to take away, remove: *qlqch à qlqn,* sth from sn.

other*:* see *autre* and *tout* ii.

ou, or: spelt **without** accent.

où, where, when (**with** accent). **Relative adverb**
   i. **where:** refers **only** to things: *la ville où nous habitons,* the town where we live; *le pays d'où il vient,* the country from which he comes; *c'est où je l'ai rencontrée,* it is where I met her
   ii. *où* = '**when**' after a word expressing the idea of 'time when': *le temps/jour/heure/année où je l'ai trouvé,* the time/day/hour/year (when) I found it
   iii. *d'où* = '**from which**': *d'où on peut conclure,* from which one may conclude.

oublier, to forget: *de faire qlqch,* to do sth; *oublier avoir fait qlqch,* to forget having done sth; *s'oublier à faire qlqch,* to lose account of time doing sth; *s'oublier jusqu'à faire qlqch,* to forget oneself to such an extent as to do sth.

ought: see *devoir.*

ouïr, to hear. Now used **only** in the infinitive, in the past participle: *ouï, ouïe*, and in compound tenses with auxiliary *avoir:* I heard say that, *j'ai ouï dire que*.

our: see *notre:* **ours**: see *le nôtre*. **Note**: a friend of ours, *un de nos amis*.

out, outside, out of: to go out, *sortir;* to go outside, *aller dehors;* to be outside, *être au dehors;* outside the house, *en dehors de la maison;* out of doors, *dehors, hors de la maison;* out of sight, *hors de vue;* to read out of a book, *lire dans un livre;* to take out of a drawer, pocket, etc, *prendre dans un tiroir/une poche*, etc; to drink out of a glass, etc, *boire dans un verre*, etc.

outre, beyond: now used in such phrases as: *outre-mer*, across the sea; *outre-Manche*, across the English Channel; *outre-monts*, over the mountains (the other side of the mountains – especially said of the Alps); *en outre*, besides, moreover; *outre que*, besides that.

outre, noun (fem): goat-skin, leather bottle.

outré, outrée, exaggerated: *outré de*, indignant at/about sth.

ouvrir, to open: *qlqch à qlqn: ouvrir son cœur/sa maison à qlqn*, to open one's heart/house to sn; *ouvrir un compte à qlqn*, to open an account for/grant credit to sn. Pres: *ouvre, ouvres, ouvre, ouvrons, ouvrez, ouvrent*. Imperf: *ouvrais, -ais, -ait, -ions, -iez, -aient*. Fut: *ouvrirai, ouvriras, ouvrira, ouvrirons, ouvrirez, ouvriront*. Past hist: *ouvris, ouvris, ouvrit, ouvrîmes, ouvrîtes, ouvrirent*. Imperat: *ouvre, ouvrons, ouvrez*. Pres subj: *ouvre, ouvres, ouvre, ouvrions, ouvriez, ouvrent*. Imperf subj: *ouvrisse, ouvrisses, ouvrît, ouvrissions, ouvrissiez, ouvrissent*. Pres part: *ouvrant*. Past part: *ouvert, ouverte, ouverts, ouvertes*. Aux: *avoir*.

over: above: see *dessus:* to rule over, *régner sur;* it is over = ended, *c'est fini;* one over, *un(e) en plus;* white all over, *tout blanc*.

own

    i. **verb**, to own
        a. possess: *posséder*. Like *céder: je possède, je posséderai*, etc
        b. to acknowledge: *avouer, reconnaître*. Like *connaître*
        c. own up, confess: *avouer, confesser*
    ii. **adjective**: *propre:* written with his own hand, *écrit(e) de sa propre main;* here are his own words, *voici ses propres mots* (**or** *paroles);* a house of my/his/her/one's own, *une maison à moi/à lui/à elle/à soi;* at his/her own house, *chez lui/elle;* to hold one's own, *tenir sa place;* to live on one's own, *vivre seul*.

-oyer, -uyer, **verbs**: verbs so ending change *-y-* to *-i-* before *e*-mute endings, and in future stem: for example see *employer*, to use, eg: *j'emploie, nous employons, ils emploient, j'emploierai*, etc. See also *envoyer*, to send, which has an irregular future stem: *j'enverrai*.

P

page, **masculine** = pageboy: **feminine** = page of a book.

paître, to graze on, feed upon: *paître de qlqch*, to graze on sth; *mener paître, faire paître*, to lead to pasture; *envoyer qlqn paître*, to send sn packing. Pres: *pais, pais, paît, paissons, paissez, paissent*. Imperf: *paissais, -ais, -ait, -ions, -iez, -aient*. Fut: *paîtrai, -as, -a, -ons, -ez, -ont*. No past hist. Imperat: *pais, paissons, paissez*. Pres subj: *paisse, paisses, paisse, paissions, paissiez, paissent*. No imperf subj. Pres part: *paissant*. No past part.

palpiter, to palpitate, to throb: *de qlqch*, with sth.

se pâmer de rire, joie, etc, to die of, split one's sides with, burst with laughing, joy, etc.

par, by, per, via, on account of: *par force*, by force; *par ici*, this way; *aller par (le) chemin de fer*, to go by rail; *voyager par mer*, travel by sea; *par avion*, by plane/by air; *deux fois par semaine*, two times/twice a week; *passer par Londres*, to go via London; *de par*, by, eg: *de par la volonté du peuple*, by the will of the people.

paraître, to appear, seem: *paraître faire qlqch*, seem to be doing sth. Like **connaître**. Aux: **être** for describing state or condition: **avoir** to describe an action performed.

pardonner, to forgive: *pardonner qlqn*, to forgive sn; *de qlqch*, for sth; *pardonner qlqch à qlqn*, to forgive sn for sth; *d'avoir fait qlqch*, for having done sth; *il est pardonné*, he is forgiven. (See note to **obéir**.)

parer

    i. **to adorn**: *qlqn/qlqch*, sn/sth; *de qlqch*, with sth; *se parer de qlqch*, to adorn oneself with sth

    ii. **to ward off, parry**: *parer qlqn contre qlqch* **or** *de qlqch*, to guard sn against sth; *parer à qlqch*, to provide against sth/avert sth.

parler, to speak, to talk: *faire parler quelqu'un*, to make sn speak; *parler (le) français, parler (l')anglais*, to speak French, English (before a language the definite article is often dropped); *parler haut*, to speak loud; *parler hautement pour*, to speak up for; *sans parler*, without speaking; *parler de faire qlqch*, to speak of doing sth.

participer, to take part/share: *à qlqch*, in sth.

Participles: formation and usage see VERBS ¶42, ¶43. **Agreement of past participles**: see VERBS ¶44. **Passive participles** see VERBS ¶8.

partir, to depart, to leave. Pres: *pars, pars, part, partons, partez, partent*. Imperf: *partais, -ais, -ait, -ions, -iez, -aient*. Fut: *partirai, -as, -a, -ons, -ez, -ont*. Past hist: *partis, partis, partit, partîmes, partîtes, partirent*. Imperat: *pars, partons, partez*. Pres subj: *parte, partes, parte, partions, partiez, partent*. Imperf subj:

partisse, partisses, partît, partissions, partissiez, partissent. Pres part: *partant.* Past part: *parti, partie, partis, parties.* Aux: *être.* (Formerly, **but** not now, *avoir* was also used.)

Partitive Article: see ARTICLES ¶5, ¶6, ¶7.

parvenir, to reach, attain, succeed in, manage: *parvenir à qlqch,* to attain to sth; *parvenir à faire qlqch,* to manage to do sth, succeed in doing sth.

pas, used after a verb with *ne* before the verb for 'not', eg: *je parle,* I speak; *je ne parle pas,* I do **not** speak. In compound tenses *pas* follows the auxiliary: *il n'a pas parlé,* he has **not** spoken: *pas* is also used for 'not' **without** *ne* when there is no verb, eg: *pas moi!* not I! *pas du tout,* not at all; *pas assez,* not enough; *pas beaucoup,* not much; *pas trop,* not too much; *pas un seul morceau,* not a single bit, etc: *pas* is also used together with *que* to mean 'no one but', 'nothing but', eg: *je ne pense pas qu'à toi,* I think of no one but you; *il ne s'agit pas que de ton bonheur,* it is a question of nothing but your happiness (there is no question of anything but . . .): *pas* as a negative can be replaced by *point*, with the same meaning, **but** usually used for greater emphasis. When used with an infinitive, **both** *ne* and *pas* precede the verb: *'se taire' veut dire: ne pas parler, ou ne pas divulguer un secret, ou bien ne pas faire de bruit,* 'to keep quiet' means not to speak, **or** not to divulge a secret, **or** also not to make a noise. See *ne* and *que.*

***pas*, omission of**: in a negative *ne* may at times be used **without** *pas* (or *point*), this occurs:

    i.   **mainly** in certain fixed phrases, including: *il n'importe,* it doesn't matter; *à Dieu ne plaise!* God forbid! *n'ayez crainte,* don't be afraid (see *ne*)

    ii.   when two negatives or two statements are linked by *ni: il ne boit ni mange,* he neither drinks nor eats

    iii.   in a **subjunctive clause** in the **negative** following a main clause in the negative or interrogative: *je ne connais personne qui ne veuille être ici,* I don't know anyone who does not wish to be here; *y a-t-il une d'elles qui ne le fasse?* is there one of them who does not do it?

    iv.   **with the verbs**: *cesser, oser* and *pouvoir* when they are followed by an infinitive: *il n'ose le faire,* he doesn't dare do it

    v.   **after** *savoir* when it means to be uncertain: *il ne sait ce qu'ils vont faire,* he doesn't know what they are going to do **and** in *'je ne saurais'* meaning 'I couldn't' (= 'I shouldn't know how'); *je ne saurais le faire,* I couldn't do it ('I shouldn't know how to do it')

    vi.   usually **after** *si* meaning 'if': *si je ne me trompe,* unless I am mistaken (= if I don't deceive myself)

    vii.   **after** the conjunction *depuis que,* **or** one having the same meaning of 'since', introducing a compound tense: *il y a deux mois depuis que je ne vous ai vu,* it's two months since I saw you.

    viii.   **in phrases** starting with words meaning 'it's not that', such as: *ce n'est que* **or** *non que,* eg: *ce n'est qu'il ne soit toujours gentil,* it's not that he isn't always kind (**or** *non qu'il ne soit toujours gentil,* not that he isn't always kind).

passer, to pass: *passer une maison,* pass (by) a house; *passer un examen,* to pass an exam; *passer son temps à faire qlqch,* to pass one's time doing sth; *passer qlqch à qlqn,* pass/hand sth to sn: **pass by, call on:** *passer voir qlqn,* to drop in on sn/call on sn; *se passer de qlqch,* to do without sth. **Conjugated**

    i.   with *avoir* when 'to pass sth' is meant: *elle lui a passé le sucre,* she passed (to) him the sugar; *il a passé par bien des épreuves,* he has passed through many trials (= a statement of fact about the past: sth that has happened); *sa beauté a passé,* her/his beauty has left her/him (= statement of what the beauty has done)

    ii. with *être* when a state of being or change of condition is indicated and in reflexive: *il est passé par bien des épreuves,* he's a man who has known many trials (= describing what he is now, has by now become); *sa beauté est passée,* his/her beauty has passed (= statement of his/her present condition): *être* **must** be used when a 'change of position' is involved, whether real or figurative: *où je suis passé j'espère mon fils passera, lui aussi,* where I have passed (the way I have gone) I hope my son, he too, will pass; *il m'a arrêté lorsque je suis passé devant lui,* he stopped me when I passed in front of him; *se passer,* to pass by; *l'heure s'est passée* vite,* the hour passed quickly (*agrees): = **to happen, take place:** *ceci s'est passé à Paris,* this happened in Paris.

se passionner de/pour qlqch, to become enamoured with sth.

Passive: see VERBS ¶7 and ¶8.

Past Tenses: see VERBS ¶14, ¶17, ¶20 – 27, ¶31, ¶32.

pas un, more emphatic than *aucun* to express 'not one' – 'not a single one': further strengthened if necessary by **seul**: *pas un (seul) petit morceau,* not a (single) little bit. As **indefinite pronoun,** eg: *–Combien? –Pas un(e)!* 'How many?' 'Not (a single) one!' *pas un ne revint,* not one returned.

payer, to pay: *payer qlqn/qlqch,* to pay sn/sth; *j'ai payé le boucher,* I have paid the butcher; *j'ai payé la dette,* I have paid the debt; *payer qlqch à qlqn,* to pay sn for sth; *j'ai payé l'entrée à mon ami,* I have paid for the entrance for my friend; *payer qlqch de qlqch,* to pay for sth with sth; *il a payé son inflexibilité de sa liberté,* he has paid for his stubbornness with his freedom. **Sample verb for verbs ending in -*ayer*.** The -*y*- may be retained throughout and -*ayer* verbs are then like any other regular -*er* verb: **but** some writers change the -*y*- to -*i*- before *e*-mute and in the future stem. Pres: *paie/paye, paies/payes, paie/paye, payons, payez, paient/payent.* Imperf: *payais, -ais, -ait, -ions, -iez, -aient.* Fut: *paierai/payerai,* etc. Past hist: *payai, payas, paya, payâmes, payâtes, payèrent.* Imperat: *paie/paye, payons, payez.* Pres subj: *paie/paye, paies/payes, paie/paye, payions, payiez, paient/payent.* Imperf subj: *payasse, payasses, payât, payassions, payassiez, payassent.* Pres part: *payant.* Past part: *payé, payée, payés, payées.* Aux: *avoir.*

pécher, to sin. Like *céder*, the *-ch-* being considered as one consonant: *je pèche, je pécherai*, etc. **Distinguish from** *pêcher*, to fish. The *-ê-* remains unaltered throughout (with circumflex).

pécheur, pécheresse, sinner (**note** masculine and feminine forms). **Distinguish from** *pêcheur, pêcheuse*, fisherman, fisherwoman (**note** masculine and feminine).

peigner, to comb: *se peigner*, to comb one's hair. Regular *-er* verb.

peindre, to paint. Like *craindre*. Pres: *peins, peint, peignons*, etc. Imperf: *peignais*, etc. Fut: *peindrai*, etc. Past hist: *peignis*, etc. Pres part: *peignant*. Past part: *peint*.

peine, **noun** (fem): punishment, affliction, grief, difficulty: *la peine capitale*, capital punishment; *sous peine de mort*, under pain of death; *il ne vaut pas la peine*, it is not worth while, not worth the trouble; *un homme de peine*, a labourer, a drudge; *donnez-vous la peine de vous asseoir*, please take a seat; *sans peine*, without difficulty. **Adverb**: *à peine*, hardly, scarcely: *il était à peine arrivé, quand il monta à sa chambre*, he had hardly arrived, when he went up to his room; *il sait à peine lire*, he can hardly read; *à peine son ami était-il* arrivé qu'**il lui montra le livre*, hardly had his friend arrived when he showed him the book. (*Note: when a clause is introduced by *à peine* a subject pronoun follows the verb, **or** a pronoun is inserted after the verb if the subject is a noun: **'when' can be *quand, lorsque* **or** *que*.)

peler, to peel (fruit, etc). Like *mener*: *je pèle, je pèlerai*, etc.

pencher, to lean, to tend, to incline: *pencher à* **or** *vers qlqch*, to tend towards sth; *pencher à faire qlqch*, incline towards doing sth; *se pencher*, to lower oneself, bow down; *se pencher sur qlqch*, to turn one's attention to sth.

pendre, to hang, suspend: *à qlqch*, from sth; *aux arbres*, from the trees; *au mur*, on the wall; *pendu à ses paroles*, hanging on his words. Conjugated like *vendre*.

pendule, **masculine** = pendulum: **feminine** = clock (in house). (**Note:** a public clock = *une horloge*.)

pénétrer, to penetrate, imbue: *qlqn de qlqch*, sn with sth; *se pénétrer de qlqch*, to imbue oneself with sth. Like *céder*, *-tr-* counts as one consonant.

penser, to think: *penser à qlqn/qlqch*, to think about (= bear in mind, give thought to) sn/sth; *penser à faire qlqch*, to think of doing sth/intend to do sth; *penser de qlqn/qlqch*, to think of sn/sth (= to pass judgement on, eg: *que pensez-vous du professeur?* what do you think of the master?); *penser qlqch de qlqn/qlqch*, to think sth about sn/sth.

per: three times per day, *trois fois par jour;* three francs per kilo, *trois francs le kilo;* ten per cent, *dix pour cent*.

perdre, to lose. Pres: *perds, perds, perd, perdons, perdez, perdent*. Imperf: *perdais, -ais, -ait, -ions, -iez, -aient*. Fut: *perdrai, -as, -a, -ons, -ez, -ont*. Past hist:

perdis, perdis, perdit, perdîmes, perdîtes, perdirent. Imperat: *perds, perdons, perdez.* Pres subj: *perde, perdes, perde, perdions, perdiez, perdent.* Imperf subj: *perdisse, perdisses, perdît, perdissions, -issiez, -issent.* Pres part: *perdant.* Past part: *perdu, -e, -s, -es.* Aux: *avoir.*

permettre, to permit, allow: *qlqch à qlqn,* to permit sth to sn, permit sn sth; *permettre à qlqn de faire qlqch,* to allow sn to do sth. Impersonal: *il lui/leur est permis de faire qlqch,* it is allowed to him/them to do sth = he is/they are allowed to do sth; *se permettre de faire qlqch,* to allow oneself to do sth. Conjugated like ***mettre***.

persévérer, to persevere: *dans qlqch,* in sth; *à faire qlqch,* in doing sth. Conjugated like ***céder***: *je persévère, je persévérerai.*

persister, to persist: *dans qlqch,* in sth; *à faire qlqch,* in doing sth.

Personal Pronouns: see PRONOUNS ¶1 – 18.

personne, **noun** (fem): a person of either sex.

personne, **indefinite pronoun**, masc: someone, somebody, or, more frequently, no one, nobody. In the negative, personne takes *ne* before the verb if there is one: *je ne connais personne de* meilleur,* I know no one better (*Note: an adjective/adjectival phrase following *personne* **must** be preceded by *de*); *personne n'est arrivé* (masc), no one has arrived: if there is no verb the negative may be 'understood': *–Qui est là? –Personne!* 'Who is there?' 'Nobody!' More rarely: *personne* = sn, anyone, **but** only when used interrogatively **or** after a verb expressing doubt: *y a-t-il personne là?* is anyone there? *je doute que personne puisse le faire,* I doubt if anyone can do it. It is **not** possible to use *pas* or *point* with *ne . . . personne,* **but** *jamais* or *plus* may be included: *je ne vois jamais* (or *plus*) ***personne***, I never (or, no longer) see anyone. Used with an infinitive, *personne* follows the verb: *n'entendre personne,* to hear no one.

persuader, to persuade: *persuader qlqn de qlqch,* to persuade sn of sth; *persuader qlqch à qlqn,* to convince sn of sth; *je m'en suis persuadé,* I am convinced of/about it.

peu

i. **noun** (masc): a little, a few, a small quantity: *un peu de pain,* a little bread; *un peu du pain est sur l'assiette,* a little **of the** bread is on the plate; *les hommes sont arrivés hier, peu sont restés,* the men arrived yesterday, few have remained (*peu* is treated as masc sing **or** masc plural according to the sense)

ii. **adverb**: little (not much): *il parle peu,* he speaks little; *peu de gens sont contents,* few people are content (agreement with the noun); *dans/sous peu,* soon; *depuis peu,* recently; *peu à peu,* little by little; *aussi peu que possible,* as little as possible; *pour peu qu'il en mange* (subjunctive), however little he may eat of it; *peu s'en faut,* all but (may be used alone as a succinct comment). See ***petit*** and **less**

iii. ***peu de chose***, indefinite singular pronoun: 'little': *peu de chose peut
      nous aider*, little can help us; *j'ai peu de chose de grande valeur*, I have
      little of great value. (**Note**: *chose* in this phrase is **not** considered a
      separate noun, and is invariable: **note also** gender of *la valeur*.)

placer, to place. **Sample verb for those ending in -cer:** takes *ç* before endings
starting with *a* or *o*. Pres: *place, places, place, plaçons, placez, placent*.
Imperf: *plaçais, plaçais, plaçait, placions, placiez, plaçaient*. Fut: *placerai,
-as, -a, -ons, -ez, -ont*. Past hist: *plaçai, plaças, plaça, plaçâmes, plaçâtes,
placèrent*. Imperat: *place, plaçons, placez*. Pres subj: *place, places, place,
placions, placiez, placent*. Imperf subj: *plaçasse, -es, plaçât, plaçassions,
-ssiez, -assent*. Pres part: *plaçant*. Past part: *placé, -cés, -cée, -cées*. Aux:
avoir.

plaindre, to pity: ***se plaindre*** *de*, to complain of/about: like ***craindre*** and ***peindre***.

plaire, to please. Pres: *plais, plais, plaît, plaisons, plaisez, plaisent*. Imperf: *plaisais,
-ais, -ait, -ions, -iez, -aient*. Fut: *plairai, -as, -a, -ons, -ez, -ont*. Past hist: *plus,
plus, plut, plûmes, plûtes, plurent*. Imperat: *plais, plaisons, plaisez*. Pres subj:
plaise, plaises, plaise, plaisions, plaisiez, plaisent. Imperf subj: *plusse,
plusses, plût, plussions, plussiez, plussent*. Pres part: *plaisant*. Past part: *plu*
(invariable). Aux: ***avoir:*** *plaire à qlqn*, to please sn; *s'il vous plaît*, please, if
you please (literally: if it pleases **to** you); *il lui plaît de faire qlqch*, it pleases
him to do sth; ***se plaire*** *à faire qlqch*, to take pleasure in (doing) sth; *se plaire
l'un l'autre*, to take pleasure in one another; *elle s'est plu* à faire qlqch*, she
has taken pleasure in doing sth; *ils plaisent à la campagne*, they like being in
the countryside. When reflexive auxiliary: ***être***. *No agreement of past
participle (reflexive pronoun is indirect object).

play: verb: see ***jouer***.

plein, -e, **adjective**: full. **Adverb** (invariable): *tout plein*, quite (completely) full. **Also**
as **preposition** (invariable): *avoir l'argent plein ses poches*, to have one's
pockets full of money (*plein* = as full as can be).

pleurer, to weep: *pleurer qlqn/qlqch*, to mourn (for) sn/sth; *pleurer de joie*, to weep
for joy; *pleurer sur/pour qlqch*, to weep over/for sth.

pleuvoir, to rain: impersonal verb: *il pleut* (it is raining). Imperf: *il pleuvait*. Fut: *il
pleuvra*. Past hist: *il plut*. Pres subj: *il pleuve*. Imperf subj: *il plût*. Pres part:
pleuvant. Past part: *plu* (invariable). Aux: ***avoir***. **Although** impersonal, can be
used figuratively with another subject, eg: *les bombes pleuvent sur la ville*, the
bombs rain on to the town.

plupart, fem: the majority: when used as subject, the verb and any past participle or
adjective, will agree with whatever the majority refers to, whether actually
mentioned or understood: *la plupart (des gens) sont contents*, the majority (of
people) are satisfied (reference is to *gens* = people: masc plur): **but** the
singular of the verb, with feminine agreement, is necessary if reference is to
'the majority' itself (ie: to 'the greater part'): *j'écris un livre; la plupart est*

finie, I am writing a book; the greater part is finished (it is the greater part, not the book, which is finished); *la plupart du temps*, usually, most of the time.

Pluperfect Tense: see VERBS ¶24.

Plurals: see NOUNS ¶6, ADJECTIVES ¶4 and **Names**.

plus, more. Used in the comparative and superlative of adjectives and adverbs. See ADJECTIVES ¶7 and ADVERBS ¶4. With *ne* before the verb = no more, no longer: *il n'habite plus Paris*, he no longer lives in Paris; *plus ou moins*, more or less; *de plus en plus*, more and more; *(tout) au plus*, at the most; *bien plus*, much more; *d'autant plus*, all the more (so); *plus de . . .*, more than (a named number); *plus que . . .*, more than . . . (**before** a noun or disjunctive pronoun: *plus que vous*, more than you); *de plus*, more (**after** noun: *une heure de plus*, one hour more).

plusieurs, indefinite adjective and pronoun, invariable and plural = several: *j'ai acheté plusieurs pommes et plusieurs livres*, I bought several apples and several books; *j'en* ai encore plusieurs*, I still have several ('of them' = *en*, **must** be expressed in French).

poêle, **masculine** = stove, pall, canopy: **feminine** = pan, frying-pan (**or** *poêle à frire*).

poindre, to dawn: rare except in 3rd sing of present: *il point* **and** in future: *il poindra*, conditional: *il poindrait*. Compound tenses (*point* with *avoir*) and in the infinitive: *dès que le jour a point*, as soon as the day dawned. The parts used are conjugated like *craindre*.

porter, to carry: *porter qlqn à faire qlqch*, to incite sn to do sth; *être porté à faire qlqch*, to be inclined to do sth, have the urge to do sth.

posséder, to possess. Conjugated like *céder*: *je possède, je posséderai*.

Possessive Pronouns: see PRONOUNS ¶37, ¶38, ¶39.

Possessive Adjectives: see ADJECTIVES ¶10.

Possessive Case: see *'s, s'* (at start of **S** Section).

possible, adjective: after *le plus* and *le moins* remains singular, eg: *les plus de livres possible*, the most books possible: otherwise agrees in plural normally.

poste, **masculine** = post = position (eg: outpost, job), police station: *un poste d'incendie*, a fire station; *un poste (radiophonique)*, a radio station; *un (poste) récepteur*, a radio/TV receiving post/receiver/set. **Feminine** = mail. (**Note**: a post = an upright pole = *un poteau*.)

pour, preposition: for: see **for**.

pour que, conjunction: in order that: is followed by the subjunctive: *je lui ai donné l'argent pour qu'il puisse venir*, I have given him the money so that/in order that he may come.

pourquoi, why: *pourquoi êtes-vous si triste?* why are you so sad? *je ne sais pas pourquoi,* I don't know why.

poursuivre, to pursue. Conjugated like *suivre*.

pourtant, nevertheless, still = on the other hand: *c'est difficile, pourtant, si vous insistez . . .* , it is difficult, still, if you insist . . .

pourvoir, to provide. Pres: *pourvois, pourvois, pourvoit, pourvoyons, pourvoyez, pourvoient.* Imperf: *pourvoyais, -ais, -ait, -ions, -iez, -aient.* Fut: *pourvoirai, -as, -a, -ons, -ez, -ont.* Past hist: *pourvus, pourvus, pourvut, pourvûmes, pourvûtes, pourvurent.* Imperat: *pourvois, pourvoyons, pourvoyez.* Pres subj: *pourvoie, pourvoies, pourvoie, pourvoyions, pourvoyiez, pourvoient.* Imperf subj: *pourvusse, pourvusses, pourvût, pourvussions, pourvussiez, pourvussent.* Pres part: *pourvoyant.* Past part: *pourvu, -e, -s, -es.* Aux: ***avoir***: *pourvoir à vos besoins,* to provide for your needs.

pouvoir, to be able, 'can' = both, 'have power, ability to' and 'have permission to'. Pres: *peux* **or** *puis* (in the interrogative: *puis-je?*), *peux, peut, pouvons, pouvez, peuvent.* Imperf: *pouvais, -ais, -ait, -ions, -iez, -aient.* Fut: *pourrai, -as, -a, -ons, -ez, -ont.* Past hist: *pus, pus, put, pûmes, pûtes, purent.* No imperative. Pres subj: *puisse* (in the interrogative *puissé-je?*), *puisses, puisse, puissions, puissiez, puissent.* Imperf subj: *pusse, pusses, pût, pussions, pussiez, pussent.* Pres part: *pouvant.* Past part: *pu* (invariable). Aux: ***avoir***: *je peux le faire,* I can do it; *vous pouvez le faire maintenant,* you can/may do it now; *pourriez-vous m'aider?* could you help me, please? (Conditional tense makes it more polite = 'would you like to'.) *je ne pourrais pas le faire sans argent,* I could not do it without money; *puisse-t-il réussir!* may he succeed! For omission of *pas* with *pouvoir* in negative, followed by an infinitive see ***pas*, omission of** iv.

prédire, to predict. Like ***dire*** except 2nd plural present and imperative: *prédisez.*

préférer, to prefer. Like ***céder***: *je préfère, je préférerai.*

prendre, to take. Pres: *prends, prends, prend, prenons, prenez, prennent.* Imperf: *prenais, -ais, -ait, -ions, -iez, -aient.* Fut: *prendrai, -as, -a, -ons, -ez, -ont.* Past hist: *pris, pris, prit, prîmes, prîtes, prirent.* Imperat: *prends, prenons, prenez.* Pres subj: *prenne, prennes, prenne, prenions, preniez, prennent.* Imperf subj: *prisse, prisses, prît, prissions, prissiez, prissent.* Pres part: *prenant.* Past part: *pris, prise, pris, prises.* Aux: ***avoir***: *prendre qlqch à qlqn,* to take sth **from** sn; *prendre qlqn à faire qlqch,* to catch sn doing sth; *prendre qlqch **dans** un tiroir/une poche,* to take sth **out of/from** a drawer/pocket; *prendre qlqch **sur** une table,* to take sth from off a table; *prendre garde à qlqch,* to beware of sth; ***se prendre** à qlqch,* to start doing sth. When reflexive, auxiliary: ***être***.

se préoccuper *de faire qlqch,* to be engrossed doing sth.

préparer, to prepare: *qlqn/qlqch,* sn/sth; *à faire qlqch,* to do sth; *se préparer à faire qlqch,* to prepare oneself to do sth; *à qlqch,* for sth.

PREPOSITIONS: see Grammar Section.

près, near: *tout près*, very near; *à peu près*, approximately; *près de*, near to.

Present Participle: see VERBS ¶43 and PREPOSITIONS ¶4.

Present Tense: see VERBS ¶13.

Price: *le prix:* to price sth, *évaluer qlqch, mettre un prix à qlqch;* at a reduced price, *au rabais.* **Cost**: *il coûte trois francs la douzaine,* it costs (the price is) three francs per dozen: *le prix* **also** means: the prize.

prier, to pray, ask, beg: *prier Dieu*, to pray to God; *prier pour*, to pray for; *prier qlqn de faire qlqch*, to ask sn to do sth; *silence! je vous en prie!* kindly keep quiet!

prochain, -e, **adj**: neighbouring, nearest: *jeudi prochain*, next Thursday. **Noun** (masc only): neighbour = fellow human. **Adverb**: *prochainement*, soon. See *voisin*.

procurer, to obtain: *qlqch à qlqn*, sth for sn; *se procurer*, to get sth for oneself.

prodigieux, prodigieuse, adjective: wonderful, huge. Adverb: *prodigieusement*, wonderfully, to a prodigious amount or quantity.

prodigue, adjective: prodigal, lavish, extravagant. Adverb: *prodiguement*, lavishly, wastefully, extravagantly.

prodiguer qlqch à qlqn, to lavish sth on sn.

produire, to produce: *se produire*, to show oneself (in public). Like *conduire*.

professeur, masc: teacher, professor. **No** feminine form.

Professions: feminine forms: see NOUNS ¶2 – 4. Stating someone's profession, see PRONOUNS ¶33.

profiter, to profit: *de qlqch*, from sth; *de faire qlqch*, from doing sth; *profiter à qlqn de faire qlqch*, to profit/benefit sn (be of profit to sn) doing sth.

profond, -e, **adjective**: deep, profound. **Noun** (masc): depth, abyss: *au plus profond*, at the lowest point. **Adverb**: *profondément*, deeply, profoundly, intensely.

profus, -e, adjective: profuse. Adverb: *profusément*, profusely.

prohiber, to prohibit: *prohiber qlqch à qlqn*, to forbid sn sth; *à qlqn de faire qlqch*, sn to do sth.

promener, to walk (to lead to and fro), to parade sn/sth: *promener un chien*, to take a dog for a walk; *se promener*, to walk = to go for a walk. Like *mener*.

promettre, to promise. Conjugated like *mettre*: *qlqch à qlqn*, sth to sn; *de faire qlqch*, to do sth; *se promettre*, to promise oneself, resolve *(de faire qlqch)*.

proposer à qlqn de faire qlqch, to propose to sn to do sth.

propre, adjective: clean, proper, own: *des mains propres*, clean hands; *de sa propre main*, with his own hand; *propre à*, proper to.

provoquer qlqn à faire qlqch, to provoke sn to do sth.

PRONOUNS: see Grammar Section.

Proper Names: see **Names**.

proposer, to propose, to offer: *qlqch à qlqn*, sth to sn; *à qlqn de faire qlqch*, propose to sn to do sth; *proposer qlqn*, to propose sn, put sn forward (eg: for a post); *se proposer*, to offer oneself; *se proposer de faire qlqch*, to resolve to do sth.

proscrire, to proscribe, banish, exclude, exile. Like *écrire*.

protéger, to protect: *qlqn de/contre qlqch*, from/against sth. The *-é-* becomes *-è-* before the *e*-mute endings *-e, -es,* and *-ent*, **but** remains *-é-* elsewhere. Like *manger* for the insertion of *-e-* after *-g-* before endings starting with *a* or *o*, eg: *je protège, nous protégeons, je protégeais, je protégerai, protégeant, protégé.*

protester, to protest: *protester avoir fait qlqch*, to protest that one has done sth; *protester de son innocence*, to protest one's innocence.

provenir de, to arise from, come from. Like *venir*.

provoquer, to provoke: *qlqn à faire qlqch*, sn to do sth.

public, publique, **adjective**: public. **Adverb**: *publiquement*. **Noun**: *le public*, the public.

Punctuation: stops are: full stop, *le point;* comma, *la virgule;* colon, *les deux points;* semi-colon, *le point-virgule;* question mark, *le point d'interrogation;* exclamation mark, *le point d'exclamation;* hyphen, *le trait;* the dash (used usually at the start of quoted speech), *le tiret;* suspension points, *les points de suspension (. . .);* brackets, *les parenthèses* (fem); to put between brackets, *mettre entre parenthèses:* and inverted commas, *les guillemets (<< . . . >>)* (to open/close the inverted commas, *ouvrir/fermer les guillemets*). See **Inverted Commas** for French usage. **Note** that a comma is not used where words are separated by *et, ou,* or (usually) *ni:* when there is a list of several nouns with the last two linked by *et*, a comma must **not** be used before *et*, eg: *l'encre, le papier, le crayon et le stylo étaient . . .* The comma is not used between numbers: *il a deux francs cinquante centimes; il a travaillé pendant six heures trente minutes.* Except for use of commas (above) and of inverted commas, punctuation in French is much as in English. A hyphen is used to link a verb with a following conjunctive pronoun: to link *-même(s)* = self/selves to its preceding pronoun: to join *-ci* and *-là* to the word they qualify: and is an integral part of some compound nouns, pronouns, and numbers. In numbers the French use a point where we use a comma and a comma for a decimal point. See NUMBERS.

punir, to punish: *qlqn de qlqch*, sn for sth; *d'avoir fait qlqch*, for having done sth; *de prison*, with prison.

Q

quand, adverb and conjunction = when, if: *quand je l'ai vu*, when I saw him. Usually followed by the future tense when the future is envisaged, eg: *quand nous aurons mangé nous partirons*, when we (shall) have eaten we shall leave. Followed by the conditional when meaning 'if': *je le ferai quand j'aurais le temps*, I shall do it if I have time (= when I should have the time): *quand?* is also an interrogative adverb: *quand est-ce qu'il arrivera?* when will he arrive? **Note**: after a noun of **time**, 'when' is translated by *où*, eg: *le jour où nous sommes arrivés*. See *où* and also ***lorsque***. For use of *quand* as a conjunction after a clause starting with *c'est . . . :* see PRONOUNS, end of ¶30.

quand même, at the beginning of a phrase = even if, although: *quand même il n'y a plus d'encre je vais écrire*, even if there is no more ink I am going to write: if something is merely supposed or possible the conditional is used: *quand même il n'y aurait plus d'encre, je pourrais écrire avec un crayon*, even if there were no more ink I could (= should be able to) write with a pencil: **or** with the conditional perfect (conditional of the auxiliary + past participle): *quand même il n'aurait pas lu le livre il l'aurait acheté*, even if he had not read the book he would have bought it: *quand même* at the **end** of a phrase, **and** often also at the beginning, may mean 'all the same' or 'nevertheless': *il ne le voulait pas, mais je l'ai fait quand même*, he did not wish it, but I did it all the same; *tu ne veux pas? – quand même je vais le faire*, you don't want to? – nevertheless I'm going to do it.

qualifier, to qualify: *qualifié pour faire qlqch*, qualified to do sth.

que, has many meanings, and stands in at times for other less diligent words. The following is an assortment of its uses:

    i.   **than**: **conjunction**: *il est plus grand que vous*, he is taller than you

    ii. **that**: **conjunction**: *on dit que le roi est mort*, they say that the king is dead; *j'aime mieux que vous restiez* ici*, I prefer that you stay here (*with subjunctive); *il sait que son fils le veut et que** sa femme ne le veut pas*, he knows that his son wants it and (that) his wife doesn't want it (**the *que* must be repeated even if not repeated in English)

    iii. **since**: **conjunction** (seeing that): *a-t-il oublié sa famille, qu'il n'écrive jamais?* has he forgotten his family since he never writes?

    iv. **whether** (if): **conjunction**: *je doute qu'il puisse le faire*, I doubt whether (if) he is able to do it: takes the subjunctive: see subjunctive in VERBS ¶33

    v. **as repetition of or replacement for another conjunction**: *quand nous l'aurons trouvé, et que* nous l'aurons mis à sa place . . .* (*for *quand*), when we have found it, and (when we) have put it in its place . . . ; *montrez-le-moi que* je puisse le voir de plus près* (*for *pour que***), show it to me, in order that/so that I may have a closer look (**pour que, subordinating conjunction which takes the subjunctive: see CONJUNCTIONS ¶5 = 'that I may see it from more near'

    vi. **relative pronoun**: whom/which, as in 'the man whom . . .'; the book which/that': see PRONOUNS ¶35 and ¶40ff: see also *ce que*, and **what**

vii. **interrogative pronoun: what**? *que dites-vous?* what do you say? *que fait-il?* what is he doing? See **Interrogative**, PRONOUNS ¶48 and also *qu'est-ce que* in *qui est-ce qui?* below

viii. *que* + **subjunctive**, to express a wish (adverb): *que Dieu vous bénisse!* may God bless you! See VERBS ¶33ii

ix. *que* with *ne* before verb = **only**: **adverb**: *il n'a que deux amis,* he has only two friends: see *ne* and **only**

x. **adverb**: how many! *que de gens!* how many people!

quel, quelle, interrogative and exclamatory adjective

i. which(?) what(?): *quelle chambre voulez-vous?* which room do you want? *quels livres avez-vous lus?* which books have you read? *quelle heure est-il?* what time is it (= what/which hour is it)? *dans quelle boîte avez-vous pris les clefs* (or *clés* – both feminine)? from which box have you taken the keys?

ii. *quel* can be used separated from its noun by *être,* eg: *quel est son avis?* what is his advice?

iii. *quel* may be governed by a preposition: *de quel rang est cet officier?* of what rank is this officer?

iv. *quel* is used in indirect questions: *je ne sais pas quel il est,* I don't know which he is

v. *quel* is used in exclamations: *quelle (bonne) idée!* what a (good) idea! *quel dommage!* what a pity! See also ADJECTIVES ¶12.

quel que, quelle que, two words, followed by *être* = whatever: agrees with following noun: *quelle que soit* la difficulté il fera son devoir,* whatever may be the difficulty he will do his duty; *quels que soient* les problèmes qu'il puisse** rencontrer,* whatever may be the problems he may encounter (*the following verb is in the subjunctive, **but not necessarily the verb of the subsequent clause, which will depend on the meaning: if the meaning had been 'the problems he had encountered' – as a fact – the clause would have been: *qu'il avait rencontrés*).

quelque

i. **adverb**: invariable, qualifying an adjective or adverb = **however**: *quelque sage qu'ils soient*,* however wise they may be; *quelque bien que vous travailliez*,* however well you (may) work (* subjunctive): **before a number = some, approximately**: *il a quelque vingt vaches,* he has some twenty cows

ii. **adjective** (when followed by a noun or adjective + noun) = **some, a few**, eg: *je l'ai fait, avec quelque alarme,* I did it, with some alarm: can take plural *-s: achetons quelques grands choux,* let us buy several big cabbages (*quelque* does **not** elide except in *quelqu'un, quelqu'une*).

quelque chose, two words, pronoun and sometimes noun: masculine*: meaning 'something': *quelque chose de bon,* something good; *il se croit quelque chose,* he thinks he's sn (**une chose,* thing, used alone, is feminine, eg: *quelques petites choses*).

quelquefois, adverb: one word, invariable = sometimes.

quelqu'un

    i.   **invariable indefinite pronoun** = someone, somebody: *il y a quelqu'un dans le jardin,* there is someone in the garden

    ii. **adjective:** when followed by *de** + an adjective – *quelqu'un* is itself an adjective, and agrees: *Madame Brun est quelqu'une *d'intéressante,* Mrs Brown is someone who arouses interest

    iii. **variable pronoun:** *(quelqu'un(e), quelques-un(e)s):* when followed by *de,* or when after a verb preceded by *en* as indirect object*: *quelqu'un* is a pronoun agreeing with whatever it stands for: *quelqu'un des** gens dans le jardin l'a trouvé,* (some)one of the people in the garden found it; *quelqu'une des** filles dans le bureau l'a écrit,* (some)one of the girls in the office wrote it; *j'ai quelques-unes de** ces fleurs,* I have some (ones) of these flowers; *j'en** ai quelques-un(e)s,* I have some (of them – gender depending on what is referred to). *Except when used as an invariable indefinite pronoun as in i. above, *quelqu'un* **always** either precedes *de* **or** follows a verb preceded by *en.*

quereller (**Note:** one '*r*', two '*ll*'s), **intransitive:** to quarrel: **transitive:** to quarrel with: *quereller son ami,* to quarrel with his friend; *ne quereller personne,* to have no quarrel with anyone: **also:** *se quereller avec qlqn* **or** *faire une querelle à qlqn,* to quarrel with sn; *chercher une querelle à qlqn,* to pick a quarrel with sn.

Questions: see **Interrogative,** and also PRONOUNS ¶45 – 49, and *qui est-ce qui?* etc, below.

qui, **relative pronoun:** see PRONOUNS ¶40ff. **Interrogative pronoun:** see PRONOUNS ¶45ff and *qui est-ce que?* below.

quiconque, indefinite pronoun

    i. **whoever:** usually subject of the sentence or clause in which it is used, which clause may also be the direct or indirect object of a preceding clause, eg: *quiconque (= celui qui) a fait ceci sera puni,* whoever has done this will be punished; *il prêche à quiconque veut l'écouter,* he preaches to whomever will listen to him. Usually masculine singular, **but** if clearly referring to a female person requires a feminine (singular) agreement, eg: if a statement is made to a group of women or girls: *quiconque est trop fatiguée peut rester ici,* whoever is too tired can remain here **or** *je donnerai un pensum à quiconque (de vous qui) est méchante,* I shall give an imposition to whichever one (of you who) is naughty

    ii. **'anyone'** when coming at the end of a sentence with its following clause 'understood', eg: *il travail mieux que quiconque,* he works better than anyone (understood: 'else who works'). In this sense *quiconque* is masculine singular.

qui est-ce qui?

    i.   ***qui est-ce qui?*** = **who**? eg: *qui est-ce **qui** parle?* who is speaking (who is it who speaks)? ***qui-est ce que?*** = **whom**? eg: *qui est-ce **que** vous voyez?* whom do you see? (who is it whom you see?)

    ii.   ***qu'est-ce qui?*** = **what**? as subject of verb, eg: *qu'est-ce qui se trouve sur la table?* what is on the table? (what is it which finds itself on the table?) ***qu'est-ce que?*** = **what**? used as object of verb: *qu'est-ce qu'il fait?* what is he doing? (what is it that he does?) **Note**: the interrogative inversion occurs in *est-ce*, hence the following subject and verb are **not** also inverted: **note** also that *qui* does **not** elide; *que* **does** elide: therefore *qu'* is **always** an elided *que*. In these phrases the first *qui* always refers to a person or persons (= who): the second *qui* can refer to persons or things (= who, which/that, the subject of the verb): the first *que (qu')* refers to things (= what): the second *que (qu')* can refer to either persons or things (= whom, or that, or which, as the object of the verb). There are **no** plural **or** feminine forms.

quite = altogether: *tout à fait:* quite young, *tout jeune, toute* jeune, tout jeunes, toutes* jeunes.* *Note: when qualifying a **feminine** noun or adjective which starts with a consonant or *h*-aspirate, *tout* agrees in gender and number (in spite of its being here an adverb): elsewhere *tout* remains invariable (as an adverb should). See ***tout*** ii.

quitte *de qlqch*, free from sth: *quitte envers qlqn,* quits with sn; *être quitte de qlqch,* to be free from sth (some task).

quoi, what: see PRONOUNS ¶49.

quoi que, two words = whatever, no matter what: as object: *quoi que vous dites,* no matter what you say; *quoi qu'en eussent pensé* mes amis,* whatever my friends might have thought of it (*pluperfect subjunctive). As subject (rare): *quoi qui vous afflige,* whatever may afflict you.

quoique, one word, subordinating conjunction: although: *quoique malade elle s'est levée,* although ill she got up; *quoique elle fût* malade elle s'est levée,* although she was ill, she got up (*requires the subjunctive when followed by a verb, here the imperfect subjunctive of *être: fusse, fût, fussions,* etc).

R

rabattre, to bring down, lower (price), turn down (a collar), beat up, beat down, beat game (deer, etc): *se **rabattre** (sur),* to fall back (upon), to change course. Like ***battre***.

racheter, to buy back, to buy again. Like ***mener***.

raconter, to tell, to relate, to recount: *avoir fait qlqch,* having done sth.

raffoler de qlqn/qlqch, to dote on sn/sth.

railler, to ridicule, to laugh at: *railler qlqn de qlqch,* to ridicule sn about sth, to laugh at sn about sth.

raire, to bellow (like a stag): defective verb, **only** in the following. Pres: *rais, rais, rait, rayons, rayez, raient.* Imperf: *rayais,* etc. Fut: *rairai,* etc. Pres subj: *raie, raies, raie, rayions, reyiez, raient.* Pres part: *rayant.* Past part: *rait* (invariable). **Alternatives**: *raller* and *réer,* both regular but rare.

ramener, to lead, to lead again, lead back, restore, turn back, pull back: *ramener qlqn faire qlqch,* to bring sn back to doing sth; *ramener à soi,* to attribute to oneself. Like *mener.*

ranger, to put in order, arrange: *se ranger,* to take one's place, to make room for sn, to behave more correctly. Like *manger.*

rappeler, to recall, remind: *rappeler qlqch à qlqn,* to remind sn of sth; *qlqn à faire qlqch,* sn to do sth; *se rappeler,* to remember; *se rappeler qlqn/qlqch,* to remember sn/sth; *avoir fait qlqch,* having done sth. Like *appeler,* with double –*ll*– before *e*-mute endings, and in future stem.

rather: in English, has a variety of uses and meanings: some of the more usual, with their French equivalents, are: I would rather do sth, *j'aimerais mieux faire qlqch;* I would rather not, thank you, *merci, mais j'aimerais mieux en être dispensé;* I rather like him/it, *je l'aime assez bien;* rather well done, *assez bien fait;* he is rather poor, *il est assez pauvre;* rather you than me, *plutôt vous que moi;* he is rich, or rather, rather rich, *il est riche, ou plutôt, assez riche.*

ravoir, to get again: used **only** in this infinitive form.

re-, as a prefix to French verbs, as in English, means 'again'. Verbs with this prefix are normally conjugated like their base verb: thus: *reboire,* to 'redrink', 'drink again' is like *boire,* to drink. **Only** those verbs starting *re-* which are unlike their base verb or which present other problems are individually entered.

recevoir, to receive: **sample for verbs ending in** *-oir*. Pres: *reçois, reçois, reçoit, recevons, recevez, reçoivent.* Imperf: *recevais, -ais, -ait, -ions, -iez, -aient.* Fut: *recevrai, recevras, recevra, recevrons, recevrez, recevront.* Past hist: *reçus, reçus, reçut, reçûmes, reçûtes, reçurent.* Imperat: *reçois, recevons, recevez.* Pres subj: *reçoive, reçoives, reçoive, recevions, receviez, reçoivent.* Imperf subj: *reçusse, reçusses, reçût, reçussions, reçussiez, reçussent.* Pres part: *recevant.* Past part: *reçu, reçue, reçus, reçues.* Aux *avoir.* Of verbs ending in *-oir,* those in *-evoir* are regular: like *recevoir* (but the masc sing of the past participle of *devoir* has a circumflex: *dû*): *recevoir* has ç before *a, o* and *u,* in accordance with normal spelling rules, to keep the -*c*- soft, and this appears in the few other verbs ending in *-cevoir.* All *-oir* verbs which do not have *-ev-* in the infinitive have some irregularity and are listed separately: *-oir* verbs, regular or irregular, are few, but most are common and important, like *avoir, devoir, pouvoir, savoir, vouloir.*

rechigner, to sulk: *devant qlqch*, about sth; to be reluctant, *à faire*, to do sth.

Reciprocal Verbs are, in form, the same as reflexive verbs, **but** the meaning is not, eg: *se laver*, to wash oneself (reflexive): *se battre*, to fight each other **or** *se regarder*, to look at each other (reciprocal). The context should make clear which meaning applies for those verbs which can be both reciprocal and reflexive. See VERBS ¶10.

réclamer, to reclaim: *qlqch à qlqn*, sth from sn, to demand sth; *de qlqn*, of/from sn; *se réclamer de qlqn/de qlqch*, to appeal to sn/sth.

recommander, to recommend: *qlqn/qlqch à qlqn*, sn/sth to sn; *recommander à qlqn de faire qlqch*, to enjoin/bid sn to do sth; *se recommander à qlqn*, to ask sn for his assistance, to turn to sn for help, refer to sn; *se recommander de qlqn*, to invoke sn's support, sn's testimony.

récompenser, to recompense, reward: *qlqn de qlqch*, sn for sth.

reconnaissant, -e, grateful, thankful: *envers qlqn*, towards sn; *de qlqch*, for sth; *être reconnaissant(e) à qlqn d'avoir fait qlqch*, grateful to sn for having done sth.

reconnaître, to recognise. Like ***connaître***.

reconquérir, to reconquer. Like ***acquérir***.

recourir *à qlqn, à qlqch*, to have recourse to sn, to sth.

se récrier *d'admiration, de surprise, de mécontentement*, to exclaim with admiration, surprise, discontent; to protest, *contre/sur qlqch*, about sth.

recrue, fem: recruit: **always** feminine whether man or woman.

reculer, to draw back, to recoil: *devant qlqch*, from sth; *reculer à faire qlqch*, to shrink from doing sth.

redevable, indebted, obliged: *être recevable à qlqn de qlqch*, to be indebted to sn for sth.

redoubler, to redouble: *ses cris, ses efforts*, one's cries, one's efforts; *redoubler de soins*, to be more careful than ever; *redoubler une classe*, to do the same year over again (at school); *le fièvre redouble*, the fever grows worse.

redouter, to fear: *redouter qlqn/qlqch*, to fear sn/sth; *redouter de faire qlqch*, to fear doing sth.

réduire, to reduce, to abate, to break down into component parts, to constrain: *qlqn à faire qlqch*, sn to do sth. Like ***conduire***.

réfléchir, to reflect (both as in reflected light and to think it over), ponder: *à qlqch*, about sth; *sur qlqch*, on sth; *j'y réfléchirai*, I'll think it over, think about it; *le miroir réfléchit la lumière*, the mirror reflects the light; *se réfléchir*, to be reflected, eg: *les arbres se réfléchissent dans l'eau*, the trees are reflected in the water.

Reflexive Pronouns and Verbs: see PRONOUNS ¶3, ¶4, ¶6 and VERBS ¶9, ¶23. **Omission of reflexive pronouns**: see PRONOUNS ¶14. When **past participle agrees with a reflexive pronoun**, see VERBS ¶9. See also **Reciprocal Verbs**.

refuser, to refuse: *refuser un cadeau*, to refuse a gift; *de faire qlqch*, to do sth; *refuser qlqch à qlqn*, to refuse sn sth; *se refuser à qlqch*, to deprive oneself of sth; *se refuser à faire qlqch*, not to consent (**or** to be indisposed) to do sth; *se refuser à une demande*, to be disinclined to accede to a request.

regarder, to look at: *regarder qlqch*, to look at sth; *regarder qlqn faire qlqch*, to watch sn doing sth; *regarder à qlqch*, to pay special attention to sth. When followed by an infinitive with pronoun objects: see PRONOUNS ¶12.

régler, to regulate. Like *céder*, the *-gl-* counting as one consonant, eg: *je règle, nous réglons, ils règlent, je réglerai*, etc; *se régler sur qlqn/qlqch*, to regulate oneself, be guided by, sn/sth.

regorger, to overflow, flood: *de qlqch*, to teem, abound with sth. Like *manger*.

regretter, to regret: *regretter qlqch*, to regret sth; *de faire qlqch*, doing sth; *d'avoir fait qlqch*, having done sth. **No** accents: has *-tt-* throughout.

se réjouir de (faire) qlqch, to rejoice in/at (doing) sth.

Relative Clauses are those subordinate clauses which describe a person, thing or event spoken of in the main clause, eg: in 'This is the house, which I bought', the main clause is 'This is the house'; the relative clause is 'which I bought', describing 'house'. The pronoun 'which', introducing the relative clause, is a **relative pronoun**. French relative pronouns are given in PRONOUNS ¶41, ¶42 – *qui*, ¶43 – *lequel* and ¶44 – *dont*. **Rules** for the agreement of the relative pronoun with its antecedent and with adjectives and participles in the relative clause are given in PRONOUNS ¶42. Use of subjunctive in relative clauses see '**uses of subjunctive**' VERBS ¶33. See also: *où*, relative adverb = where, when.

relever, to raise up again, to restore: *relever un bateau*, refloat a boat; *relever ses manches*, to turn up/back one's sleeves; *relever d'un vœu*, to annul a vow; *relever une sentinelle*, to relieve a sentry; *relever qlqn de qlqch*, to relieve sn of sth; *relever de qlqn/qlqch*, to be dependent upon sn/sth; *se relever de qlqch*, to manage to escape from sth. Like *mener*.

rembourser, to repay: *rembourser qlqch à qlqn*, to repay sth to sn; *rembourser qlqn de qlqch*, to reimburse sn for sth.

remédier à qlqch, to remedy sth.

remercier qlqn de qlqch (or *pour*), to thank sn for sth: *qlqn d'avoir fait qlqch*, sn for having done sth.

remettre *qlqch à qlqn,* to hand sth over to sn: *se remettre à (faire) qlqch,* to restart (doing) sth; *se remettre de qlqch,* to recover from sth; *s'en remettre à qlqn,* to leave (sth) to sn (to attend to). Conjugated like *mettre.*

remplir, to fill: *qlqch de qlqch,* sth with sth; *se remplir de . . . ,* to fill oneself with . . .; *rempli(e) de . . . ,* filled with, full of . . .

rendre, to render, return, give back: *se rendre,* to make oneself, to make each other, to betake oneself, to surrender, to be expressed/translated. Like *vendre.*

renoncer *à qlqch,* to renounce sth. Like *placer,* with cedilla under '*c*' before -*a* and -*o* endings.

renseigner *qlqch à qlqn,* to inform sn of sth, tell sn sth: *se renseigner sur qlqch,* to obtain information about sth, to enquire about sth.

rentrer *faire qlqch,* to go home (in order) to do sth.

renvoyer, to send back: *renvoyer qlqn faire qlqch,* to send sn (back/away) to do sth; *renvoyer qlqn,* to dismiss sn (a worker, servant, etc); *renvoyer qlqn à qlqch,* to refer sn to sth. Like *envoyer,* with -*y*- changing to -*i*- before *e*-mute, and irregular future stem: *je renvoie, je renverrai.*

se repentir *de qlqch,* of sth: *se repentir d'avoir fait qlqch,* to repent having done sth.

répéter, to repeat. Like *céder.* Pres: *je répète.* Fut: *je répéterai.*

répondre, to reply, to answer: to sth: *répondre qlqch,* to answer sth; *répondre à qlqn, à qlqch,* to answer sn, to reply to sth, to correspond (fit/match) with sth; *répondre de qlqn/qlqch,* to answer for, accept responsibility for, sn/sth, to stand guarantor for. Like *vendre.*

reposer, to replace, reposition, to repose, take a rest: *reposer qlqn de qlqch,* to give sn a rest from sth; *se reposer,* to take a rest; *se reposer sur ses lauriers,* to rest on one's laurels (cease further effort); *se reposer sur qlqn de (faire) qlqch,* to rely upon sn/have confidence in sn for (his doing) sth.

reprendre, to retake, to reprimand, blame. Like *prendre.*

réprimander *qlqn d'avoir* (**or** *pour avoir*) *fait qlqch,* to reprimand sn for having done sth.

reprocher *qlqch à qlqn,* to reproach sn for sth: *se reprocher qlqch,* to reproach oneself **for** sth; *il se reproche sa témérité,* he reproaches himself **for** his temerity.

répugner, to be repugnant: *il leur répugne de le faire qlqch,* they find it repugnant to do; *l'homme me répugne,* I find the man repugnant.

réputé, *être réputé(e) pour être . . . ,* to have the reputation for being.

responsable, responsible: *pour qlqn,* for sn; *de qlqch,* for sth; *être responsable vis-à-vis de qlqn,* to be responsible to sn.

requérir, to require, to beg. Like *acquérir.*

réserver *qlqch à qlqn,* to reserve sth for sn: *se reserver de faire qlqch,* to reserve to oneself the right to do sth.

résider *à* or *dans un endroit, une maison,* to reside at or in a place, a house. Pres part: *résidant.* **Noun:** *un résident,* a government agent residing in a colony, etc, a resident of some country of which he is not a native; *une résidente,* the wife of a government agent in a colony, etc.

se résigner, to resign oneself, submit: *à (faire) qlqch,* to (doing) sth.

résister *à (faire) qlqch,* to resist (doing) sth.

résoudre, to dissolve, decompose, to resolve (= determine): *de faire qlqch,* to do sth; *se résoudre à faire qlqch,* to make up one's mind to do sth; *se résoudre en* . . ., to dissolve in(to) . . . Pres: *résous, résous, résout, résolvons, résolvent.* Imperf: *résolvais, -ais, -ait, -ions, -iez, -aient.* Fut: *résoudrai, -as, -a, -ont, -ez, -ont.* Past hist: *résolus, résolus, résolut, résolûmes, résolûtes, résolurent.* Imperat: *resous, résolvons, résolvez.* Pres subj: *résolve, résolves, résolve, résolvions, résolviez, résolvent.* Imperf subj: *résolusse, résolusses, résolût, résolussions, résolussiez, résolussent.* Pres part: *résolvent.* Past part: *résolu, résolue, résolus, résolues.* Aux: *avoir.*

resplendir *de qlqch,* to glitter with sth.

ressembler *à qlqn/qlqch,* to resemble sn/sth. (**Note** the double *-ss-*.)

ressortir, to go out again, to bring out: *faire ressortir ses défauts,* to bring out one's defects; *il ressort de là que* . . . , it follows/results from that, that . . . Like *sortir.* (Pres: *ressors, ressors, ressort, ressortons, ressortez, ressortent.* Pres part: *ressortant.* Past part: *ressorti.* Aux: *être.*) **Distinguish from** *ressortir à,* to be under the jurisdiction of/within the competence of. Like *finir.* (Pres: *ressortis, ressortissons.* Imperf: *ressortissais.* Pres part: *ressortissant.* Past part: *ressorti.* Aux: *avoir.*)

rester *faire qlqch,* stay to do/stay and do sth: *il lui reste à faire qlqch,* there remains sth for him to do; *il lui reste à écrire la lettre,* there remains for him to write the letter; *il reste à savoir si* . . . , there remains to find out if/remains to be seen whether . . . Aux: *être.*

restreindre, to limit, to restrict: *se restreindre (à faire qlqch),* to restrain oneself (from doing sth), to limit one's expenses. Conjugated like *craindre.*

retenir, to retain, to detain: *retenir qlqn à dîner,* to keep sn back for dinner; *se retenir de,* to refrain from; *se retenir à qlqch,* to cling to sth. Like *tenir.*

retirer *qlqch à qlqn,* to withdraw sth from sn.

retourner, to return: *retourner faire qlqch,* to return the letter; *tourner et retourner,* to turn over and over; *retourner faire qlqch,* to return to do sth; *retourner à,* to return to. Aux: *avoir* when transitive (give back sth/return sth): *être* when intransitive (to go back/come back).

retrancher *qlqch à qlqn,* to withdraw sth from sn: *retrancher qlqn à qlqch,* to cut sth from sth.

réussir, to succeed (be successful): *son projet a réussi,* his plan has been successful; *il a réussi à son examen,* he has succeeded in his exam/passed his exam; *il réussit à lui parler,* he succeeds in speaking to him; *il y réussit,* he succeeds in it, he is successful at it; *réussir à faire qlqch,* to succeed in doing sth; *il lui réussit en tout,* he succeeds in everything; *le portrait a réussi,* the portrait is a success. **Note:** spelling of imperf: *réussissais,* etc.

revenir, to return: *revenir faire qlqch,* to return in order to do sth; *revenir à dire qlqch,* to amount to saying sth; *revenir à ses études,* to return to one's studies; *revenir sur qlqch,* to change one's opinion about sth, retract (one's opinion, promise, etc), to reconsider sth; *en revenir à (faire) qlqch,* to revert to (doing) sth; *revenir au même,* to come to the same thing; *revenir à qlqn de droit,* to revert to sn by right; *revenir de qlqch,* to recover from sth (shock, illness, etc); *je n'en reviens pas,* I can't get over it/am very surprised by it. Like **venir.** Aux **être.**

rêver, to dream: *rêver de . . . ,* to dream about, long for . . . ; *rêver à . . .,* ponder on, reflect upon; *rêver de (faire qlqch),* to dream about (doing sth).

revêtir *qlqn/qlqch,* to clothe sn/sth: *de qlqch,* with/in sth; *revêtir un habit,* to put on a coat. Like **vêtir.**

revoir, to see again, to meet again: *au revoir!* = good-bye! 'be seeing you'; *jusqu'au revoir,* until we meet again, 'so long'; *se revoir,* to see each other again; *à revoir,* to be examined, to be looked into (for correction, etc). Like **voir.**

rien, indefinite pronoun

i.   something, anything: *ce sera ta faute si rien est cassé,* it will be your fault if anything is broken; *y a-t-il rien de* si utile?* is there anything so useful? *Note: an adjective/adjectival phrase following *rien* **must** be preceded by *de*

ii.   usually *rien* is used with *ne* before the verb to mean 'nothing'. In a simple tense it is then placed after the verb: *il ne voit rien,* he sees nothing: in a compound tense it is usually placed after the auxiliary: *il n'a rien vu,* he has seen nothing: **but** *rien* may come later if the sense requires: *il n'a vu d'abord rien d'autre** qu'un tas de bois,* he saw (has seen) first nothing but a pile of wood (**see **Note** above in i)

iii.   *rien* may combine with other words used in a negative construction, eg: *il ne voit plus rien,* he no longer sees anything (he sees nothing any more); *celui qui n'a jamais fait rien, ne gagne rien,* he who has never done anything earns nothing

iv.   when there is no verb *rien* normally means 'nothing', eg: *—Mais qu'a-t-il dit? —Rien!* 'But what did he say?' 'Nothing!'

v.   *rien que,* 'nothing but': requires *ne* before the following verb: *rien que la mort ne pourrait l'arrêter,* nothing but death could stop him.

rien, **noun** (masc): *un rien*, a nothing, a bagatelle, a trifle: *un rien pouvait lui faire peur*, a mere trifle could frighten him.

riens moins que, nothing less than, no less than: *cet homme n'est rien moins qu'un héros*, this man is nothing less than a hero; *cet homme ne cherche rien moins que de vous tuer*, this man seeks nothing less than to kill you.

rire, to laugh: *rire de qlqn/qlqch*, to laugh at sn/sth; *rire aux éclats*, to burst out laughing; *mourir de rire*, to die of laughing; *rire dans sa barbe*, to take a secret pleasure in sth; *faire rire qlqn*, to make sn laugh; *se rire de qlqn/qlqch*, to make fun of sn/sth. Pres: *ris, ris, rit, riez, rient* (note **no** -s- in the plural stem). Imperf: *riais, riais, riait, riions, riiez, riaient*. Fut: *rirai, riras, rira, rirons, rirez, riront*. Past hist: *ris, ris, rit, rîmes, rîtes, rirent*. Imperat: *ris, rions, riez*. Pres subj: *rie, ries, rie, riions, riiez, rient*. Imperf subj: *risse, risses, rît, rissions, rissiez, rissent*. Pres part: *riant*. Past part: *ri* (invariable). Aux: *avoir*. **Beware** of spelling in plural of pres and pres subj.

rire, **noun** (masc): *un rire*, a laugh.

risque, masc: risk: *à tout risque*, at all risks; *au risque de*, at the risk of; *courir un risque*, to run a risk; *à vos risques et périls*, at your risk.

risquer, to risk: *risquer sa vie*, to risk one's life; *risquer de faire qlqch*, to run the risk of doing sth; *risquer de tomber*, to risk falling; *se risquer à faire qlqch*, to venture on sth.

road: *la route:* motor-way = *autoroute* (fem): roadway = *la chaussée:* street = *la rue:* path, way = *le chemin:* footpath, lane = *le sentier*.

rompre, to break (into fragments), break apart – usually as a deliberate act or result of action (*casser* being to break by accident), to burst, to stave: *le prisonnier rompt ses fers*, the prisoner breaks his chains; *le fleuve rompt ses digues*, the river bursts its dykes; *rompre la glace*, to break the ice = overcome the initial difficulties, etc; *rompre qlqn à qlqch*, to break sn in to sth, inure sn to sth; *rompu de fatigue*, tired out. Like **vendre**, except for the **-t** at the end of the third person singular of the present indicative: *il rompt* (so also other verbs in -*pre;* all other regular -*re* verbs have the stem only, with **no** ending in 3rd sing, eg: *vendre – il vend*).

rougir, to redden, to blush: *rougir de faire qlqch*, to blush at doing sth (be ashamed at doing sth).

rouler, to roll. Used for 'travel' or 'go' or 'drive' when speaking of a vehicle on wheels: *la Renault roule vite*, the Renault goes/travels quickly; *les cyclistes roulent moins vite*, the cyclists ride more slowly; *rouler à droite/gauche*, to drive on the right/left: **also**: *rouler un projet/une idée*, to 'turn over' an idea; *rouler un client*, to diddle a client. Aux: *avoir* in all senses except *être* when reflexive; *se rouler*, to turn over or roll about, eg: in bed or on the grass.

S

's, s' showing possession: there is **no** possessive case for French nouns: 'the boy's book' must be turned round to: 'the book of the boy', *le livre du garçon;* John's book, *le livre de Jean:* see *de* and ARTICLES.

sa = 'his', 'her', 'its' before a feminine singular noun: *sa maison* = his/her/its house. *sa* can **only** be used before nouns starting with a consonant or *h*-aspirate, as in: *sa haine,* his/her/its hatred. Before a vowel or *h*-mute, *son* is used, whatever the gender: *son ami, son amie,* his/her he-friend, she-friend; *son histoire* (fem), his/her story/history. See ADJECTIVES ¶10.

saillir

  i. to gush. Like *finir,* but used only in infinitive, in 3rd persons singular of simple tenses and in pres part, *jaillir* is more commonly used.

  ii. to project, stand out: occurs only in 3rd sing and plur of all tenses, and in both participles. Pres: *saille, saillent.* Imperf: *saillait, -aient.* Fut: *saillera, sailleront.* Past hist: *saillit, saillirent.* Pres subj: *saille, saillent.* Imperf subj: *saillît, saillissent.* Pres part: *saillant.* Past part: *sailli, saillis, saillie, saillies.* Aux: *avoir.*

saisir, to seize: *saisir une idée,* to grasp an idea; *saisir une viande,* to cook meat quickly; *saisir un tribunal d'une affaire,* to submit a case to a court of law; *se saisir de qlqch,* to seize upon sth; *saisi(e) de peur,* seized with fear. Like *finir.* Aux: *avoir :* **except** reflexive: *être.*

same: adjective: *même:* the same thing, *la même chose;* all/just the same, *tout de même;* 'and the same to you!' *et moi de même!* it's all the same/all one to me, *cela m'est égal.* See *même.*

sans, without: followed by the infinitive of verbs when translating English present participle: *sans parler,* without speaking; *sans doute,* without (a) doubt; *sans bruit,* without a sound (indefinite article not used); *sans l'aide de,* without the help of (definite article used as in English); *sans faire de fautes,* without making a fault, faultlessly; *sans faire des fautes,* without making faults; *sans guère de chance d'en sortir,* with hardly a chance of escaping therefrom: *sans que,* conjunction requiring the subjunctive: *sans que je l'aie su,* without my knowing it ('without that I had known it'); *sans qu'on en s'aperçoive,* without one's noticing it: *sans quoi* = otherwise, eg: *sans quoi je ne l'aurais pas fait,* otherwise I should not have done it

satisfaire, to satisfy: *satisfaire qlqn,* to satisfy sn; *satisfaire à ses* obligations, to fulfil one's obligations. Like *faire.*

sauf

  i. **adjective**: fem = *sauve:* safe, unhurt

  ii. **preposition**: save, except, excepting: *sauf erreur ou omission,* errors excepted. See **except** ii and *hors.*

savoir, to know (a fact), eg: *savoir l'âge de qlqn*, to know the age of sn; *savoir le chemin*, to know the way; *savoir sa leçon*, to know (have learnt by heart) one's lesson; *savoir faire qlqch*, to know how to do sth; *savoir comment faire*, know what to do, how to behave; *que je sache*, as far as I know; *pas que je sache*, not as far as I know; *je ne saurais le faire*, I can't do it, I wouldn't know how to do it. **Distinguish from** *connaître*, to be acquainted with (someone, some place). Pres: *sais, sais, sait, savons, savez, savent*. Imperf: *savais, -ais, -ait, -ions, -iez, -aient*. Fut: *saurai, -as, -a, -ons, -ez, -ont*. Past hist: *sus, sus, sut, sûmes, sûtes, surent*. Imperat: *sache, sachons, sachez*. Pres subj: *sache, saches, sache, sachions, sachiez, sachent*. Imperf subj: *susse, susses, sût, sussions, sussiez, sussent*. Pres part: *sachant*. Past part: *su, sue, sus, sues*. Aux: *avoir*. **Noun:** *un savant*, a learned man or woman: *une femme savante*, a blue stocking. **Adjective:** *savant, savante*, learned.

Season: the seasons, *les saisons* (fem): in season, *de saison;* out of season, *hors de saison;* in the spring, *au printemps;* in summer, *en été* (masc); in autumn, *en automne* (masc); in winter, *en hiver* (masc); during the winter, *pendant l'hiver* (masc); at the beginning of summer, *au début de l'été* (masc); at the end of autumn, *à la fin de l'automne* (masc); a season ticket, *un billet de saison*. **Verb:** to season = *assaisonner*.

sec, sèche, adjective: dry. Adverb: *sèchement*, drily, abruptly (of speaking).

sécher, to dry. Takes *-è-* in stem before *e*-mute endings, eg: *sèche, sèchent:* **but** retains *-é-* elsewhere, eg: *sécherai*. Like *céder*, *-ch-* acting as one consonant.

seem: *avoir l'air:* agreement after: see *avoir*.

self: see *même*, and PRONOUNS, end of ¶15.

semer, to sow (seeds, etc). Like *mener*, eg: *sème, sèment, sèmerai*, etc.

semi, adjective: *semi-* is invariable before an adjective or noun **and** joined by hyphen: *semi-automatique*, semi-automatic; *une semi-voyelle*, a semi-vowel.

sentinelle, fem: sentry: always **feminine** whether a man or woman.

sentir, to feel, to smell: *sentir qlqn/qlqch faire qlqch*, to feel sn/sth doing sth; *ne pouvoir sentir qlqn*, not to be able to stand sn, feel dislike for sn; *je ne me sens pas bien*, I do not feel well. Pres: *sens, sens, sent, sentons, sentez, sentent*. Imperf: *sentais, -ais, -ait, -ions, -iez, -aient*. Fut: *sentirai, -as, -a, -ons, -ez, -ont*. Past hist: *sentis, sentis, sentit, sentîmes, sentîtes, sentirent*. Imperat: *sens, sentons, sentez*. Pres subj: *sente, sentes, sente, sentions, sentiez, sentent*. Imperf subj: *sentisse, sentisses, sentît, sentissions, sentissiez, sentissent*. Pres part: *sentant*. Past part: *senti, sentie, sentis, senties*. Aux: *avoir*.

Sequence of Tenses: see VERBS ¶34 and in *si* clauses: see *si* i.

servir, to serve: *servir la rente*, to pay the interest; *servir de mère à qlqn*, to act as mother to sn; *servir qlqch à qlqn*, to serve sth to sn/sn with sth; *servir à qlqn*, be useful to sn; *servir à qlqch*, to serve as (be useful as) sth; *servir à faire qlqch,* be useful for doing sth; *à quoi sert cela?* what is the use of that, what is that for? *à quoi sert-il?* what's the use of it, what's it for? *ne servir à (or de) rien,* to be of no use; *se servir de qlqch,* to use, employ, help oneself to sth. Pres: *sers, sers, sert, servons, -vez, -vent.* Imperf: *servais, -ais, -ait, -ions, -iez, -aient.* Fut: *servirai, -as, -a, -ons, -ez, -ont.* Past hist: *servis, servis, servit, servîmes, servîtes, servirent.* Imperat: *sers, servons, servez.* Pres subj: *serve, serves, serve, servions, serviez, servent.* Imperf subj: *servisse, servisses, servît, servissions, servissiez, servissent.* Pres part: *servant.* Past part: *servi, servie, servis, servies.* Aux: *avoir,* **except** reflexive: *être.*

servant: *serviteur* = **masc**: *servante* = **fem**. In the home, usually = *un, une domestique* (masc **and** fem), a domestic servant.

seul, seule, single, sole, only: when meaning 'one only' comes before the noun: *il y a un seul Dieu,* there is only one God, a single God: when meaning 'alone', 'nothing but', follows the noun **or** a disjunctive pronoun: *cette pensée seule l'effraie,* this thought alone frightens him; *ma parole seule suffira,* my word alone will suffice; *lui seul l'a fait,* he alone has done it; *nous seuls l'avons fait,* we alone have done it. (See also **only** i and for *seulement:* see **only** ii.)

several: *plusieurs:* **no** feminine form: precedes the plural noun: we have several houses, *nous avons plusieurs maisons;* I have sold several of them, *j'en* ai vendu* plusieurs* (*past participles do **not** agree with *en*): several (a variety of) = *divers,* eg: there are several (different kinds of) flowers in the garden, *il y a divers fleurs dans le jardin.*

she: see PRONOUNS ¶3, ¶4, ¶6, ¶7.

should: see **Conditional** and **also** conditional tense in VERBS ¶18.

si

    i. **subordinating conjunction**: if, whether: introduces a dependent clause which may either precede or follow the main clause. If the main clause is conditional the *si* clause will be imperfect or pluperfect (with auxiliary in imperfect): *il m'a dit qu'il irait si sa santé le permettait,* he told me that he would go if his health permitted it; *il m'a dit qu'il irait s'il n'avait pas perdu son argent,* he told me he would go if he had not lost his money. If the main clause is in a tense other than conditional the clause following *si* (= if) can be in any tense that fits the meaning **other than** the future or conditional: *je ne sais pais s'il vient,** I don't know if he will come*; *si vous ne venez* pas avec moi, je n'irai pas seul,* if you will not come* with me I shall not go alone. (*French present, English future in the 'if' clause, in both examples.) In an indirect question, when *si* = **whether**, *si* can be followed by either future or conditional: *je ne sais pas si mon projet vous plaira,* I don't know whether my plan will please you; *je ne suis pas certain si je le ferais,* I am not certain whether I should do it. **Note** that *si* is elided **only** before: *il* and *ils – s'il, s'ils,* **but** not elsewhere: *si elle, si elles, si on, si un ami,* etc. See also: **if only**

ii. **adverb** (a) *si* = **so**: *il est si grand,* he is so tall; *ne parlez pas si vite,* don't talk so quickly; *il n'est pas si pauvre qu'on ne puisse lui demander quelque chose,* he is not so poor that one cannot (= may not) ask him for sth (b) *si* = **although** (with subjunctive): *si pauvre qu'il soit, il vous donnera qlqch,* although he's so poor he'll give you sth (= poor though he be . . .)

iii. **'yes'** in contradiction: *–Il ne pleut pas. –Mais si, il pleut toujours.* 'It isn't raining.' 'Yes it is, it's still raining.'

sien, sienne, **possessive pronoun** = his, her, its: see PRONOUNS ¶38.

siffler qlqn, to whistle to sn: *siffler un chien,* to whistle to a dog.

signifier, to signify, to mean, to notify: *ce mot latin signifie en français . . . ,* this Latin word means in French . . . (**but** *'ce mot veut dire'* for 'this word means' is a more usual idiom); *signifier à qlqn de faire qlqch,* to notify sn to do sth.

since

i. *depuis:* I have not seen him since yesterday, *je ne l'ai pas vu depuis hier;* since I started this work I have not seen him, *depuis que j'ai commencé ce travail je ne l'ai pas vu;* since the end of the war, *depuis la fin de la guerre;* it is a long time since I saw you, *il y a longtemps que je ne vous ai vu;* it is not long since that happened, *il n'y a pas longtemps que cela est arrivé*

ii. *puisque:* since you do not wish to do it I'm going, *puisque tu ne veux pas le faire je m'en vais;* I shall do it since you wish it, *je le ferai puisque vous le voulez.*

Slave (national), **noun**: Slav of either sex: **adjective**: *slave,* masc or fem.

soigneux, soigneuse, **adjective**: careful: *soigneux de ses vêtements,* careful with his clothes. **Verb**: *soigner,* to look after, care for, nurse.

solliciter qlqn à (or *de) faire qlqch,* to solicit, urge, beseech sn to do sth.

some: he has some books, *il a des livres;* he has some bread, *il a du pain:* see ARTICLES ¶5 – 8. See also *quelque* i and *de* iii.

somebody, someone: see *quelqu'un.*

somehow: somehow or other, *d'une manière ou d'une autre.*

something: see *quelque chose.*

some time (in the past): *autrefois* (one word), *jadis* (pronounced *jardeess*): some time (in the future), *un jour, un de ces jours.*

sometime: a sometime President, *un ancien Président.*

sometimes: *quelquefois* (one word, invariable).

somewhat: *quelque peu, un peu, assez.*

somwhere: *quelque part:* somewhere else, *autre part.*

somme, **masculine** = sleep, nap: **feminine** = sum, total (**note**: *nous sommes,* we are).

sommer qlqn de faire qlqch, to summon sn to do sth.

son, sa, ses, **possessive adjective**: his, her, its: see ADJECTIVES ¶10.

songer de qlqch, to dream of sth: *songer à qlqch,* to bear sth in mind. Like *manger.*

sonner, to ring: *sonner la messe,* to ring for Mass; *entendre sonner,* to hear a/the bell ringing; *minuit vient de sonner,* midnight has just struck/it has just struck midnight; *sonner une trompette, un cor,* etc, to blow a trumpet, a horn, etc.

sortir, verb: intransitive. Like *dormir*

    i. **intransitive**: to go out, to come out, to emerge, to go for a walk: *il sort de chez lui,* he comes out of his house; *sortir faire qlqch,* to go out to do sth; *sortir de faire qlqch,* to have just finished doing sth; *sortir de l'hiver,* to emerge from winter; *sortir de Saint-Cyr,* to pass out from (the military academy of) Saint-Cyr; *ses yeux lui sortaient de la tête,* his eyes were popping out of his head. Aux: *être*

    ii. **transitive** (with a direct object): to bring out: *sortir un livre,* to bring out a book; *sortir qlqn d'embarras,* to get sn out of his embarrassment; *sortir un cheval de l'écurie,* to lead a horse from the stable. In this sense: auxiliary: *avoir*

    iii. **impersonal**: *il sortit,* it produces, a legal term: also: to exhale: *il sort une douce odeur,* a sweet scent exudes. Aux: *avoir*

    iv. *se sortir de,* to get oneself out from (some awkward predicament): *elle s'est sortie* d'une difficulté inattendue* (**sortie* agrees with reflexive pronoun), she got (herself) out of an unexpected difficulty; *il s'en est sorti,* he has got out of it, he has pulled through (eg: an illness).

sot, sotte, adjective and noun: stupid, a stupid person, dolt.

se soucier de (faire) qlqch, to be uneasy about (doing) sth.

soudain, -e, adjective and adverb: sudden, suddenly. **Also**: adverb: *soudainement,* suddenly.

souffrir, to suffer: *à faire qlqch,* from doing sth (physical pain); *souffrir de voir, entendre,* etc, *qlqch,* to suffer (mentally) through seeing, hearing, etc, sth; *souffrir à qlqn de faire qlqch,* to suffer (= allow) sn to do sth. Like *ouvrir.* Pres: *je souffre, nous souffrons.* Fut: *je souffrirai.* Past hist: *souffris.* Pres part: *souffrant.* Past part: *souffert, soufferte.* Aux: *avoir.*

souhaiter qlqch à qlqn, to wish sn sth: *souhaiter que,* wish that (with subjunctive), eg: *je souhaite qu'on le fasse,* I wish that one do it (wish it be done).

soûler qlqn de qlqch, to intoxicate, satiate sn with sth: *se soûler de qlqch,* to get drunk with sth.

soumettre, to submit. Like *mettre.*

soupçonner *qlqn de qlqch*, to suspect sn of sth.

souper, to have supper: *souper de qlqch*, to sup on sth.

*soupirer après (*or *pour) qlqn/qlqch*, to sigh/long for sn/sth.

sourire, to smile: *sourire de qlqch*, to be amused by sth; *sourire à qlqn*, to smile on sn. Like *rire*. **Noun**: *un sourire*, a smile.

sous, under, beneath: *un oreiller sous la tête*, a pillow under the (one's) head; *sous Louis XIV*, under (in the reign of) Louis XIV; *sous ses ordres*, under his orders; *sous mon nom*, in my name; *sous ce rapport*, in this respect; *sous clef*, under lock and key; *sous peine de mort*, under pain of death; *sous une semaine*, in/under/within a week; *sous peu*, before long, very shortly.

souscrire, to subscribe, endorse, underwrite. Like *écrire*.

soustraire, to withdraw, to subtract: *qlqch de qlqch*, sth from sth; *soustraire qlqn à qlqch*, to protect/preserve sn from sth. Like *traire*.

soutenir, to uphold, to sustain, maintain, assert: *soutenir d'avoir fait qlqch*, to maintain that one has done sth. Like *tenir*.

se souvenir de qlqn/qlqch, to recall, remember sn/sth: *elle s'est souvenue* d'avoir fait qlqch*, she remembered having done sth. Like *venir*. *The past participle agrees with the reflexive pronoun.

se spécialiser dans qlqch, to specialise in sth.

still

    i.   **yet**: *encore:* he is still speaking, *il parle encore;* your house is big, but mine is still bigger (yet bigger), *ta maison est grande, mais la mienne est encore plus grande;* he is still unmarried, *il est encore garçon/célibataire.* 'Have you still not done it?' 'Not yet.' ('Still not.'), *—Ne l'avez-vous pas fait encore? —Pas encore*

    ii. **'on and on'**: *toujours:* he is still talking, he goes on talking (ceaselessly), *il parle toujours;* it is still raining, it goes on raining, *il pleut toujours*

    iii. **nevertheless**: see *pourtant*.

stimuler qlqn à faire qlqch, to stimulate sn to do sth.

SUBJUNCTIVE: see VERBS ¶28 – 33 and ¶34ii. **For subordinating conjunctions followed by subjunctive**: see CONJUNCTIONS ¶5.

subsister de qlqch, to live on sth.

substituer qlqch à qlqch, to substitute sth for sth: *se substituer à qlqn*, to take the place of sn.

subtiliser qlqch à qlqn, to sneak sth from sn.

subvenir à qlqn/qlqch, to help, assist, relieve sn/sth.

succéder à *qlqn/qlqch*, to follow/succeed, take the place of sn/sth: *le jour succède à la nuit*, day follows night (**note**: to succeed = to be successful = *réussir*). Like *céder*.

succomber à *(*or *sous) qlqch*, to succumb to, yield to sth.

suffire, to suffice, to be adequate: *suffire à qlqch*, to be adequate for sth; *suffire à faire qlqch*, to be equal to doing sth; *suffire pour qlqch*, be sufficient for doing sth; *cela suffit*, that's enough; *il suffit de faire cela*, it's enough to do that; *il suffit que*, it is sufficient that (usually with subjunctive); *se suffire*, to be self-sufficient, to be able to manage on one's own, by oneself. Pres: *suffis, suffis, suffit, suffisons, suffisez, suffisent*. Imperf: *suffisais, suffisais, suffisait, suffisions, suffisiez, suffisaient*. Fut: *suffira, suffiras, suffira, suffirons, suffirez, suffiront*. Past hist: *suffis, suffis, suffit, suffîmes, suffîtes, suffirent*. Imperat: *suffis, suffisons, suffisez*. Pres subj: *suffise, suffises, suffise, suffisions, suffisiez, suffisent*. Imperf subj: *suffisse, suffisses, suffît, suffissions, suffissiez, suffissent*. Pres part: *suffisant*. Past part: *suffit* (**no** feminine). Aux: *avoir*.

suggérer qlqch à qlqn, to suggest sth to sn. Like *céder*.

Suisse (national), (masc) = Swiss male: *Suissesse* = Swiss female (persons).

suisse, **adjective**: masc or fem: Swiss. **Noun**: *un suisse*, beadle, church caretaker, Swiss cheese, member of the Vatican Swiss Guards (*la garde suisse pontificale*). As **adverb**: *faire suisse*, to eat or drink on one's own.

suivre, to follow. Pres: *suis, suis, suit, suivons, suivez, suivent*. Imperf: *suivais, -ais, -ait, -ions, -iez, -aient*. Fut: *suivrai, -as, -a, -ons, -ez, -ont*. Past hist: *suivis, -is, -it, -îmes, -îtes, -irent*. Imperat: *suis, suivez, suivons*. Pres subj: *suive, -es, -e, -ions, -iez, -ent*. Imperf subj: *suivisse, -es, suivît, -issions, -issiez, -issent*. Pres part: *suivant*. Past part: *suivi, -e, -s, -es*. Aux: *avoir*.

Superlative: see ADJECTIVES ¶7 and ADVERBS ¶4.

suppléer, to supply, to supplement, to take sn's place: *suppléer qlqn*, to replace sn; *suppléer à qlqch*, compensate for sth.

supplier, to beg, beseech: *qlqn de faire qlqch*, to beg sn to do sth.

sur, preposition: on: *sur la table*, on the table; *la fenêtre donnait sur le jardin*, the window gave on to the garden (looked out on to); *un discours sur la loi*, a discourse on (about) the law; *la clef est sur la porte*, the key is in the door; *six mètres sur quatre*, six metres by four; *sur le soir*, about evening; *il va sur ses dix ans*, he is round about ten years old; *il est revenu sur Paris*, he turned back towards Paris; *grimper sur un arbre*, to climb a tree; *juger sur les apparences*, to judge by appearances; *tirer sur*, to fire on; *sur ce*, upon this, whereupon; *sur quoi*, upon which. See also **on**. **Distinguish from** *sur, sure*, adjective = sour **and** *sûr, sûre*, adjective (**with accent**) = sure, certain: *j'en suis sûr(e)*, I am sure of it.

surprendre qlqn à faire qlqch, to catch sn doing sth: *surprendre un voleur*, to catch a thief. Like *prendre*.

survivre à qlqn/qlqch, to survive (outlive) sn/sth. Like *vivre*. Aux: *avoir*.

susceptible, susceptible, touchy: *susceptible d'amélioration*, susceptible of/to improvement.

suspecter qlqn de qlqch, suspect sn of sth: *d'avoir fait qlqch*, of having done sth.

suspendre qlqch, to suspend (= put a stop on) sth: *suspendre qlqch à qlqch*, to suspend (= hang) sth on/to/from sth. Like *prendre*.

T

-t- **inserted**, eg: *parle-t-il?* See **Interrogative** iii.

tache, fem: a stain, spot (**no** accent). **Distinguish from** *tâche*, fem: a task (with accent).

taire, to conceal, to keep secret: *se taire*, to keep silent, to say nothing, hold one's tongue, keep a secret. Pres: *tais, -s, -t, taisons, -ez, -ent*. Imperf: *taisais, -ais, -ait, -ions, -iez, -aient*. Fut: *tairai, -as, -a, -ons, -ez, -ont*. Past hist: *tus, tus, tut, tûmes, tûtes, turent*. Imperat: *tais, taisons, taisez*. Pres subj: *taise, -es, -e, taisions, -iez, taisent*. Imperf subj: *tusse, tusses, tût, tussions, tussiez, tussent*. Pres part: *taisant*. Past part: *tu, tue, tus, tues*. Aux: *avoir: taire la vérité*, to conceal the truth.

se taire, *je me tais*, etc, I keep silent. Imperative: *tais-toi! taisez-vous!* keep quiet! shut up! *elle s'est tue**, she kept quiet: *past participle agrees with direct object reflexive pronoun.

tant, so many, so much: *il y a tant (de* choses) pour vous*, there are so many (things) for you; *nous avons tant de* pain*, we have so much bread (*note the *de* before the noun; **but** the partitive article, *du, de la, des*, is used if the meaning is 'so many **of the**, so much **of the** . . .'); *elle a encore tant des pommes que vous lui avez données**, she still has so many of the apples which you gave her (*données agrees with *que*, relative pronoun standing for *pommes*). In a negative comparison *tant* can be used for 'as many': *il n'a pas tant* (or *autant*) *de pommes que vous*, he has not as many apples as you (have); *tant mieux*, so much the better; *tant pis*, so much the worse; *tant soit peu*, ever so little; *tant pour cent*, so much percent.

tard, adverb: late: *il est tard* **or** *il se fait tard*: see **late**.

tarder, to delay, tarry, be long: *tarder à faire qlqch*, to be long in doing sth, to put off doing sth; *il me tarde de faire qlqch*, I long to do sth, I can't wait to do sth.

tarir, to dry up: *ne pas tarir sur qlqch*, not to stop talking about sth.

tâter, to touch, to feel: *tâter le terrain*, feel one's way; *tâter de qlqch*, to try one's hand at sth.

taxer qlqn/qlqch, sn/sth: *qlqn de qlqch*, accuse sn of sth (tax sn with . . .).

teindre *qlqch de* . . . , to dye, colour, stain, tint sth with . . . Like ***craindre***. Pres: *je teins, il teint, nous teignons,* etc. Fut: *teindrai.* Past hist: *teignis,* etc, *teignant, teint(e)(s).*

***tel, telle, tels, telles,* adjective**: as, such (as), like: *avec une telle force,* with such force: **pronoun**: *telle est la loi,* such is the law; *'tel(le) quel(le)'* = *tel(le) qu'il/elle est,* such as it is. See **as**.

télégraphier/téléphoner *à qlqn,* to wire (telegraph) sn/to telephone sn: *à faire qlqch,* to do sth.

témoin, masc: witness: 'she is a witness' = *elle est témoin.*

temps, (masc) time in general: *je n'ai pas le temps,* I haven't the time; *le temps passe vite,* (the time passes quickly; *le temps solaire,* solar time; *de temps en temps,* from time to time, sometimes; *le temps* = the weather, see **Weather**). (For time by the clock see **Time**; for time, as in six times = *six fois,* see **Time** and ***fois***).

tendre
  i.   to stretch, tender/offer, to pitch (a tent), lay (a trap): *tendre une* main, to offer assistance
  ii. to tend to, be inclined to: *tendre à (faire) qlqch,* to tend towards (doing) sth. Like ***vendre***.

tenir, to hold. Pres: *tiens, tiens, tient, tenons, tenez, tiennent.* Imperf: *tenais, -ais, -ait, -ions, -iez, -aient.* Fut: *tiendrai, -as, -a, -ons, -ez, -ont.* Past hist: *tins, tins, tint, tînmes, tîntes, tinrent.* Imperat: *tiens, tenons, tenez.* Pres subj: *tienne, tiennes, tienne, tenions, teniez, tiennent.* Imperf subj: *tinsse, tinsses, tînt, tinssions, tinssiez, tinssent.* Pres part: *tenant.* Past part: *tenu, -e, -s, -es.* Aux: ***avoir***: *tenir qlqch de qlqn/qlqch,* to derive sth from sn/sth (owe sth to . . .); *tenir de qlqn,* to take after sn; *tenir à qlqn/qlqch,* to stick to sn/sth; *tenir à faire qlqch,* to be anxious, keen to do sth; *être tenu de faire qlqch,* be under the/an obligation to do sth; *tiens!* really! is that so? indeed! *tenez!* hold on a moment, listen; *se tenir à qlqch,* to hold on to sth (physically or figuratively); *tenez-vous là,* stay there.

tenter, to try, to attempt, to undertake, to tempt: *tenter de faire qlqch,* to try to do sth; *tenter une expédition,* undertake an expedition; *être tenté de faire qlqch,* to be tempted to do sth; *tenter qlqn,* to tempt sn.

Tenses: see VERBS ¶13ff.

terminer *qlqch par qlqch,* to end (up) sth with sth: *se terminer par qlqch,* to conclude (eg: a speech) with sth; *terminer en* . . . , to end in (eg: 'a verb ends in . . .').

than: comparisons = *que:* he is bigger than his brother, *il est plus grand que son frère;* he has more/fewer books than I (have), *il a plus de/moins de livres que moi:* **more than/less than** = *plus de/moins de:* more than/fewer than three hundred people work there, *plus de/moins de trois cents gens y travaillent;*

more than one boy has done it (verb in singular in French and English), *plus d'un garçon l'a fait;* more than one **of the** boys have done it, *plus d'un des garçons l'ont fait* (verb in plural in French and English).

thank: see *remercier:* thank you for sth, *merci pour* qlqch;* thank you for your charming letter, *merci pour votre lettre charmante;* thank you for having done sth, *merci d'avoir fait qlqch* (*the use of *pour* instead of *de* is now in frequent use).

that

    i.   **demonstrative adjective**: (plural = those): *ce, cet, cette, ces:* see ADJECTIVES ¶11

    ii. **conjunction**: *que:* he said that you have done it, *il a dit que vous l'avez fait: que* elides before vowel or *h*-mute: that he has . . . , *qu'il a . . .* After the conjunction *que,* the subjunctive is often used: see SUBJUNCTIVE ¶5 and CONJUNCTIONS ¶3, ¶4, ¶5

    iii. **demonstrative pronouns** (eg: give me that): *celui, cela:* see PRONOUNS ¶19, ¶21.

their: **possessive adjective**: *leur, leurs* (**no** feminine form): their book, *leur livre* (masc); their house, *leur maison* (fem); their books and their houses, *leurs livres et leurs maisons.* See ADJECTIVES ¶10.

theirs: *le/la leur, les leurs* or *à eux, à elles:* the book is theirs, *le livre est le leur* or *à eux, à elles;* the house is theirs, *la maison est la leur* or *à eux/elles;* the books/houses are theirs, *les livres/maisons sont les leurs* or *à eux/elles: le leur,* does **not** show the gender of the owners: *à eux* and *à elles* distinguish the gender of the owners where the use of *le leur* might be ambiguous. See PRONOUNS ¶17, ¶38.

them is usually translated by *les* as a direct object pronoun before the verb: I see them, *je les vois;* I do not see them, *je ne les vois pas;* I give them to you, *je vous les donne.* In a compound tense the past participle agrees with *les* in number, and in gender if known: *il les a acheté(e)s:* 'to them' in its **dative sense** of 'giving to' (not 'going to') = *leur,* eg: he gives it to them, *il le leur donne.* The disjunctive pronouns for 'them' (or 'they') = *eux, elles* (usually used only for persons): these can be used if it is necessary to indicate the gender of those to whom something is given, eg: he gives it to them (masc), *il le donne à eux* (masc: as opposed to giving it to them: fem = *à elles*). When translating 'them' after any preposition other than the dative 'to' and also when there is no verb, the disjunctive pronouns: *eux, elles,* **must** be used, eg: **with** them (masc), *avec eux;* **for** them (fem), *pour elles;* they but not **them,** *elles mais pas eux* (the females thus distinguished from the males). Compare **theirs** above, and see PRONOUNS ¶3ff and ¶15 – 17.

there

    i.   'at/in/on/to that place' and 'there is', 'there are': see *y*

    ii. when emphasising 'there rather than elsewhere' **or** 'there' as the opposite of *ici,* here = *là,* eg: not here – there! *pas ici – là! là* is **also** used in compounds, eg: therein, *là-dedans;* that man there, *cet homme-*

là (*cet homme* alone does not distinguish between the man 'there' and the man 'here')

iii. the answer to the question 'where?' may be either *là!* **or** *voilà!* **voilà** is **also** used for 'there' when sn awaited arrives: 'there you are!' *ah! vous voilà!* and when handing over something, eg: 'there you are,' *le voilà!* (or *la* or *les voilà!* as sense requires)

iv. note the French for: 'there remains . . .', *il reste;* a railway ticket 'there and back', *un billet d'aller et retour;* 'then and there', *en temps et lieu* (= in time and place); it is there I saw him, *c'est là que je l'ai vu.*

therefore: see *aussi, ainsi, donc,* and in CONJUNCTIONS ¶2 and ¶4.

they: conjunctive pronoun: *ils, elles:* see PRONOUNS ¶3 and ¶4.

this, these: **adjective**: *ce, cet, cette, ces:* see ADJECTIVES ¶11: **pronoun**: *celui, celle, ceux, celles, ceci:* see PRONOUNS ¶19 and ¶21.

though, although: conjunction: introducing a dependent clause: even if = *quand même,* eg: though/even if he comes, *quand même il viendrait* (with the conditional); I shall pay, though (= but/however) you must help me, *je payerai, mais/cependant vous devez m'aider;* I shall pay, though I am poor, *je payerai, tout pauvre que je suis* **or** *quoique/bien que je sois pauvre* (with subjunctive: see CONJUNCTIONS ¶4 for *quand* and ¶5 for *bien que* and *quoique,* and also the separate entries *quand même, quoique* and *bien* iii).

through

i. from one side to the other, *à travers, au travers de* (the two phrases are synonymous): the soldiers marched through the town, *les soldats ont marché à travers la ville* **or** *au travers de la ville;* he was trying to see it through the window-pane, *il tentait de le voir au travers de la vitre*

ii. by way of, by means of, *par:* he passed through (went via) Paris, *il a passé par Paris;* you have to pass through a little yard, *on doit passer par une petite cour*

iii. because of something happening, *par suite de:* he had to walk through having lost his money, *il devait aller à pied par suite d'avoir perdu son argent.*

tien, possessive pronoun: *le tien,* yours (thy): see PRONOUNS ¶38.

tiens! = indeed! really! is that so! (from *tenir*).

till, until

i. **conjunction**: *jusqu'à ce que:* introduces a clause in the subjunctive: she will stay there until he comes, *elle y restera jusqu'à ce qu'il vienne;* he will not leave until you give it to him, *il ne s'en ira pas jusqu'à ce que vous le lui donniez.* **Alternatively**, *que* may be used: wait until he comes/wait for him to come (before doing sth), *attendez qu'il vienne*: **not until**, not before: *pas avant,* eg: don't start until (before) noon, *ne commencez pas avant midi;* I shall not arrive until late, *je n'arrivera pas que tard.* See also *jusque* and CONJUNCTIONS ¶5

ii. **preposition**: *jusque* + *à* (or, less frequently, with some other preposition): I shall work until three o'clock, *je vais travailler jusqu'à trois heures;* he has travelled till (= as far as) Rome, *il a voyagé jusqu'à Rome;* until then, *jusqu'alors;* until January, *jusqu'en janvier;* until the month of June, *jusqu'au mois de juin.*

Time: in general, see *temps.*

Time of day: the time (by the clock), *l'heure qu'il est:* 'it is' = *il est . . . :* it is one o'clock, *il est une heure;* it is two o'clock, *il est deux heures;* three, etc, up to eleven o'clock, *il est deux, trois,* etc . . . , *onze heures;* it is twelve o'clock, midday, *il est midi;* it is midnight, *il est minuit:* **minutes past** the hour, eg: four minutes past six, *six heures quatre;* twenty minutes past noon, *midi vingt:* **minutes to** (before) the hour are given with *moins,* less (= minus), eg: ten to seven, *sept heures moins dix:* **half past** = *et demi(e)* (note: *demie* is in the feminine if the word *heure(s)* precedes it): half past one, half past two, *une heure et demie, deux heures et demie.* **But:** half past midday, *midi et demi;* half past midnight, *minuit et demi* (both with **no** -*e*): **a half hour**/half an hour = *une demi-heure:* **the quarter** = *le quart:* **a quarter past** five, *cinq heures et quart;* **a quarter to** one, *une heure moins le quart* or *une heure moins ún quart:* **a quarter of an hour** = *un quart d'heure:* **a.m.** = *du matin:* **p.m.** = *de l'après-midi* (of the afternoon); *du soir* (of the evening); *de la nuit* (of the night). Good morning, *bonjour.* Good afternoon, *bonjour, bonsoir.* Good night, *bonne nuit:* **at** nine o'clock, *à neuf heures:* **about** nine o'clock, *vers neuf heures:* **to strike** (**the hour**), *sonner (l'heure):* midnight has struck/it is past midnight, *minuit est sonné;* six o'clock has struck, *six heures sont sonnées* **or** *il est six heures sonnées.* On hearing the clock strike: what time is that? *quelle heure est-ce?* that's midnight striking, *c'est minuit qui sonne.* **The twenty-four hour** clock is used as in English, but with '*heure(s)*': twelve hours, midday = *douze heures;* twelve hours, midnight = *zéro heure;* thirteen hours = *treize heures,* etc; fourteen forty = *quatorze heures quarante;* twelve (midday) fifteen = *douze heures quinze;* half past twelve midnight = *zéro heure trente.*

to: usually *à:* see *à:* but 'to' may be translated in other ways, eg: to a country, if **feminine** = *en:* if **masculine** = *à:* see **Countries:** to, towards (motion) = *vers:* to, towards (behaviour, attitude) = *envers:* to the home/place of = *chez:* in order to = *pour:* from time to time = *de temps en temps:* from place to place = *de lieu en lieu:* (to) go to prison = *aller en prison:* (to) put to flight = *mettre en fuite:* near to = *auprès de:* up to (as far as) = *jusqu'à:* (to) come to (= recover consciousness) = *reprendre connaissance.* **See the above prepositions in separate entries.**

'**to**': **before an infinitive**: the correct French preposition used to introduce an infinitive after another verb, as in 'I want **to** work', 'I hope **to** pay', 'I try **to** hear' etc, varies in French: sometimes the infinitive follows with **no preposition**: sometimes it is introduced by *à:* sometimes by *de:* occasionally by *pour* or some other preposition. There is no satisfactory guiding rule, **but** those verbs which do not translate the English 'to' by *à* (as in 'he learns to read', *il apprend à lire*) are listed individually, eg: *essayer **de** faire qlqch (= quelque chose)*, to try **to** do sth – indicating that the English 'to' before an infinitive is translated by **de**. Some verbs require no preposition: these are shown followed directly by *faire* (to do), eg: *vouloir faire*, to wish **to** do – indicating that **no preposition** is used before an infinitive. Others are shown followed by the correct preposition for that verb.

toi, disjunctive personal pronoun = thou, thee, you: see PRONOUNS ¶15 – 17: for *toi* replacing *te* in the imperative, see PRONOUNS ¶9.

tomber, to fall. Aux: *être* (change of position). **But**: *tomber un adversaire*, to floor/ground an adversary – auxiliary: *avoir*.

ton, ta, tes = your (thy): see ADJECTIVES ¶10.

too

    i.   as in 'too much' = **trop***:* he has too much bread, *il a trop de* pain* (**de* is necessary unless it means 'of the', eg: he has too much **of the** black bread, *il a trop **du** pain noir*); too (heavy) for, *trop (lourd) pour;* too much = to be unwanted, *être de trop*

    ii.   meaning 'also', as in 'he came too', see *aussi*.

toucher, to touch, to interfere with, to be concerned with/relevant to: *toucher qlqch*, to touch sth, be adjacent to sth; *toucher à qlqch*, to be in contact with sth; *toucher qlqch du doigt*, to touch sth with a finger; *toucher son salaire*, to draw one's wages; *toucher du piano/de l'orgue*, to play the piano/organ (*jouer de . . .* is also used: see *jouer*); *son malheur me touche*, his misfortune touches me; *cela ne me touche pas*, that doesn't concern me.

toujours

    i.   **always**: *il est toujours content de le faire*, he is always pleased to do it

    ii.   **still, yet**: *est-ce que tu m'aimes toujours?* do you still love me? *il pleut toujours*, it is still raining

   iii. **nevertheless**, all the same: *faites-le toujours, et nous verrons après*, do it nevertheless/all the same, and we shall see afterwards; *mais écrivez-moi toujours*, but write to me all the same

   iv. **continually**, still, on and on: *il parle toujours*, he is still speaking (speaks on and on).

tour, **masculine** = *un tour*, a tour (= trip), a turn ('go', revolution of wheel, etc), a short walk, a (malicious) trick, a turn of expression: **feminine** = *une tour*, a tower (building).

se tourmenter de qlqch, to worry about sth; *se tourmenter à* (or *pour*) *faire qlqch*, to take great pains to do sth.

tous les deux: see *tout* i(f) below.

tout

    i.   **as adjective**: all, every, the whole: agrees with the noun: *tout, toute, tous* (**note** the masc plur has no *-t-*), *toutes*, and may be used: (a) immediately **before a noun**: *pour toute éternité,* for all eternity (b) frequently **with the definite article before a noun**: *tous les livres,* all the books; *toute la journée,* the whole day/all the day (c) *tout* can be an **adjective** – qualifying a demonstrative adjective preceding a noun: *toute cette eau,* all this water (d) **adjective** – qualifying a possessive adjective preceding a noun: *tout mon malheur,* all my misfortune (e) when used before the name of a town, meaning either the whole town or all its inhabitants, *tout* is invariable: *tout Paris croyait que . . . ,* all Paris believed that . . . (f) with *deux* = 'both' ('all the two'), *tous les deux, toutes les deuz* or *tous deux, toutes deux,* eg: *Madame Brune et sa fille (elles*) sont toutes les deux arrivées hier,* Mrs Brune and her daughter both (fem) arrived yesterday; *ils sont arrivés tous les deux hier,* both (masc) arrived yesterday; *tous deux sont arrivés,* both have arrived; *il faut acheter tous les deux,* both must be bought; *le petit gourmand a mangé tous deux,* the little glutton has eaten both. Similarly: *tous (les*) trois,* etc, all three, etc (*optional)

ii.   **adverb**: all, wholly, very, completely: *il est tout fatigué,* he is very tired: **by exception** *tout,* although an adverb, when qualifying an adjective which qualifies a feminine noun, takes a feminine ending, and, in the plural, a feminine plural ending, **if** it comes before a consonant or *h*-aspirate: *Jeanne est toute contente,* Joan is very pleased; *elles sont toutes honteuses (h*-aspirate), they are very ashamed: **but** *tout* remains invariable before a vowel or *h*-mute: *Jeanne est tout étonnée,* Joan is very surprised; *elle est tout heureuse,* she is very happy (*h*-mute); *tout plein,* quite full; *tout doux!* gently! *tout prêt,* all/quite ready; *tout à fait,* altogether, entirely; *tout fait,* ready made; *tout à vous,* yours truly (somewhat informal); *cette question est tout autre – c'est une tout autre question,* this question is quite different – it's a quite different question: *tout* being an adverb qualifying *autre,* so does **not** agree: **but** in: *je répondrai à toute autre question que vous pouvez me poser,* I shall answer every other question that you can ask me, *toute* is an adjective qualifying question = *toute question autre que . . . ,* every question other than (those so far put)

iii. **noun**: masc: all, everything: *il a dit tout,* he has said all; *à tout prendre,* taking everything into consideration; *après tout,* after all; *il a risqué le tout pour si peu,* he has risked everything for so little; *par-dessus tout,* above all, above everything; *propre à tout,* suitable for everything, fit for anything; *voilà tout, c'est tout,* that's all

iv. *tous, toutes,* **pronoun (always** plural: *tous sont arrivés,* all have arrived (if all are feminine: *toutes, sont, arrivées*)); *je les ai vus tous*,* I have seen them all (*pronounced 'touss' when a pronoun).

tout en, with the present participle used as verb noun (gerund) = while, whilst: *tout en parlant,* while speaking.

tout le monde: everyone, everybody: takes the verb in the singular: *tout le monde, était là,* everybody was there.

toward(s): referring to both place and time = ***vers****: ils vont vers Paris*, they go towards Paris; *ils arrivent vers trois heures*, they arrive towards (about) three o'clock; *vers la fin de la journée*, towards the end of the day: with regard to = ***envers*** *(or vers), à l'égard de* **or** *pour:* he is loyal towards his friends, *il est loyal envers ses amis;* they are well disposed towards us, *ils sont bien disposés envers nous* **or** *ils sont bien disposés à notre égard* **or** *à l'égard de nous* **or** . . . *ils sont bien disposés pour nous.*

traduire, to translate, to express, interpret: *traduire un livre en français*, to translate a book into French; ***se traduire***, to become, to be expressed; *sa joie se traduit par ces actions*, his joy is expressed by these deeds. Conjugated like ***conduire***.

trafiquer *en qlqch*, to deal dishonestly in sth.

traire, to milk (a cow, goat, etc). Pres: *trais, trais, trait, trayons, trayez, traient*. Imperf: *trayais, -ais, -ait, -ions, -iez, -aient*. Fut: *trairai, -as, -a, -ons, -ez, -ont*. No past historic. Imperat: *trais, trayons, trayez*. Pres subj: *traie, traies, traie, trayions, trayiez, traient*. No imperf subj. Pres part: *trayant*. Past part: *trait, traite, traits, traites*. Aux: ***avoir***.

traiter, to treat, to handle: *traiter à manger*, to treat sn to a meal; *traiter une question*, deal with a question; *traiter en enfant/imbecile*, to treat as a child, as an idiot.

trancher, to cut off: *trancher court*, to cut short; *trancher net*, to speak plainly; *trancher du grand*, to give oneself airs; *trancher une difficulté*, to settle a difficulty; *trancher sur qlqch*, to contrast with sth/stand out against sth; *trancher sur tout*, to be dogmatic about everything.

transformer *qlqch en qlqch*, to transform sth into sth.

transcrire, to transcribe. Like ***écrire***.

Transitive, Intransitive, *transitif, intransitif, intransitif indirect*: see NOUNS ¶5.

transmettre, to transmit. Like ***mettre***.

transpercer, to transfix, transpierce: *de qlqch*, with sth. Conjugated like ***placer***.

travail, masc: plur: *travaux:* work, labour, employment, study: *travail* (= painful effort), work of art; *le travail manuel*, manual labour; *le travail intellectuel*, mental work; *un travail historique*, an historical work (= book/study); *une femme en travail*, a woman in labour; *les travaux publics*, public works; *les travaux forcés*, forced labour (punishment).

travailler, to work, to labour, to study, to fashion/make, work on: *travailler à faire qlqch*, endeavour to do sth; *travailler son style*, to work in one's own style; *se travailler à faire qlqch*, strain/make an effort to do sth. (**Note**: my watch works well (= functions), *ma montre marche bien*.)

tréma, the French name for diæresis (¨): used in a few words in French to mark two vowels pronounced separately, as in *Noël*, Christmas and in ***haïr***.

trembler, to tremble: *de froid/peur*, with cold/fear; *trembler de faire qlqch*, tremble at the thought of doing sth.

tressaillir, to shake, start (= be startled): quake with fear, *de peur*. Pres: *tressaille, -es, -e, -ons, -ez, -ent*. Imperf: *tressaillais*, etc. Fut: *tressaillirai*, etc. Past hist: *tressaillis, -is, -it, -îmes, -îtes, tressaillirent*. Pres subj: *tressaille, -es, -e, -ions, -iez, -ent*. Imperf subj: *tressaillisse, -es, tressaillît, tressaillissions, -issiez, tresaillissent*. Pres part: *tressaillant*. Past part: *tressailli*. Aux: ***avoir***.

triste, sad: *il a l'air triste*, he looks sad; *des tristes nouvelles*, sad news; *des couleurs tristes*, dull colours. Adverb: ***tristement***, sadly.

tromper, to deceive: ***se tromper***, to (make a) mistake; *se tromper de route*, to mistake the road, take the wrong road; *je me suis trompé*, I made a mistake; *se tromper sur qlqch*, to make a mistake about sth.

trop, too much, too many: see **too** above.

true: see *vrai*.

tuer, to kill (literally or figuratively): *faire tuer qlqn/qlqch*, to have sn/sth killed.

turc, fem: *turque* (**no 'c'** in fem): Turkish. **Noun**: Turk, with capital 'T': *Turque*.

twice: *deux fois*: see *fois*.

U

un, une, indefinite article = a, an: **also** the number 'one' (**but** for the pronoun 'one' see *on*). The plural of the indefinite article *un* is *des*: *il a un livre*, he has a book; *il a des livres*, he has some books: **but** after a negative *de* is used: *il n'a pas de livre*, he does not have a book; *pas un(e)* = not one (agrees with whatever is referred to): **but** *page un* = page one (**note**: *page* is feminine, but this means 'page with number one'); *le un* = the figure one (**no** elision); *l'un(e) et l'autre*, the one and the other; *l'un l'autre*, each other; *un et un font deux*, one plus one make two. See NUMBERS in Grammar Section.

under: *sous*: under the tree, *sous l'arbre*; under Louis XIV, *sous Louis XIV*; under my name, *sous mon nom*; under pain of death, *sous peine de mort*: underneath, below, beneath = *au-dessous de*: under the table, *au-dessous de la table*; under/below the clouds, *au-dessous des nuages*: he has under ten children, *il a moins de dix enfants*; that costs under ten francs, *cela coute moins de dix francs*. See *dessous*.

unless: *à moins que*: subordinating conjunction, with the following clause in the subjunctive: if the following verb is affirmative *ne* precedes it, eg: unless he does it, *à moins qu'il ne le fasse*: if the following verb is negative, **both** *ne* and *pas* are used, eg: unless he does **not** do it, *à moins qu'il ne le fasse pas*: other negatives can be used as the sense requires, eg: unless he writes **only** two, *à moins qu'il n'écrive que deux*: *à moins de* is used before an infinitive or noun with no subjunctive in the following clause, eg: unless one is strong it is not possible to do it, *à moins d'être fort on ne peut pas le faire*; I shall not punish him unless he makes a serious mistake, *je ne le punirai pas à moins qu'il ne fasse une faute grave:* or I shall not punish him **but for** a serious mistake, *je ne le punirai pas à moins d'une faute grave.* See *ne.*

until: see **till.**

up: phrases in English ending in 'up' such as 'go up,' 'shut up', 'hard up', etc, **must** be changed before translating to some other form, such as 'to climb' or 'to ascend', 'to enclose', 'to imprison,' 'poor', etc, eg: 'he goes up', *il monte;* 'he is hard up', *il est pauvre;* 'to end up', *fînir;* 'to start up', *commencer;* 'fed up', *mécontent(e),* etc.

us: *nous:* pronoun: see PRONOUNS ¶1 – 4.

usé, usée, adjective: worn (out), threadbare, hackneyed.

used to can be expressed by the imperfect (see VERBS ¶14) **or** by *avoir l'habitude de . . .* **or** *être accoutumé à . . . ,* whichever best conveys the intended meaning.

user, to use, to wear out: *user qlqch,* to use sth; *user ses vêtements,* to wear out one's clothes; *user de qlqn/qlqch,* to make use of sn/sth; *user de son talent,* to make use of one's talent; *en user bien/mal avec qlqn,* to use sn well/badly; *se user vite,* to wear out quickly.

usurper, to usurp: *qlqch sur qlqn,* sth from sn; *usurper sur qlqn/qlqch,* to encroach upon sn/sth.

V

vaincre, to vanquish. **Note** that *-c-* appears only in the infinitive, the singular of present and imperative, in the future stem and in the past participle. Pres: *vaincs, vaincs, vainc* (**no** *-t,* **but** interrogative = *vainc-t-il?*), *vainquons, -quez, -quent.* Imperf: *vainquais, -ais, -ait, -ions, -iez, -aient.* Fut: *vaincrai, -as, -a, -ons, -ez, -ont.* Past hist: *vainquis, vainquis, vanquit, vainquîmes, vainquîtes, vainquirent.* Imperat: *vaincs, vainquons, vainquez.* Pres subj: *vainque, -ques, -que, vainquions, -quiez, -quent.* Imperf subj: *vainquisse, -quisses, -quît, -quissions, -quissiez, vainquissent.* Pres part: *vainquant.* Past part: *vaincu, -ue, -us, -ues.* Aux: *avoir.*

valoir, to be worth: *ce livre vaut d'être lu,* this book is worth reading; *il sait ce qu'il vaut,* he knows what he (or it) is worth; *Paris vaut une visite,* Paris is worth a visit; *ne rien faire qui vaille,* to do nothing worth while; *vaille que vaille,* whatever it may be worth/for better or worse: **most frequently used in impersonal form,** eg: *il vaut la peine de le faire,* it is worth while doing it; *il ne vaut pas la peine de l'essayer,* it's not worth the trouble trying it; *il vaut la peine qu'on le fasse,* it is worth while doing it (= that one may do it); *il vaut mieux* (sometimes: *mieux vaut*) *faire qlqch,* it is preferable to do sth, eg: *il vaut mieux le faire maintenant que d'attendre,* it is preferable/it is better to do it now than to wait; *il autant vaut* (**or** *il vaut autant*) *que vous le fassiez,* its all the same whether you do it/you may as well do it; *il autant vaudrait qu'il soit* *fait*, it would be just as well that one should do it. Pres: *vaux, vaux, vaut, valons, valez, valent*. Imperf: *valais, -ais, -ait, -ions, -iez, -aient*. Fut: *vaudrai, -as, -a, -ons, -ez, -ont*. Past hist: *valus, valus, valut, valûmes, valûtes, valurent*. Imperat: *vaux, valons, valez*. Pres subj: *vaille, vailles, vaille, valions, valiez, vaillent*. Imperf subj: *valusse, valusses, valût, valussions, valussiez, valussent*. Pres part: *valant*. Past part: *valu, value, valus, values*. Aux: ***avoir***.

se vanter *de qlqch*, to pride oneself on sth: *d'être qlqch*, on being sth; ***se vanter*** *de faire qlqch*, to boast of doing sth.

vapeur, **masculine** = steamship: **feminine** = vapour, steam.

vaquer, to stop fulfilling one's functions temporarily: *vaquer à ses affaires*, to apply oneself to one's business.

vedette, small naval vessel, military scout, film/stage star (he **or** she): **always** fem.

veiller, to watch over: *veiller qlqn*, to attend to, sit up with, watch over sn; *veiller sur qlqn/qlqch*, to look after, take care of sn/sth; *veiller à faire qlqch*, to take care to do sth.

vendre, to sell, to sell for, to deal in: *vendre du fromage*, to sell, deal in cheese; *une maison à vendre*, a house for sale; *vendre* (**or** *se vendre*) *dix francs*, to sell for ten francs; *vendre* (**or** *se vendre*) *pour rien*, to sell for nothing; *vendre chèrement sa vie*, to sell one's life dearly; *vendre ses complices*, to betray one's accomplices. **Sample for verbs ending in -re**. Pres: *vends, vends, vend, vendons, vendez, vendent*. Imperf: *vendais, -ais, -ait, -ions, -iez, -aient*. Fut: *vendrai, -as, -a, -ons, -ez, -ont*. Past hist: *vendis, vendis, vendit, vendîmes, vendîtes, vendirent*. Imperat: *vends, vendons, vendez*. Pres subj: *vende, vendes, vende, vendions, vendiez, vendent*. Imperf subj: *vendisse, vendisses, vendît, vendissions, vendissiez, vendissent*. Pres part: *vendant*. Past part: *vendu, -e, -s, -es*. Aux: ***avoir***.

venger *qlqn de qlqch*, to avenge sn for sth: *venger qlqch sur qlqn*, to take revenge on sn for sth; *se venger de qlqn/qlqch*, to exact revenge from sn/for sth; *se venger sur qlqn de qlqch*, to revenge oneself/take revenge on sn for sth. Takes '*e*' after '*g*' before '*a*' and '*o*', eg: *il vengeait, nous vengeons*.

venir, to come: *venir faire qlqch*, to come to do sth (come and do sth); *venir à faire qlqch*, to happen/chance to do sth, arrive at the point of doing sth; ***venir de*** *faire qlqch*, to have just done sth, eg: *je viens de le trouver*, I have just found it; *(c'est) à venir*, (it's) to come; *en venir à qlqch*, to arrive at sth, to have recourse to sth; *vouloir en venir à faire qlqch*, to aim at doing sth; *faire venir qlqch*, to order sth (to be sent/fetched); *venir à bout de faire qlqch*, to succeed in doing sth; *où voulez-vous en venir?* what are you aiming at? Pres: *viens, viens, vient, venons, venez, viennent*. Imperf: *venais, -ais, -ait, -ions, -iez, -aient*. Fut: *viendrai, -as, -a, -ons, -ez, -ont*. Past hist: *vins, vins, vint, vînmes, vîntes, vinrent*. Imperat: *viens, venons, venez*. Pres subj: *vienne, viennes, vienne, venions, veniez, viennent*. Imperf subj: *vinsse, vinsses, vînt, vinssions,* *vinssiez, vinssent.* Pres part: *venant.* Past part: *venu, venue, venus, venues.* Aux: *être.*

vêtir, to clothe: *vêtir qlqn de qlqch,* to clothe sn with/in sth; ***se vêtir (de qlqch),*** to dress oneself, clothe oneself (in sth). Pres: *vêts, vêts, vêt, vêtons, vêtez, vêtent.* Imperf: *vêtais, -ais, -ait, -ions, -iez, -aient.* Fut: *vêtirai, -as, -a, -ons, -ez, -ont.* Past hist: *vêtis, vêtis, vêtit, vêtîmes, vêtîtes, vêtirent.* Imperat: *vête, vêtons, vêtez.* Pres subj: *vête, vêtes, vête, vêtions, vêtiez, vêtent.* Imperf subj: *vêtisse, vêtisses, vêtît, vêtissions, vêtissiez, vêtissent.* Pres part: *vêtant.* Past part: *vêtu, vêtue, vêtus, vêtues.* Aux: ***avoir.***

***veuf, veuve*, adjective**: widowed, deprived of: *veuf de,* bereft of. **Noun**: widower, widow: *épouser la veuve,* to be guillotined (popular).

vexer, to vex, annoy, tease: *vexer qlqn,* to annoy, tease sn; *être vexé de/par qlqch,* to be vexed/annoyed at/by sth; *se vexer de qlqch,* to get annoyed with sth; *il se vexe facilement,* he gets easily annoyed.

victime, victim (**always** feminine gender whether male or female).

vieillot, vieillotte, oldish.

vieux, vieil, fem = ***vieille:*** adjective: old: *vieil* is used before singular masculine nouns starting with a vowel or *h*-mute, eg: *un vieil arbre,* an old tree. Masculine plural **always *vieux.*** Feminine plural, *vieilles.* See ADJECTIVES ¶3ii and ¶4 ii.

viser qlqn/qlqch, to take aim at sn/sth: *viser à faire qlqch,* to aim at doing sth. **Also**: to put a visa on (a passport).

vite, adjective and adverb: fast, quick, quickly: *au plus vite,* as fast as possible. **No separate adverbial form in normal use.**

vivre, to live, to dwell: *vivre de,* to live on. Pres: *vis, vis, vit, vivons, vivez, vivent.* Imperf: *vivais, -ais, -ait, -ions, -iez, -aient.* Fut: *vivrai, -as, -a, -ons, -ez, -ont.* Past hist: *vécus, vécus, vécut, vécûmes, vécûtes, vécurent.* Imperat: *vis, vivons, vivez.* Pres subj: *vive, vives, vive, vivions, viviez, vivent.* Imperf subj: *vécusse, vécusses, vécût, vécussions, vécussiez, vécussent.* Pres part: *vivant.* Past part: *vécu, -e.* Aux: ***avoir:*** *vivre à la campagne,* to live in the country(side); *vivre seul,* to live alone; *apprendre à vivre à quelqu'un,* to punish sn for bad behaviour; *vive le roi!* long live the king!

Voice: active and passive: see VERBS ¶2.

***voile*, masculine** = veil: **feminine** = sail, sailing-ship: *mettre à la voile,* to set sail.

voir, to see. Pres: *vois, vois voit, voyons, voyez, voient.* Imperf: *voyais, -ais, -ait, voyions, -iez, -aient.* Fut: *verrai, verras, verra, verrons, verrez, verront.* Past hist: *vis, vis, vit, vîmes, vîtes, virent.* Imperat: *vois, voyons, voyez.* Pres subj: *voie, voies, voie, voyions, voyiez, voient.* Imperf subj: *visse, visses, vît, vissions, vissiez, vissent.* Pres part: *voyant.* Past part: *vu, vue, vus, vues.* Aux: ***avoir:*** *voir qlqn/qlqch faire qlqch,* to see sn/sth doing sth; *voir à faire qlqch,* to see about doing sth, to arrange for sth to be done; *voir son médecin,* to see one's doctor; *faire voir qlqch à qlqn,* to show sth to sn; *aller voir qlqn,* to go and visit sn; *je vais voir si cet habit me va,* I am going to see if this coat suits/fits me; *cela se voit tous les jours,* that's sth that happens every day/frequently; *voir faire qlqch,* to see sth done; *on lui voit beaucoup d'amies,* he appears to have a lot of girl friends; *oui, je vois bien,* yes, I understand; *voyons!* let's see!

voisin, voisine, neighbour (the person next door), 'neighbour' in general, 'fellow human being': see ***prochain.***

voler

    i. **to fly** (in the air), to move very quickly, to pass very quickly: *le temps vole,* time flies. (Regular *-er* verb, auxiliary: ***avoir.***)

    ii. **to steal:** *qlqch à qlqn,* sth from sn. (Regular.)

vouloir, to wish, want. Pres: *veux, veux, veut, voulons, voulez, veulent.* Imperf: *voulais, voulais, voulait, voulions, vouliez, voulaient.* Fut: *voudrai, voudras, voudra, voudrons, voudrez, voudront.* Past hist: *voulus, voulus, voulut, voulûmes, voulûtes, voulurent.* Imperat: *veux, voulons, voulez* (polite form: *veuille, veuillez*). Pres subj: *veuille, veuilles, veuille, voulions, vouliez, veuillent.* Imperf subj: *voulusse, voulusses, voulût, voulussions, voulussiez, voulussent.* Pres part: *voulant.* Past part: *voulu, voulue, voulus, voulues.* Aux: ***avoir:*** *vouloir faire qlqch,* to want/wish to do sth; *veuillez vous asseoir* (**no** hyphen, *vous* is reflexive pronoun of *asseoir*), please sit down; *je vous prie de vouloir bien manger,* do please eat; *je vous prie de bien vouloir vous taire,* kindly keep quiet: **notice the difference in meaning between *vouloir bien* and *bien vouloir:*** *vouloir qlqch de qlqn,* to want sth from sn; *en vouloir à qlqn (de qlqch), to* have a grudge against sn/feel malice towards sn (for/on account of sth); *que voulez-vous (de moi)?* what do you want (of/from me)? *oui, je veux bien,* yes, certainly I will/I'd like to/yes, all right (or similar expression); *vouloir du bien/du mal à qlqn,* to wish sn well/ill; *qu'est-ce que cela veut dire?* what does that mean? For use with subjunctive see VERBS ¶33x.

vous, you: **conjunctive and reflexive pronoun,** see PRONOUNS ¶3, ¶4, ¶6, ¶7. **Disjunctive pronoun,** see PRONOUNS ¶15, ¶16, ¶17.

voyager, to travel. Conjugated like ***manger.***

voyageur, **masc** = traveller: **fem** = *voyageuse.* **Also** adjective = travelling.

vrai, vraie, **adjective**: true, real: *un vrai ami,* a true (reliable, steadfast) friend; *voilà sa vraie place,* that's his real (proper) place; *une histoire vraie,* a true story; *à dire vrai* **or** *à vrai dire,* to speak openly/frankly; *pour de vrai,* really/truly; *est-il mort pour de vrai?* is he really dead? **Noun**: *le vrai,* truth: *il aime le vrai,* he loves truth.

vue, **fem**: view, eyesight: *avoir une bonne vue,* to have good eyesight.

W

want

    i.   wish: see *vouloir*

    ii. need: see *falloir, besoin.*

Weather: it is fine, *il fait beau (temps);* it is mild, *il fait doux;* it is bad weather, *il fait mauvais (temps);* it is sunny, *il fait du soleil;* it is foggy, *il fait du brouillard;* there is a sea fog, *il fait du brume, il brume;* it is windy, *il fait du vent;* it is breezy, *il fait du brise;* it is hot, *il fait chaud;* it is cold, *il fait froid;* it is raining, *il pleut;* it is snowing, *il neige;* it is freezing (hard), *il gèle (dur);* it is thawing, *il dégèle;* what is the weather like? *quel temps fait-il?*

well: to get well: *guérir* **or** *se guérir* (see *guérir*). I don't feel well, *je ne me sens pas bien;* I am (very) well, *je me porte (très) bien.* 'Well, now . . .' *Or,* . . . (when continuing telling a story after a pause). See *bien.*

what: *ce que, que, quoi, quel:* what I say is true, *ce que je dis est vrai;* what's that? *qu'est-ce que c'est que cela?* what would you? *que voulez-vous?* what did you say? *comment?* **or** *quoi?* **or**, more politely: *plaît-il?* with what, *avec quoi;* I don't know what to say/to do, *je ne sais pas quoi dire/faire* **or** *que dire/faire; quel bruit!* what a noise! See *que* vii, *quel, qui est-ce qui* and PRONOUNS ¶49.

what ever is that/it? = *qu'est-ce que c'est?*

whatever: *tout ce qui* (subject), *tout ce que* (object): as subject: whatever is on the table, *tout ce **qui** se trouve sur la table:* as object: whatever you say is true, *tout ce **que** vous dites est vrai:* none whatever, *aucun* (see *aucun, aucune*); nothing whatever, *rien du tout;* it is of no use whatever, *cela sert (absolument) à rien;* whatever you may think of it, *quoi que* vous en pensiez* (*followed by the subjunctive).

when: see CONJUNCTIONS ¶4 and *quand, lorsque,* and *où* ii.

whether: see *si* i, second half of paragraph.

which: see PRONOUNS ¶40ff: **which?** see PRONOUNS ¶45 – 47.

while, whilst

    i.   at the same time as, *en* + **present participle** (used as verb noun or gerund: see VERBS ¶43iii), eg: the soldiers sang while marching, *les soldats chantaient en marchant: **tout** can be inserted to emphasise that both are concurrent: she speaks while working (even as she works), *elle parle **tout** en travaillant;* whilst accepting what is offered, *tout en acceptant ce qui est offert;* he eats while he reads, *il mange pendant qu'il lit*

    ii. ' by way of contrast', *tandis que,* eg: John is tall while Joan is little, *Jean est grand tandis que Jeanne est petite.* See CONJUNCTIONS ¶4.

who (?), whom (?), whose (?): see PRONOUNS ¶40ff, ¶46ff.

will, shall: see future tense of VERBS ¶15 and ¶16.

will = wish: see *vouloir*.

with: *avec*: *de:* with a pencil, *avec un crayon;* filled with, *rempli de;* to cover with, *couvrir de,* see **couvrir;** what will he do with . . . ? *que va-t-il faire de . . . ?* Describing personal appearance with = *à*, eg: the man with the white beard, *l'homme à la barbe blanche;* a coat with brown stripes, *un habit à rayons bruns;* a house with two storeys, *une maison à deux étages.* Describing the attitude of body, limbs, etc, 'with' is **not** translated, eg: he walks with his eyes shut, *il marche, les yeux fermés;* with open arms, *les bras ouverts.*

without: *sans:* he came without a hat, *il est venu sans chapeau;* he is quite without money, *il est tout à fait sans argent;* he works without making any noise, *il travail sans qu'il fasse aucun bruit* (= 'without that he make any noise': with subjunctive **or** *sans bruit* **or** *sans faire du bruit* – both = silently).

would

    i.   he **would** do something if he could = **conditional tense**: see VERBS ¶18

    ii. when he was a child he **would** play in the garden = 'used to', 'was accustomed to': in this sense 'would' is expressed by the **imperfect tense**: see VERBS ¶14

    iii. I would (= should) like to do it, *je voudrais bien le faire;* he would not do it (= he didn't want to do it), *il ne voulait pas le faire:* see *vouloir*, to wish, to want

    iv. I thought I would do sth, *j'ai eu l'idée de faire qlqch*

    v. would that I could (do sth)! = 'if only I could' (do sth)! = *si seulement je pouvais (faire qlqch)!*

Y

y

    i.   adverb and conjunctive pronoun = there, in/to/at/on that place/thing. When a noun object of a verb is governed by a preposition expressing the idea of 'place where' or 'therein', 'thereto' (such as *en* = in: *dans* = in: *sur* = on: *sous* = under), the pronoun used to replace that noun will be *y*, eg: *il travail dans son jardin* (he works in his garden): '*dans son jardin*' (replaced in English by '**in it**') = *y: il y travail* (he works **in it**): similarly: *il veut aller à la ville* (he wants to go to the town): 'to the town' is replaced in English by '**there**': in French '*à la ville*' becomes *y: il veut y aller* (he wants to go **there**). After a few verbs, such as *penser à,* to think about: *se fier à,* to trust: *croire en,* have faith in: *y* may stand for a person: 'about/in him/her/us/you/them', eg: *ne vous y fiez pas,* don't trust him (= don't trust yourself **to** him: *fier* governs *à*); *je crois en Dieu* (I believe in God), '*en Dieu*' is replaced by *y: j'y crois* (I believe in Him); *ne touchez pas aux animaux,* (don't touch the animals), is replaced by: *n'y touchez pas* (don't touch them – *toucher à* means 'to touch with the hand', 'put the hand **on**'). A **whole phrase** can similarly be replaced by *y*, eg: in '*il s'est obstiné à le faire*' (he insisted **on doing it**), the phrase '*à le faire*' (on doing it) is replaced by *y*: *il s'y est obstiné* (he insisted on it). For position of *y* used with other conjunctive pronouns see PRONOUNS ¶2ff.

ii.   *il y a*, there is, there are: subject is always *il*: the verb always 3rd sing: tense can change: *il y avait*, there was/were; *il y aura*, there will be; *il y a eu*, there has/have been; *il n'y a pas*, there is/are not; *y a-t-il?* is/are there? *n'y a-t-il pas?* is/are there not? Any tense of *avoir* can be used with *y* as indirect pronoun object always placed immediately before the verb.

year: see *an, année*.

-yer, **verbs**: **-ayer**, **verbs**: see *payer*, **-oyer** and **-uyer**, **verbs**: see *employer*. Exceptions: *envoyer*, to send: *renvoyer*, to send back (see both).

yes: usually: *oui*: more emphatically: *mais oui*: a contradictory 'yes' = *si*: 'It is not raining.' 'Yes it is.' *–Il ne pleut pas. –Si!*

yet: conjunction: but, however, nevertheless: *cependant, mais, néanmoins, pourtant, toutefois*: he is poor, yet he has a car, *il est pauvre, cependant il a une auto;* not yet, *pas encore*.

you: see PRONOUNS ¶3ff. To speak to sn using the familiar '*tu*' instead of the more formal '*vous*', is *tutoyer* ('to *tu* sn').

your: see ADJECTIVES ¶10.

yours: see PRONOUNS ¶37 – 39. A friend of yours, *un de vos amis;* yours sincerely (at end of letters), familiar form, *tout à toi, tout à vous;* yours affectionately, *à toi* or *à vous de tout cœur*. For formal letter endings see **Correspondence**.

Z

zéro, nought, and 'love' in tennis: *zéro* is used for '0' when giving individual figures, eg: 6708 (six, seven, nought, eight) = *six, sept, zéro, huit* (and when thus spoken separately the final consonant for each number is sounded: *seess, set, zeeroh, weet*). See NUMBERS. In the twenty-four hour clock *zéro heure* is used for twelve midnight, eg: 12.30 a.m. in 24-hour clock, is *zéro heure trente*. See **Time of Day**.

Grammar

ADJECTIVES

1. **An adjective is a word that qualifies a noun.** French adjectives 'agree' with the noun they qualify, usually having different endings for use with masculine, feminine and plural nouns. (See ¶5.) The most usual way to form the feminine of an adjective is to add *-e* to the masculine; the plural is usually formed by adding *-s* to the masculine or feminine singular. There are many exceptions: see below and individual entries in Reference Section.

2. **Feminine of adjectives**
   i. **All feminine singular adjectives end in** *-e*. As many adjectives end in *-e* in their masculine form, a noun qualified by an adjective ending in *-e* is not necessarily feminine
   ii. if an adjective ends in *-e* in the masculine it remains unchanged when qualifying a feminine noun: *un livre* **rouge**, a red book; *une robe* **rouge**, a red dress
   iii. **adjectives not ending in** *-e* (**including** those ending in *-é*, with accent) normally add *-e* when qualifying a feminine noun: *un livre* **vert**, a green book; *une robe* **verte**, a green dress; *Jean, né à Paris, Jeanne, née à Lyon*, John, born in Paris, Joan, born in Lyons
   iv. **other adjectives form their feminine by changing their endings as follows:**

MASC → FEM		MASC	FEM	
-er	*-ère*	*dernier*	*dernière*	last
-eil	*-eille*	*pareil*	*pareille*	similar
-el	*-elle*	*cruel*	*cruelle*	cruel
-en	*-enne*	*ancien*	*ancienne*	old
-et	*-ette*	*muet*	*muette*	dumb
-eur *	*-eure*	*meilleur*	*meilleure*	better
-eur **	*-euse*	*trompeur*	*trompeuse*	deceitful
-f	*-ve*	*neuf*	*neuve*	new
-il	*-ille*	*gentil*	*gentille*	kind
-ier	*-ière*	*dernier*	*dernière*	last
-ot	*-ote*	*dévot*	*dévote*	devout
-teur	*-trice*	*moteur*	*motrice*	motive
-x	*-se*	*furieux*	*furieuse*	furious

* Mainly comparatives
** Usually formed by adding *-eur* to the stem of present participle of a verb, eg: *tromper*, to deceive, *trompant*

3.   **Irregular feminines of adjectives**

   i.   **The following have feminine forms which either follow special rules or are irregular:**

MASC	FEM		MASC	FEM	
aigu	*aiguë*	sharp	*las*	*lasse*	weary
bas	*basse*	low	*long*	*longue*	long
bénin	*bénigne*	good-natured	*malin*	*maligne*	sly, shrewd
blanc	*blanche*	white	*pâlot*	*pâlotte*	palish, wan
bon	*bonne*	good	*public*	*publique*	public
bref	*brève*	short	*sec*	*sèche*	dry
frais	*fraîche*	fresh	*secret*	*secrète*	secret
gras	*grasse*	fatty	*sot*	*sotte*	stupid
gros	*grosse*	fat, corpulent	*vieillot*	*vieillotte*	oldish

   For further information and usage see individual alphabetical entries

   ii. **the feminines of adjectives which have a second masculine singular form** used before a vowel or *h*-mute are formed from this secondary form, doubling the final *-l* and adding *-e:*

MASC	MASC BEFORE VOWEL	FEM
beau	*bel*	*belle*
fou	*fol*	*folle*
mou	*mol*	*molle*
nouveau	*nouvel*	*nouvelle*
vieux	*vieil*	*vieille*

   eg: *un beau jour,* a fine day; *un bel homme,* a handsome man; *une belle dame,* a beautiful lady; *de beaux hommes, de belles dames*

   iii. **nouns with no feminine form**, such as *professeur*, teacher, have **no** feminine, eg: *une femme professeur*, a woman teacher (see ¶5iv).

4.   **Plural of adjectives**

   i.   **Normally** the plural of both masculine and feminine forms of an adjective is made by adding *-s* to the singular: *grand, grands, grande, grandes*

   ii. as all feminine singular adjectives end in *-e*, all plural feminine adjectives end in *-es*

   iii. **the following masculine singular endings change in the plural as shown:**

   a.   **endings** in *-s* or *-x* do **not** change in masc plural, eg: *gris* (grey); *vieux* (old)

   b.   **endings** in *-eau* add *-x*, eg: *beau, beaux:* **also** *Hébreu, -x*

   c.   **endings** in *-ou* and also *bleu* (blue); *feu* (late = deceased) add *-s*, eg: *fou, fous,* mad; *mou, mous* soft; *bleu, bleus.* See NOUNS ¶15iii

   d.   **most endings** in *-al* change this to *-aux*, eg: *loyal, loyaux*

e. **a few endings** in *-al* add *-s*, eg: *banal, banals,* trite, banal; *bancal, bancals,* bandy-legged; *fatal, fatals,* fatal; *final, finals,* final; *natal, natals,* native; *naval, navals,* naval (There is some variation in usage for these.)

f. *tout, -e* (all, every) has masculine plural *tous,* feminine plural *toutes*

g. **adjectives with two masculine forms,** like *vieux, vieil,* have plurals formed from the first form **only**: *un vieil ami, deux vieux amis,* an old friend, two old friends. See 3ii above.

5. **Agreement of adjectives**

i. **Adjectives 'agree' with the noun they qualify**: that is, they take the same form in gender and number; where the same adjective qualifies **two or more nouns** the adjective will be in the plural; if qualifying nouns of different genders the adjective will be masculine plural

ii. **exceptional adjectives**: for rules of agreement for the following see each in its alphabetical entry: *cent, demi, feu, grand, mi, nu, possible, semi, tout, vingt.* See NUMBERS in this section for *mille:* see also **Colour**

iii. **compound adjectives**: normally both elements agree: *les enfants sourds-muets,* the deaf-mute children. If the first element is invariable or used adverbially it cannot be changed, **but** the second element will agree normally: *l'avant-dernière page,* the last but one page; *une femme anglo-indienne,* an Anglo-Indian woman; *des enfants nouveau-nés,* **newly** born children (*nouveau* assumes the role of adverb here). If one **colour** is combined with another to form a single compound adjective, **neither colour agrees,** eg: *des cravates vert pomme,* apple-green cravats. This also applies when there are two colours linked by *et: une étoffe blanc et noir,* a white and black cloth. In practice, however, these rules are **not** always adhered to

iv. **nouns which have no feminine form when used as adjectives** agree in number **only**: *les femmes professeurs,* the women teachers.

6. **Position of adjectives**

i. **Adjectives usually follow the noun they qualify, but** this rule may be broken for euphony, emphasis or special effect. There are also a number of adjectives which normally precede the noun (see iii below), and some which change their meaning according to their position (see ¶14)

ii. more especially, adjectives which normally FOLLOW the noun they qualify are those of **nationality, group** (religion, politics, etc), **shape** (or other physical quality such as **colour and taste**) (with the exception of those listed below in iii; see also iv below). **Present and past participles** used as adjectives also follow the noun

iii. adjectives which **precede** the noun they **qualify are the short and common adjectives**: *beau, bon, gentil, grand, gros, haut, joli, long, mauvais, meilleur, nouveau, petit,* and also adjectives which have a special masculine form before a vowel, eg: *vieux, vieil* (see ¶2iv above): and *meilleur* is included because it is the comparative of *bon:* but –

   iv.   adjectives qualified by an adverb **follow** the noun even if, when used alone, they would precede it: *un chien vraiment mauvais,* a really fierce dog (*mauvais* if not qualified by *vraiment* would precede *chien*)

   v.   **when two adjectives are used** they retain their normal position even if one precedes and the other follows: *une grande maison rouge*

   vi.   adjectives qualifying **compound nouns** will normally be placed before the first noun **or** after the second noun according to which of the two they actually qualify: and agreement will be with that noun, eg: *une grande maison de campagne,* a big country house (the house is big not the countryside); *une malle en cuir brun,* a trunk of brown leather (*cuir* is masculine; *brune* could have been used at the end in this case if it referred to *malle,* its gender making this clear. It would **not** have been clear if both nouns were of the same gender)

   vii.   **adjectives may change their meaning according to their position** (see ¶14 below).

7.   **Comparison of adjectives**

   i.   Adjectives form their **comparison** with *plus* = more, and their **superlative** with *le (la, les) plus* = the most, the definite article agreeing with the noun, and *que* = than (when needed), eg: *grand(e)(s),* big; *plus grand(e)(s) (que),* bigger (than); *le (la, les) plus grand(e)(s),* the biggest. Similarly: *moins* = less: *moins grand(e)(s) (que),* less big (than); *le (la, les) moins grand(e)(s),* the least big: and *aussi . . . que* = as . . . as: *aussi grand que,* as big as

   ii.   **a few adjectives have irregular comparisons,** eg: *bon* = good; *meilleur(e)(s)* = better; *le/la/les meilleur(e)(s)* = best: *mauvais* = bad, regular form; *plus mauvais(e)(s)* = worse; *le/la/les plus mauvais(e)(s)* = worst **or** irregular form, *pire** = worse; *le/la/les pire(s)* = worst (*this second form is especially, **but** not exclusively, used for **morally worse/worst** (adjective)): *petit* = small, regular form; *plus petit(e)(s)* = smaller; *le/la/les plus petit(e)(s)* = smallest (used mainly for size) **and** irregular form, *moindre* = less; *le/la/les moindre(s)* = least (used mainly for importance)

   iv.   **note:** if two or more superlatives are used for one noun the **definite article must be repeated for each,** eg: *l'homme le plus savant et le plus sage,* the most learned and wisest man.

8.   **Adjectives used as adverbs**

Some adjectives can be used as adverbs, mainly in conjunction with specific verbs in set phrases, eg: *voler bas,* fly low; *sentir bon,* smell good; *voir clair,* see clear(ly); *marcher tout droit,* walk quite straight/straight ahead; *coûter cher,* cost dearly/a lot; *arrêter court,* stop short. **Other adjectives that can be similarly used include:** *creux,* hollow; *doux,* sweet, soft; *dur,* hard; *faux,* false; *fort,* strong; *gras,* fat, plump, fatty; *gros,* big, large; *haut,* high, tall; *juste,* exact; *lourd,* heavy; *mauvais,* bad. **When these adjectives are thus**

used as adverbs they do not agree, except in a few idiomatic phrases. See *tout* in Reference Section

9.   **Nouns used as adjectives**

In English, nouns are frequently used as adjectives, eg: 'a country house'. In French, when a noun is used to describe another noun the two are usually connected

    i.   **by the preposition** *de: une maison de campagne,* a country house; *une montre d'or,* a gold watch (made of gold)

    ii.   **by the preposition** *à,* used to express **purpose**: *une brosse à cheveux,* a hair brush (a brush for the hair) **or** expressing the idea of 'with': *une charrette à deux roues,* a two-wheel cart (a cart with two   wheels)

    iii.   by the preposition *en,* to express 'made of': *une malle en cuir,* a leather trunk. This use of *'en'* tends to emphasise the importance of the material referred to.

10.   **Possessive (pronominal) adjectives**

These are used before nouns with which they agree:

FOR NOUNS IN . . .	MASC SING	FEM SING	MASC/FEM PLUR
my	*mon*	*ma**	*mes*
your (if using *tu*)	*ton*	*ta**	*tes*
his, her, its, one's	*son*	*sa**	*ses*
our	*notre*	*notre*	*nos*
your (using *vous*)	*votre*	*votre*	*vos*
their	*leur*	*leur*	*leurs*

* before feminine nouns beginning with a vowel or *h*-mute *mon, ton* and *son* are used, eg: *mon absence* (fem), my absence; *ton amie,* your (thy) girl friend; *son herbe* (fem), its grass

Note that agreement in gender is with the thing possessed: *sa maison* can mean his/her/its house. To make it clear if there is doubt whether it is 'his' or 'her': house a **disjunctive pronoun** can be added: *à lui* (to him) **or** *à elle* (to her): *c'est sa maison à lui,* 'it is his house to him' = it is **his** house. **There are no special feminine forms for**: *notre/nos, votre/vos, leur/leurs (leur* does **not** take *-e*): their house = *leur maison* (fem); their houses = *leurs maisons.*

11.   **The demonstrative adjectives** for both 'this' and 'that' **always** precede the noun they qualify **and** agree with it in gender and number, eg: this/that, masculine singular = *ce* (or *cet* before a vowel or *h*-mute): *ce chien,* this/that dog; *cet homme,* this/that man; *cet ami,* this/that he-friend (*ce,* when an adjective, is *cet* before a vowel or *h*-mute, **not** *c'*): this/that, feminine singular = *cette: cette maison,* this/that house; *cette action,* this/that action: **there is only one plural**: *ces chiens, ces hommes, ces maisons, ces actions.* **To distinguish** 'this' from 'that', **and** 'these' from 'those', where this is necessary to avoid ambiguity, the suffixes *-ci* or *-là* are added: *ce livre-ci,* this

book here (the nearer); *ce livre-là,* that book there (the farther). These suffixes are **invariable** whatever the gender or number of the noun may happen to be.

12. **The interrogative adjective** asks 'which?' or 'what?' person or thing: it precedes the noun with which it agrees in gender and number: masculine singular = *quel?* feminine singular = *quelle?* eg: *quel homme? quelle femme?* which man? which woman? masculine plural = *quels?* feminine plural = *quelles?* eg: *quels hommes? quelles femmes?* which men? which women? *quelle heure est-il?* what time is it (what hour is it)? These forms can be used **without a noun** if followed by the verb *être: quels sont ces hommes?* who are these men? *quel est ce bruit?* what is this/that noise? *Quel(le)(s)* is **also** used as an **exclamation** (= 'what a . . . !'): *quel dommage!* what a pity! *quelle quantité!* what a lot! See *quel* and also **interrogative adjective** in Reference Section.

13. **Indefinite adjectives** meaning 'some', 'any', 'each', etc, agree with the following noun in gender and number. Those which end in *-e* in the masculine singular have the same form in both genders; the others vary in the formation of their feminine. Plurals add *-s* to the masculine or feminine singular — **except** *tout:* **masc plur:** *tous.* They are:

	SINGULAR		PLURAL	
	MASC	FEM	MASC	FEM
no	*aucun*	*aucune*	*aucuns*	*aucunes*
other	*autre*	*autre*	*autres*	*autres*
each	*chaque*	*chaque*	(**no** plural)	
a certain/certain	*certain*	*certaine*	*certains*	*certaines*
many/many a	*maint*	*mainte*	*maints*	*maintes*
same	*même*	*même*	*mêmes*	*mêmes*
no/not any	*nul*	*nulle*	*nuls*	*nulles*
several	(**no** singular or feminine)		*plusieurs*	*plusieurs*
what/what a!	*quel!*	*quelle!*	*quels!*	*quelles!*
whatever	*quelconque*	*quelconque*	*quelconques*	*quelconques*
some	*quelque*	*quelque*	*quelques*	*quelques*
such	*tel*	*telle*	*tels*	*telles*
all	*tout*	*toute*	***tous***	*toutes*

see each of these adjectives in the Reference Section for examples of its use, especially *tout,* frequently also used as pronoun and adverb.

14. **Adjectives which change their meaning with their position**
Some adjectives are used **both** before and after the noun, according to their meaning. These are:

	BEFORE NOUN	AFTER NOUN
ancien	former, ex- . . .	old, ancient
bon	good (satisfactory)	(morally) good
brave	worthy	brave
certain	some (or other)(a)certain . . .	certain = sure
cher	dear = well loved	dear, expensive
dernier	(the) last (of several)	last (Monday, etc)
différent	various (when plural)	different
divers	divers (with plural)	different, differing, diverse
grand	great = famous, great (size)	tall (**not** grand)
méchant	worthless, no good	wicked, bad-tempered
nouveau	new = another	new = brand new
pauvre	poor = wretched	poor = without money
prochain	next (in time or place)	next to come, near-by
propre	own ('his own book')	clean
seul	(a) single (person/thing)	alone, only the . . .
triste	sad = unhappy	of wretched quality
vrai	(the) real, true = genuine	true (a true story)

see individual entries for further information about these adjectives.

15. **Participles used as adjectives always** follow the noun, and agree in the normal way. **Present participles always** end in *-ant* and their feminine is formed by adding *-e: parlant, parlante:* the **plurals** add *-s* to masculine or feminine singular: *parlants, parlantes.* The same applies to **regular past participles** when used as adjectives, eg: *parlé, parlée, parlés, parlées,* spoken; *fini, finie, finis, finies,* finished; *vendu, vendue, vendus, vendues,* sold; *reçu, reçue, reçus, reçues,* received. For **irregular past participles** see the individual verbs concerned in the Reference Section.

16. **Numerical adjectives**: see under NUMBERS, below, in this section.

ADVERBS

1. Adverbs qualify verbs, adjectives or other adverbs. They answer or ask the questions – How? How much? Where? When? **Except in a very few cases adverbs are invariable**. Many are formed from corresponding adjectives, as in English: rapid – rapidly.

2. **Formation of adverbs from corresponding adjectives**
   i. If the adjective ends in a vowel, *-ment* is added to form the adverb: *sage, sagement,* wise, wisely; *poli, poliment,* polite, politely; *résolu, résolument,* resolutely (see iv below)

ii. if the adjective does **not** end in a vowel *-ment* is added to the feminine:
certain: fem = *certaine* – adverb = *certainement,* certainly

iii. **in some adverbs the final *-e* of the adjective changes to *-é*** before
adding *-ment:*

aveuglément	blindly	*importunément*	importunately
commodément	conveniently	*incommodément*	inconveniently
communément	commonly	*obscurément*	obscurely
confusément	confusedly	*opportunément*	opportunely
diffusément	diffusely	*précisément*	precisely
énormément	enormously	*profondément*	profoundly
expressément	expressly	*profusément*	profusely
exquisément	exquisitely	*uniformément*	uniformly
immensément	immensely		

iv. a few adverbs, formed from adjectives ending in *-u*, change this to *û-*
before adding *-ment:*

assidûment	assiduously	*goulûment*	gluttonously
congrûment	properly, suitably	*incongrûment*	incongruously
crûment	bluntly, crudely	*indûment*	unduly, unlawfully
dûment	duly	*nûment*	nakedly, openly

v. the following are **special cases:**

ADJECTIVE	ADVERB	
gentil	*gentiment*	nicely, in a kind way
grave	*gravement* **and** *grièvement*	seriously
impuni	*impunément*	with impunity
prodigue	i. *prodiguement* ii. *prodigieusement*	lavishly, prodigally, prodigiously
traître	*traîtreusement*	treacherously

vi. some adverbs are the **same as their adjectives**: *fort* = strong, loud,
strongly, loudly, very; *vite* = quick, quickly; *soudain* = sudden,
suddenly **or** less stylishly = *soudainement*

vii. some adverbs **differ considerably from their adjectives**:

ADJECTIVE		ADVERB	
bon	good	*bien*	well
mauvais	bad	*mal*	badly*
meilleur	better	*mieux*	better
petit	little, small	*peu*	(a) little**
* also **noun**: masc = an evil, an ache ** also **noun**: masc = a little			

3. **Classification of adverbs**

   i. **Adverbs of manner** (answering the question 'How?'):

ainsi	thus	*gratis*	free
aussi	also (see ***aussi***)	*impromptu*	impromptu
autrement	otherwise	*incognito*	incognito
bien	well	*lentement*	slowly
bonnement	simply, naively	*mal*	badly
certainement	certainly	*mieux*	better
comme	as, like	*naturellement*	naturally
comment	how	*pis*	worse
debout	upright, standing	*plutôt*	preferably
doucement	softly, quietly	*quasi*	almost
ensemble	together	*recta*	punctually
exprès	purposely	*tout* (when adv)	very, quite
facilement	easily	*vite*	quickly
fort	very much, loudly, strongly	*volontiers*	willingly
		vraiment	truly, really
franco	free of charge		

note: there are a few other adverbs of manner, including musical terms, eg: *allegro, forte, piano*. **And these phrases**:

à genoux	kneeling	*à toute vitesse*	at full speed
à haute voix	aloud	*à voix basse*	in a low voice/whisper
à pied	on foot	*tout à fait*	altogether, quite
à propos	aptly	*tout d'un coup*	all at once

   ii. **adverbs of quantity** (answering 'How many?' 'How much?'):

assez	enough	*peu*	few
aussi	besides (many meanings: when conjunction = also)	*plus*	more
		presque	most
		que de . . .!	How many . . . !
combien	how many/much	*quelque*	some (vague number)
davantage	further, farther		
environ	approximately	*tant*	so many
fort	a great deal, loudly, etc	*tellement*	so much
		tout	(so) very, etc
guère	(with *ne*) not many/much	*très*	very
		trop	too much
moins	less		

iii.   **adverbs of time** (answering 'When?'):

alors	then	*jadis*	of old, formerly
après	after	*jamais*	never
auparavant	before	*longtemps*	for a long time
aussitôt	at once	*lors*	then
autrefois	formerly	*maintenant*	now
avant	before	*naguère(s)*	not long
bientôt	soon	*parfois*	now and then
déjà	already	*puis*	then
depuis	since	*quand*	when
derechef	once more	*quelquefois*	sometimes
des fois	now and then	*sitôt*	so soon (as)
désormais	henceforth	*soudain*	suddenly
dorénavant	henceforth	*souvent*	often
encore	still, yet, again	*subito*	suddenly
enfin	at last	*tantôt*	soon, by and by
ensuite	then, next	*tard*	late (in time)
entre-temps	meanwhile	*tôt*	soon
incontinent	forthwith	*toujours*	always

and adverbs connected with days:

après-demain	the day after tomorrow	*demain*	tomorrow
aujourd'hui	today	*hier*	yesterday
avant-hier	day before yesterday		

and the following adverbial phrases:

à jamais	for ever	*de bonne heure*	early
à l'instant	instantly	*de nouveau*	again, once more
à nouveau	afresh, anew	*de temps en temps*	from time to time
à présent	nowadays	*jusque-là*	till then/there
d'abord	at first, first of all	*tout à coup*	all of a sudden
		tout à l'heure	soon, presently
dans la suite	afterwards, eventually	*(tout) de suite*	at once, immediately

iv.   **adverbs of place** (answering the question 'Where?'):

ailleurs	elsewhere	*ci*	here
alentour	around	*contre*	near, near by
arrière	behind	*dedans*	within
attenant	next to, close by	*dehors*	outside
autour	around	*derrière*	behind

dessous	beneath, below	*où*	where (also: when)
dessus	above, over	*outre*	beyond
devant	in front of, before	*partout*	everywhere
ici	here	*près*	near, near by
là	there	*proche*	near, close by
loin	far, far off		

and the following adverbial phrases:

à côté	near by, at the side	*en avant*	ahead, in front
à droite	on the right, right	*en bas*	below, downstairs
à gauche	on the left, left	*en face*	opposite
à la maison	at home	*en haut*	above, upstairs
au-dedans, *en-dedans*	inside	*en plein air*	out of doors
		là-bas	down there
au-dehors, *en-dehors*	outside	*là-dedans*	therein
		là-haut	up there
au-dessous	lower than, below	*n'importe où*	no matter where
au-dessus	higher than, above	*quelque part*	somewhere or other
en arrière	behind		

v. **adverbs of doubt or uncertainty** (may answer 'How?'):

apparemment	apparently	*sans doute*	doubtless, without doubt
peut-être	perhaps, maybe		
		vraisemblablement	in all probability
probablement	probably		

vi. **adverbs of negation**: see **Negative** in Reference Section

vii. **interrogative adverbs**: see this entry in Reference Section.

Note: the adverbs listed are a selection. The meaning of adverbial phrases, which may be constructed as needed, is usually clear: only a few in everyday use are given. Meanings of both adverbs and adverbial phrases given above indicate their general sense; most have other meanings according to context; some can be used as prepositions or adjectives. Important adverbs will be found in the Reference Section.

4. **Position of adverbs**

i. **Adverbs of place** normally follow the verb, or the past participle in compound tenses: *on travaille ici,* one works here; *ils sont descendus en bas,* they have gone downstairs

ii. **adverbs of precise time** (eg: *hier,* yesterday; *demain,* tomorrow) usually follow the verb or past participle in compound tenses, **but** may also be used for effect at the beginning of a sentence: *il arrivera demain,* he will arrive tomorrow; *elle est venue hier,* she came yesterday; *demain nous verrons tout,* tomorrow we shall see everything

iii. **other shorter adverbs** come after the verb or, in a compound tense, after the auxiliary: *il travaille bien,* he works well; *ils sont déjà partis,* they have already left; *il s'est alors tu,* he then said nothing

iv. **longer adverbs** normally follow the verb or, in compound tenses, the past participle: *il parle lentement,* he speaks slowly; *il a parlé lentement,* he spoke slowly

v. **adverbs can** be placed elsewhere for emphasis, **but,** except for *ne* and *assez,* **not** between the subject and verb.

5. **Comparison of adverbs**

i. The **comparative** of an adverb is formed by putting either ***plus*** (= more), ***moins*** (= less) or ***aussi*** (= as) in front of it, eg: *vite,* fast, quickly; *plus vite,* faster, more quickly; *moins vite,* less fast, less quickly. The **superlative** is formed by putting *le* before the comparative: *le plus vite,* fastest, most quickly: 'than' and 'as' (after *aussi*) both = ***que,*** eg: *plus vite que,* faster than . . .; *aussi vite que,* as fast as . . . The *le* is **invariable**

ii. a few adverbs have irregular comparatives, from which their superlatives are formed regularly:

ADVERB		COMPARATIVE		SUPERLATIVE	
beaucoup	much	*plus*	more	*le plus*	most
bien	well	*mieux*	better (adverb)	*le mieux*	best
mal	badly	*plus mal* or *pis**	worse	*le plus mal* or *le pis**	worst
peu	little	*moins*	less	*le moins*	least

* *pis* and *le pis* are used mainly in set phrases

Note: as for superlatives of adjectives, where there are two or more adverbs together the *le* of the superlative adverb **must** be repeated before each adverb: *c'est lui qui a parlé le plus vite et le plus fort,* it is he who spoke the fastest and loudest.

6. **Interrogative adverbs** are those adverbs from other groups used to **ask** (instead of answer) the questions: 'How?' 'When?' 'Where?' 'How Many?' 'Why?', etc, such as: *comment?* how? *quand?* when? *combien?* how many? *pourquoi?* why? See these in Reference Section.

ARTICLES

1. There are three articles in French: the **definite article** (*le, la, les* = the), the **indefinite article** (*un, une* = a, an; *des,* some, any) and the **partitive article** (*du, de l', de la, des* = some, any).

2. **The definite article**

The definite article = 'the', expressed by *le* before a masculine singular noun; *la* before a feminine singular noun; *l'* before a noun of either gender if it starts with a vowel or *h*-mute (see '*h*-mute' entry below) and by *les* before any noun in the plural: *à + le* becomes *au; à* with *la* or with *l'* remains as *à la,* or *à l; à + les* becomes *aux; de + le* becomes *du; de* with *la* or *l'* remains *de la* or *de l'; de + les* becomes *des* = of the, and is the same in form as the partitive article (= some, any – see ¶3 below). The definite article after all prepositions other than *à* and *de* is not affected.

3. **Definite article usage**

The definite article is used where 'the' would be used in English. It is **also used**:

    i.   **before abstract nouns**, eg: power corrupts, *le pouvoir corrompt;* they love life, *ils aiment la vie.* (See **Abstract Nouns** in Reference Section.)

    ii.   **when speaking of a noun in general terms**, eg: dogs chase cats, *les chiens chassent les chats;* life is beautiful, *la vie est belle*

    iii.   **usually before an adjective or noun preceding a title**: good little Peter, *le bon petit Pierre;* King Louis XIV, *le roi Louis XIV.*

    iv.   **after** *Monsieur, Madame, Mademoiselle* when these come before a title: *M. le Maire; M. le Curé* (but **not before** *Monsieur, Madame, Mademoiselle, maître, monseigneur, lord, milord, saint,* when followed by a name: *Madame Dupont, milord Grandhomme, maître Lesavant, saint Jeanne d'Arc*)

    v.   **before** names of countries, geographical areas, etc: *la France, la Provence,* **but** not after 'to' or '**from**' a country if feminine: *en* or *de France.* If the country is masculine the definite article is retained: *au/du Brésil,* **to/from** Brazil. **Note**: *de la France* = **of** France

    vi.   the **definite article** is also used **before** the names of languages: English, French, Japanese: *l'anglais, le français, le japonais:* **but** the article is usually omitted after *parler:* he speaks French, *il parle français;* do you speak English? *parlez-vous anglais?*

    vii.   the **definite article** is used when giving prices per quantity of weight: two francs a/per dozen, *deux francs la douzaine*

    viii.   to express '**on**' before days and dates: on Sunday, *le dimanche;* on Sundays (regularly), *les dimanches;* every Sunday, *tous les dimanches.*

4. **The indefinite article**

The indefinite article is used where in English 'a' or 'an' would normally be used before a singular noun, and for 'some' or 'any' before plural nouns. (**But** see ¶5 below.)

    i.   **In the singular** *un* is used before masculine nouns and *une* before feminine nouns: *un garçon, un arbre, un hangar* (shed – aspirated *h*), *un habit* (coat – *h*-mute), *une fille, une encre* (ink), *une haie* (hedge – aspirated *h*), *une herbe* (grass, herb – *h*-mute). **Note**: the '*n*' of *un* is mute before a consonant or aspirated '*h*', **but** is sounded before a vowel or *h*-mute

    ii.   **in the plural** the indefinite article (some, any) is **always** *des*. It is often omitted in English **but** is normally necessary in French (**but** see ¶5 below), eg: there are some houses in the street, *il y a des maisons dans*

la rue; there are trees in the park, *il y a des arbres dans le parc;* have
you **any** books? *avez-vous des livres?* I did not see any* cars, *je n'ai
pas vu des autos* (*see *aucun*). **Note**: the final '*s*' of des is mute before
a consonant or aspirated '*h*', **but** has a '*z*' sound before vowels and *h*-
mute.

5.   **The partitive article** in the singular = *de + le, la,* or *l'* (the plural is identical
with the plural of the indefinite article, *des*) and means 'some' **or** 'any' of
something, eg: give me **some bread**, *donnez-moi du pain;* have you **any** ink
here? *avez-vous de l'encre ici?* The partitive article **must** be repeated before
each item: he has (some) butter, cream, bread and apples, *il a du beurre, de la
crème, du pain et des pommes.* (**But** see ¶9vi below.)

6.   **Articles and the negative**
      i.   After a verb in the negative *de (d')*, **not** an article, is used, eg: there
            were no trees in the park, *il n'y avait pas d'arbres dans le parc;* she has
            no pencil, *elle n'a pas de crayon;* there is not any ink here, *il n'y as pas
            d'encre ici*
      ii.   when 'the' is intended to be expressed the *le, la, les* element of the
            indefinite or partitive article is retained, eg: haven't you one of **the** red
            pencils? *n'avez-vous pas un des crayons rouges?* he has no more of **the**
            white bread, *il n'a plus du pain blanc*
      iii. when the negative refers to the **verb**, the article remains unaffected, eg:
            in 'he never writes with the old pen', if the negative refers to 'write'
            'the' **must** be expressed: *il n'écrit jamais avec le vieux stylo;* he does
            not carry **an** umbrella **like mine** (this does not mean he carries 'no'
            umbrella at all), *il ne porte pas un parapluie comme le mien*
      iv.   after a negative which is only partial the partitive article (*du, de l', de la*
            or *des*) remains, eg: whereas the negative is all-embracing (absolute) in:
            on ne voit jamais d'autos dans cette rue, one never sees any cars in this
            street: the negative is only partial in: *on ne voit presque jamais des
            autos dans cette rue,* one hardly ever sees (any) cars in this street.

7.   **Before an adjective**, where 'some' is meant, *du, de l', de la* or *des* are
normally replaced by *de (d')*, eg: one eats good meat here, *on mange de bonne
viande ici.* The indefinite article *un, une,* is **not** affected by a negative
statement which does not imply the idea of 'some' or 'any': he does not have
a big house, *il n'a pas une grande maison.*

8.   **After an adverb of quantity** (such as *assez,* enough/sufficient; *beaucoup,*
many; *peu,* few; *tant,* so many/so much) *de* is used alone, eg: there are
many/few books on the table, *il y a beaucoup de/peu de livres sur la table*
(**but** see *bien*).

9.   **Omission of article**
      The article (definite or indefinite) is omitted:
      i.   **before a noun used adjectively**: *une montre d'or,* a gold watch (watch
            of gold)

ii. **before a noun specifying the profession or group to which someone belongs**: *il est médecin,* he is a doctor (**except** after *c'est: c'est un Français,* he is a Frenchman: see PRONOUNS ¶36)

iii. **in a number of popular phrases**, eg: *noblesse oblige, carte blanche*

iv. **in phrases where the verb and the noun together form a single recognised idiom**, eg: *avoir peur,* to be afraid; *demander pardon,* to ask pardon; *prendre feu,* to catch fire

v. **in exclamations**: what an idea! *quelle idée!* what a pretty tree! *quel joli arbre!*

vi. **as a literary device to produce effect**: *tous – hommes, femmes, enfants* . . . , all of them – men, women, children . . . ; *il y avait beurre, crème, pain et pommes,* there was butter, cream, bread and apples. (**Note**: *le, la, l'* and *les* when coming **before a verb** are **pronouns** used as direct objects – him, her, it and them: see PRONOUNS ¶6 – 13.)

CONJUNCTIONS

1. **Co-ordinating conjunctions** join words, phrases and sentences of equal standing. **Subordinating conjunctions** join a dependent clause to a main clause.

2. **Co-ordinating Conjunctions include**:

ainsi	thus
ainsi que	as well as (= also)
aussi	so, therefore, equally (see ***aussi***)
car	for = because
cependant	however, yet
donc	therefore, then, consequently
et	and
et . . . et	both . . . and (see separate *et* entry)
mais	but
ni . . . ni	neither . . . nor (with *ne* before the verb if there is one)
or	well, well now, well then (used when continuing a story)
ou	or
ou . . . ou	either . . . or
soit . . . soit	be it . . . or
sinon	if not, or else, otherwise, unless
puis	then (*le tonnerre puis la pluie,* the thunder then the rain)
tantôt . . .tantôt . . .	sometimes (one thing) . . . sometimes (another) . . .
toutefois	however, nevertheless, still, yet

note: some of the above, and other words sometimes listed as conjunctions, are also adverbs: the distinction is **not** always easy to see. Most of the above are separately entered, in French **or** English, in the Reference Section.

3.   **Subordinating conjunctions**

These link a subordinate clause to a main clause: they are for the most part conjunctive phrases including *que, que* providing the conjunction element. They are of **two kinds**: those followed by a clause with verb in the **indicative** (any non-subjunctive tense) as in ¶4 and those which are followed by a verb in the **subjunctive** (present, imperfect or a compound tense with its auxiliary in the subjunctive), as in ¶5.

4.   **Subordinating conjunctions followed by a clause in the indicative**

ainsi que	just as, like (eg: . . . *ainsi que j'ai dit*, just as I (have) said)
alors que	when = while, whereas (eg: . . . *alors que j'attendais*, while I was waiting; . . . *alors que je ne l'ai pas dit*, whereas I didn't say it)
à mesure que **or** *à proportion que*	as (= in proportion as, to the extent that)
à peine . . . que	hardly/scarcely (did something happen) when . . .
après que	after (eg: *après qu'il l'avait vu*, after he had seen him/it)
attendu que	considering, seeing that, in as much as, since
aussitôt que	as soon as
comme	as (= while or because)
autant que	in as much as, seeing that
d'autant plus que	all the more because
de façon que, **or** *de manière que*, **or** *de sorte que*	so that (followed by the indicative when stating a **fact** resulting). (When meaning 'in order that': see ¶5 below.)
depuis que	since (the time that . . .)
dès que	from the moment that, as soon as
de même que	even if (with conditional)
lorsque	when*
maintenant que	now that
outre que	besides that, 'over and above that'
parce que	because
pendant que	while
puisque	since (= because: reason, **not** time)
quand	when (**see** note to *lorsque*, above)
selon que	according as
si	if (see *si* i and *si* ii for usage)

sitôt que	from the moment/time that, as soon as
supposé que	supposing
tandis que	while, at the same time as, whereas
tant que	as long as
vu que	seeing that
suivant que	as, according as
supposé que	supposing (that)

* after nouns of time 'when' is translated by the relative adverb *où*, eg: *le moment où il arriva*, the moment when he arrived

5.   **Subordinating conjunctions followed by clause in subjunctive** (see VERBS ¶33)

à condition que	on condition that
afin que	in order that
à moins que*	unless (*when meaning 'unless something may/does actually happen', that is, unless they (do actually) speak, *ne* must be inserted: *à moins qu'ils ne parlent*. The *ne* has no negative value. If the verb is negative it will have both *ne* and *pas*: *à moins qu'ils ne parlent pas*, unless they don't speak)
au cas que	in case, should it so happen that
avant que*	before (*ne* should be used here as for *à moins que*, **but** the rule in this case **not** always adhered to)
bien que	although
de crainte que	for fear that/lest
de façon que	so that, in such a way that (with the result that)
de manière que	so that, in such a way that (with the result that)
de peur que*	for fear that (*ne* is used as for *à moins que*)
de sorte que	in such a way that (when meaning 'with the result that')
en cas que	in case
jusqu'à ce que	until (do not confuse with *jusque* = until, preposition)
non que	not that
pour que	in order that/to the end that, eg: *il doit être très mauvais pour qu'on l'ait puni si souvent*, 'he must be very bad for that one should have punished him so often' = for him to have been so often punished
pourvu que	provided that, on condition that, if only
quoique	although
sans que	without (eg: *il est parti sans que je l'ait remarqué*, he left without my noticing it = 'without that I noticed it')

Note: some of the above will be found individually entered in the Reference Section.

NOUNS

1. Common nouns, the names of things or ideas, have a gender, masculine or feminine. Many nouns referring to persons and some animals have the grammatical gender which reflects their actual sex, eg: *un homme,* a man; *une femme,* a woman; *un lion,* a lion; *une lionne,* a lioness. **But** for a few nouns referring to persons, for many animals and for **all** plants and inanimate things, the **only** certain way of knowing the gender of a noun is to know whether it has *le* or *la* before it when preceded by the definite article, or, in the case of nouns starting with a vowel or *h*-mute, *un* or *une* when preceded by the indefinite article. More nouns ending in *-e* are feminine than masculine, **but**, as will be seen from the following, so many are masculine that the final *-e* alone is **no safe guide** to gender – just a somewhat doubtful 'best bet' if there is nothing else to go by.

2. **One gender for both sexes**
    i. A number of nouns (usually the name of a profession originally occupied by men only) **remain masculine** whatever the sex of the person concerned:

un auteur	author
un agent	agent, policeman/woman
un bébé	baby
un médecin*	doctor
un professeur	professor/teacher
un témoin	witness

> * *la médecine* = the science of medicine; a medicine (tonic pill, etc) = *un médicament:*; a 'lady doctor' = *une femme médecin* – address as: *Monsieur le Docteur, Madame le Docteur*

   ii. a few nouns are **feminine** although they can refer to persons of either sex:

une connaissance	acquaintance
une personne	person
une recrue	recruit
une sentinelle	sentry
une vedette	cinema/stage star of either sex (**also** a military scout **and** a small naval vessel)
une victime	victim

Note: *Majesté* is feminine, therefore **always** '*Sa Majesté*' whether addressing a king or a queen.

3. **Nouns used in either gender**
    The following is a selection of nouns (most ending in *-e*) that can be used in either gender:

MASC OR FEM	
adversaire	adversary
aide	assistant (when fem = assistance)
arbitre	arbitrator
artiste	artist (painter, actor, actress, etc)
bigame	bigamist
camarade	friend, chum, pal, mate
collègue	colleague
copiste	copyist
élève	pupil
enfant	child*

* *-e* in feminine, normally masculine, **but** feminine when specifically referring to a girl or girls, eg: *une charmante enfant*

MASC OR FEM	
garagiste	garage owner **or** manager
garde	guard (person)
patriote	patriot
philosophe	philosopher
pianiste	pianist
propriétaire	proprietor
touriste	tourist
AND THESE NATIONALS	
Arabe	Arab
Belge	Belgian
Russe	Russian
Slave	Slav

4. **Forming feminines from masculine**

A number of masculine nouns referring to persons can be given feminine form by changing their endings as follows:

   i. by adding *-e* to the masculine form (other than those listed in ii to vi, and in ¶5 and ¶7 below):

MASC		FEM	
ami	friend	*amie*	friend
Anglais	Englishman	*Anglaise**	Englishwoman
cousin	cousin	*cousine*	cousin
étudiant	student	*étudiante*	student
marchand	merchant	*marchande*	woman merchant
châtelain	lord of the manor	*châtelaine*	lady of the manor
voisin	neighbour	*voisine*	neighbour

* this can be done for many nationalities

   ii. the feminine can be formed by doubling the final consonant of endings in *-an*, *-en*, *-on* and adding *-e:*

MASC		FEM	
paysan	peasant	*paysanne*	peasant woman
gardien	guard	*gardienne*	guardian
patron	manger, 'boss'	*patronne*	manageress, 'boss'

   iii. the feminine can be formed by changing a final *-er* to *-ère:*

MASC		FEM	
écolier	schoolboy	*écolière*	schoolgirl
fermier	farmer	*fermière*	lady farmer

iv.   by changing a final *-x* to *-se*, eg: *un époux, une épouse,* spouse

v.   by changing a final *-f* to *-ve*, eg: *un veuf,* a widower; *une veuve,* a widow

vi.   the ending *-eur* may be changed in two ways:

    a.   to *-euse:*

MASC		FEM	
danseur	dancer	*danseuse*	dancer
pêcheur	fisherman	*pêcheuse*	fisherwoman
voyageur	traveller, passenger	*voyageuse*	traveller, passenger

    b.   **but** if the ending is *-teur* this changes to *-trice:*

MASC		FEM	
acteur	actor	*actrice*	actress
conducteur	conductor	*conductrice*	conductor
directeur	director	*directrice*	director
note: there are many nouns in this group			

5.   The above rules apply to many, **but** not to all, nouns. They also apply to adjectives (see ADJECTIVES ¶2). The most important special nouns are listed below.

6.   **Special feminine forms**

A number of nouns referring to persons and animals have special feminine forms, the following being the most important:

    i.   **family and friends**:

MASC		FEM	
beau-fils	stepson	*belle-fille*	stepdaughter
compagnon*	companion, mate, trade-union member, etc	*compagne**	female companion, etc
fils	son	*fille*	daughter
frère	brother	*sœur*	sister
garçon	boy	*(jeune) fille*	girl
gendre	son-in-law	*bru*	daughter-in-law
grand-père	grandfather	*grand-mère***	grandmother
homme	man	*femme*	woman (wife)
maître	master	*maîtresse*	mistress
mari	husband	*femme*	wife
neveu	nephew	*nièce*	niece
oncle	uncle	*tante*	aunt
papa	dad(dy)	*maman*	mum(my)

MASC		FEM	
père	father	*mère*	mother
petit-fils	grandson	*petite-fille*	granddaughter
vieillard **or** *vieux****	old man	*vieille****	old woman

* **both** can be used in compounds: *compagnon de voyage*, fellow traveller; *compagne d'infortune*, fellow sufferer, fem

** in the feminine *grand-* with hyphen takes **no** *-e*, and **no** plural *-s*

*** *vieux* and *vieille* are **also** adjectives for 'old'

ii. **status, titles, etc** (a short selection):

MASC		FEM	
duc	duke	*duchesse*	duchess
le héro	hero	*l'héroïne*	heroine
mâle	male	*femelle*	female
monsieur	Mr (sir)	*madame*	Mrs (madam)
monsieur	gentleman	*dame*	lady
patron	patron (of charity, etc)	*patronnesse*	patron (of charity, etc)
muet	mute, dumb person	*muette*	mute, dumb person
pécheur	sinner	*pécheresse*	sinner
prince	prince	*princess*	princess
roi	king	*reine*	queen
serviteur	male servant	*servant*	female servant
traître	traitor	*traîtresse*	traitress

iii. **some important animals** (amongst many): most animals have **only** one form; where two forms exist only one form is usually used in everyday speech, and this form is marked with an asterisk*; where there is no sign both forms are in common use:

MASC		FEM	
âne*	donkey	*ânesse*	donkey
bélier	ram		
mouton	wether, he-sheep	*brebis*	ewe, she-sheep
bouc	he-goat	*chèvre**	she-goat
bœuf	bullock/ox†	*vache*	cow
canard*	drake	*cane*	duck
chameau*	male camel	*chamelle*	female camel
chat* *(matou)*	tom cat	*chatte*	cat
cheval*	horse	*jument*	mare
chien*	dog	*chienne*	bitch

MASC		FEM	
*cochon** and *porc*	pig (verrat boar)	*coche* and *truie*	sow
coq	cock	*poule*	hen
*dindon**	turkey	*dinde*	turkey-hen
jars	gander	*oie**	goose
*lièvre**	hare	*hase*	hare
*lapin**	rabbit	*lapine*	rabbit
lion	lion	*lionne*	lioness
*loup**	wolf	*louve*	wolf
poulain	colt	*pouliche*	filly
*singe**	monkey	*guenon*††	female monkey
tigre	tiger	*tigresse*	tigress

† *taureau*, bull for breeding, fighting
†† **also** an ugly woman

Note: other animals either have **no** feminine form, **or** a form used only by specialists.

7.   **Gender rules**

When a gender cannot be ascertained for certain, there are a number of rules which can be used to guess the probable gender of nouns, especially of plants and inanimate things, **but** they are far from infallible, and should be treated as rough guides only:

i.   **masculine are:**

a.   **nouns ending in -*age*:**

un étage	floor (storey)
EXCEPT	
une cage	cage
une image	picture
*une page**	page (of book)

* *un page* = page-boy

un garage	garage
EXCEPT	
la nage	swimming
une plage	beach
une rage	rage, anger

b.   **nouns ending in a pronounced vowel** (other than abstract nouns ending in -*té*):

le café	café/coffee
le midi	midday
un oiseau	bird
EXCEPT	
la clé (or *clef*)	key
la dynamo	dynamo
l'eau (fem)	water

le pneu	tyre
le seau	bucket
le vélo	bike
EXCEPT	
la peau	skin
la radio	radio

and abbreviations of feminine nouns such as:

une auto (= automobile)	car	une photo (= la photographie)	photograph
une moto (= motocyclette)	motor-bike		

c. **nouns ending in *-isme*,** such as *l'héroisme, le communisme*

d. **nouns ending in a consonant, other than the endings *-çon*, *-son*, *-tion*:**

le banc	bench	le nœud	knot
un coup	blow	le nom	name
le crayon	pencil	un œuf	egg
le creux	hollow	le papier	paper
le fil	thread	le sort	fate
le nez	nose	le tas	pile

and nouns ending in *-ent*, eg: *le tempérament*, temperament

e. **important exceptions (to the above rule) include:**

la clef (or clé)	key	la mort	death
la couleur	colour	la mer	sea
la cour	court, yard	la nuit	night
la croix	cross	la paix	peace
la dent	tooth	la peur	fear
la faim	hunger	la soif	thirst
la fleur	flower	la tour*	tower
la fois	time (occasion)	la voix	voice
la forêt	forest	* le tour = turn, tour	

ii. **feminine are:**

a. **nouns (other than persons) ending in *-çon*, *-son*, *-tion*:**

la leçon	lesson	EXCEPT	
la maison	house	le poisson	fish
la question	question		

b. **nouns ending in a double consonant + *e*:**

une assiette	plate	EXCEPT	
EXCEPT		le tonnerre	thunder
le beurre	butter	le verre	glass (substance and
le mille	thousand		tumbler)
le télégramme	telegram		

c. **nouns ending in *-ée* or other vowel + *e*:**

la fée	fairy	EXCEPT	
la journée	day (period)	le Brie	a type of cheese
la rue	street	le lycée	secondary school
la sortie	exit	le musée	museum

d. **abstract nouns ending in -té:** *la santé*, health; *l'électricité* (fem), electricity

e. **nouns ending in -ance, -anse, and -ence:**

la chance	chance	EXCEPT	
la danse	dance	*le silence*	silence
la patience	patience		

8. Gender by meaning

Certain groups of word tend to have the same gender:

i. **masculine are:**

a. **trees:** *un arbre*, a tree: **and** the names of trees, eg: ***le chêne***, oak

b. **weights, measures, points of the compass:** *un gramme*, a gram; *le Nord*, the North: **except:** *la livre*, the pound (*un livre* = a book); *une tonne*, a metric ton

c. **metals:** *le fer*, iron; *l'or*, gold; *l'argent*, silver (**and** money)

d. **days, months** and **seasons:** *le lundi*, Monday; *le mai*, May; *le printemps*, spring

e. **the names of languages:** *le français*

f. **nouns ending in -a:** *le choléra*, cholera

ii. **feminine are:**

a. **flowers:** *une fleur*, a flower: **and** the names of flowers: *la rose*, the rose: **except:** *le narcisse*, the narcissus; *un mimosa*, mimosa

b. **scientific names:** *la chemie*, chemistry; *la grammaire*, grammar: **except:** *le droit*, law

9. Masculine words that look feminine

A number of masculine nouns ending in -e look feminine, among these are:

un anniversaire	birthday	*le monde*	world, people
un arbre	tree	*un musée*	museum
le bagage	luggage	*un nombre*	number
un chèque	cheque	*un ordre*	order
le commerce	commerce	*un parapluie*	umbrella
un disque	record	*un portefeuille*	wallet
un électrophone	record-player	*un pupitre*	desk
un groupe	group	*un rire*	laugh
un incendie	fire = conflagration	*le russe*	Russian (language)
		le sable	sand
un insecte	insect	*un service*	service
un légume	vegetable	*le silence*	silence*
un litre	litre	*un sourire*	smile
un lycée	secondary school	*le sucre*	sugar
un meuble	piece of furniture	*un téléphone*	telephone
un mille	mile, thousand	*le théâtre*	theatre

un timbre	stamp (post)
un utensile	utensil

le ventre	stomach
* -ence: others are feminine	

10. **Different gender – different meaning**

There are a number of nouns which change meaning according to gender, eg: *le livre*, book – *la livre*, pound (weight or money). Among the more important of these are:

MASC		FEM	
aigle	male eagle	aigle	female eagle or standard (eg: as carried by Romans)
crêpe	black mourning silk, band, veil	crêpe	pancake
critique	critic	critique	criticism
enseigne	ensign (lowest rank of officer)	enseigne	badge, banner
foudre	great leader, orator	foudre	heavy thunder, thunderbolt, lightening
garde	male person, thing guarding something or someone, warden, etc	garde	female guardian, protection, group forming a guard, wardship, hilt (see **garde** in Reference Section)
guide	guide (person, male or female or guide-book)	guide	guiding rein
manche	handle	manche	sleeve*
manœuvre	labourer	manœuvre	manœuvre
mémoire	memorandum, memoir	mémoire	memory
mode	method, way, mood (of verb)	mode	fashion
mort	dead person, corpse	mort	death
moule	mould, mesh	moule	mussel
page	page boy	page	page of book
pendule	pendulum	pendule	clock (in house)
physique	physique, bodily constitution	physique	physical science, physics
poêle	large stove	poêle	frying-pan
poste	post (job), position (eg: military), police station	poste	mail service, post office
somme	nap (short sleep)	somme	sum
tour	turn, tour, trick	tour	tower

MASC		FEM	
trompette	trumpeter	*trompette*	trumpet
vapeur	steamship	*vapeur*	steam, mist, vapour
voile	veil	*voile*	sail

* *la Manche*, the English Channel

11.   **Plural of nouns**

    i.   The normal plural of nouns is formed by the addition of **-s**, with the **exception** of proper names of persons, which do **not** take *-s:* see **Names** in Reference Section

    ii.   **nouns ending in -s, -x, and -z do not change:**

un cas	des cas	case/s
un prix	des prix	price/s
un nez	des nez	nose/s

    iii.   **nouns ending in -au and -eu add -x:**

l'eau	les eaux	water/s
un feu	des feux	fire/s
EXCEPT		
le landau	les landaus	landau/s
le bleu	les bleus	blue/s
le pneu	les pneus	tyre/s

    iv.   **nouns ending in -ou are usually regular, and add -s, but the following add -x:**

le bijou	les bijoux	jewel/s
le caillou	les cailloux	pebble/s
le chou	les choux	cabbage/s
le genou	les genoux	knee/s
le hibou	les hiboux	owl/s
le joujou	les joujoux	small toy/s, plaything/s
le pou	les poux	the louse/lice

    v.   **nouns ending in -al change to -aux:**

le cheval	les chevaux	horse/s
EXCEPT		
le bal	les bals	ball/s (gathering/s for dance/s)
le cal	les cals	callus/callosity (thickening/s of the skin)
le carnaval	les carnavals	carnival/s
le chacal	les chacals	jackal/s
le festival	les festivals	festival/s
le régal	les régals	feast/s

note: a few other rare words in *-al* are sometimes given this ending (**but** sometimes *-aux*), including: *choral, chorals* **or** *choraux,* chorals.

vi. **the plurals of words ending in -*ail* are usually regular, with plural -*ails*, but the following take -*aux*:**

l'aspirail (masc)	les aspiraux	air-hole/s
le bail	les baux	lease/s
le corail	les coraux	coral/s
l'émail (masc)	les émaux	enamel/s
le soupirail	les soupiraux	air-hole/s, vent/s
le travail	les travaux	work/s
le vantail	les vantaux	folding door/s
le vitrail	les vitraux	coloured-glass window/s

vii. **note these two exceptional plurals:**

le ciel	les cieux	sky/skies, heaven/s
un œil	des yeux	eye/s

viii. **compound nouns**: the plural of these depends on their composition, eg: in un *arc-en-ciel*, **only** the arc is put into the plural, des *arcs-en-ciel*, rainbows (arc-in-sky, arcs-in-sky): **but**: une *basse-cour*, des *basses*-cours*, farmyards: *if one part agrees with the other in the singular it **must** also do so in the plural.

ix. **collective nouns** (that is, nouns which name a group or number of persons or things) are singular for agreement purposes, **but** this rule is not always adhered to when the noun is followed by a plural noun, eg: *un grand nombre de soldats étaient . . .*, a large number of soldiers were . . . See also **Collective Nouns** in Reference Section for further examples of usage

x. **note the pronunciation of** the singular and plural forms of: *œuf, œufs*, eggs; *bœuf, bœufs*, bulls and *os*, bone, *os*, bones: in the singular of **all** three the final consonant is sounded: in the plural the final consonant of the singular and the *s* are both silent, eg: *un bœuf, des bœu(fs); un œuf, des œu(fs); un os (oss), des o(s)* (pronounced 'oh')

xi. when a number of persons each have only one of something, or if only one is intended for each individual, the French use the singular where we would use the plural, eg: *les spectateurs ont jeté **leur chapeau** en l'air*, the spectators threw their **hats** into the air; *si vous comprenez, mes enfants, levez **la main***, if you understand, children, **raise your hands**.

NUMBERS

1. **Cardinal numbers**: numerical adjectives, invariable **except** un, une:

1	un, une (the same as the indefinite article; the **only** cardinal number to agree in gender, both used alone and in **21, 31, 101**, etc	2	deux
		3	trois
		4	quatre
		5	cinq

6	*six*
7	*sept*
8	*huit*
9	*neuf* (do **not** confuse with adjective, *neuf, neuve* = new)
10	*dix**

(* the final consonant of *cinq, six, sept, huit, neuf* and *dix* is sounded in counting, before a vowel or *h*-mute, and before all months, but is otherwise not sounded before a consonant and an *h*-aspirate, eg: *le huit_mai* but *hui(t) héros, se(pt) villes* (a rule not always adhered to))

11	*onze* (**note**: *le onze*: see **Elision** v)	52	*cinquante-deux*, etc
12	*douze*	60	*soixante*
13	*treize*	61	*soixante et un(e)*
14	*quatorze*	62	*soixante-deux*, etc
15	*quinze*	70	*soixante-dix*
16	*seize*	71	*soixante et onze* (**last** number with *et*)
17	*dix-sept*	72	*soixante-douze*, etc
18	*dix-huit*	80	*quatre-vingts* (**note**: *the -s*)
19	*dix-neuf*	81	*quatre-vingt-un* (**no -s**)
20	*vingt*	82	*quatre-vingt-deux*, etc
21	*vingt et un(e)*	90	*quatre-vingt-dix*
22	*vingt-deux*, etc	91	*quatre-vingt-onze*
30	*trente*	92	*quatre-vingt-douze*, etc
31	*trente et un(e)*	100	*cent* (**not** *'un' cent*)
32	*trente-deux*, etc	101	*cent un(e)* (**not** *un cent*, **no** *et*)
40	*quarante*	102	*cent deux*, etc
41	*quarante et un(e)*	200	*deux cents*
42	*quarante-deux*, etc	201	*deux cent* un(e)* (***no -s** if followed by a number)
50	*cinquante*		
51	*cinquante et un(e)*		

1000	*mille** (***no** hyphens with *cent* or *mille*)
2,000 men	*deux mille* hommes* (***no -s**, *deux milles* = two miles/knots)
1,000,000	*un million* (with points, **not** commas, eg: *1.000.000**)
2,000,000 men	*deux millions d'hommes* (million is a noun: compare *millier* in ¶4)
a thousand million	*un milliard* (noun), also takes *de* before the noun.

***The French use points where we use commas, and a comma for the decimal point**: English: 2.5 = French: 2,5. In **dates of years** *mil* is used for 'thousand' when one or more other numbers follow it, eg: in (the year) 1901 = *en (l'an) mil neuf cent un* (or *dix-neuf cent un*): but **the year 1000** alone is *l'an mille*; **the year 2000** (with no other number after it) is *l'an deux mille*. See also *mile*, and *mille* i, ii, iii.

2. **Ordinal numbers**: also numerical adjectives: the **only** ordinals with masc and fem forms (other than the *le* or *la*) are: **first**, *le premier, la première* and **second**, *le/la second(e)*, used mainly when **no** subsequent numbers are listed: or *deuxième*, the usual form. *Le/la deuxième* **and** all other ordinals are formed by adding *-ième* to the cardinal, dropping any final *-e* the cardinal may have, *cinq* and *neuf* both being modified, thus:

trois	*troisième*
quatr(e)	*quatrième*
cinq	*cinquième*
six	*sixième*
sept	*septième*
huit	*huitième*
neuf	*neuvième*
dix	*dixième*
onz(e)	*onzième* (*le* **or** *l'onzième*: see **Elision** v in Reference Section)
douz(e)	*douzième*, etc

in **21st, 31st**, etc: '*et un*' **or** '*-un*' for '**first**' becomes *unième*, eg: *vingt et un* – *vingt et unième* (**not** *premier*)

cent un	*cent unième* (**no** *et*). **Note** also: **the two-hundredth part**: *la deux centième partie*
the thousandth	*le millième**
the millionth	*le millionième**
* these are masculine nouns when used alone but adjectives when used with a noun	

3. **Fractions** are formed by combining cardinals with ordinals:

trois cinquièmes	three fifths
deux vingtièmes	two twentieths
EXCEPT	
un quart	a quarter
trois quarts	three quarters
*un demi**	a half
*un tiers***	a third

* *demi* does **not** agree when before a noun, eg: *une demi-bouteille*, a half bottle, **but** agrees, in gender only, after a noun, eg: *deux bouteilles et demie*, two bottles and a half (**note also**: *la moitié*, half, is **not** used with arithmetical numbers, see *demi* and **half** in Reference Section)
**also used for 'third party' (third person concerned). The music interval = *une tierce*. In speaking, 'nought' is '*zéro*', see ¶6

4. **'Round numbers'** (numbers given to express approximations):

une centaine	'some hundred or so'
une dizaine	'some ten or so'
une douzaine (may mean 'twelve' or 'twelve or so')	a dozen

note: these, like other words of quantity, take *de* before the following noun (unless 'of the' is intended):

une douzaine d'œufs	a dozen eggs
une cinquantaine de voitures	some fifty cars
des milliers de soldats	thousands of soldiers
* but: ***des milliers des soldats***	thousands of **the** soldiers

5.   **Note**: a fortnight, ***une quinzaine***. (The French count the days at each end: thus a week *(une semaine)* is, for example, Sunday to Sunday = *huit jours* **or** *une huitaine*.)

6.   **Telephone numbers** are grouped in pairs: thus – 012347 would be *01-23-47, zéro un, vingt-trois, quarante-sept.*

PREPOSITIONS

1.   No one French preposition is always translated by the same one preposition in English, and the correct use of prepositions always presents a major danger for the unwary. The following list, giving the more usual translations of the commonest French prepositions, is intended as a general guide. See individual entries in the Reference Section for examples of usage:

à	to, at
au-delà or *par-delà*	beyond, on the other side (of)
avant	before (usually in time, occasionally in position)
avec	with
chez	at the house, place, etc, of
contre	against
dans	in (before a qualified noun)
de	of, from (occasionally: with)
dedans	within
dès	from the time/moment of, place of
dessous	underneath
devant	in front of, before (usually: position, occasionally: time)
durant	during
en	in (see ¶4 below and in Reference Section)
entre	between
envers	towards
ès	in the (**only** in university degrees: *docteur ès lettres*)
excepté	excepting
hormis	except, save, but (for)
hors	beyond, outside

jusque	as far as, up to (both in position and time)
malgré	in spite of
moyennant	by means of
outre	beyond (now only used in compounds: see *outre* in Reference Section)
par	by, by means of, through
parmi	among
passé	after (time)
pendant	during
plein	full (invariable as preposition)
pour	for
près	near
proche	near
sans	without
sauf	but for
selon	according to
sous	beneath
suivant	following
supposé	supposing
sur	on
touchant	touching, concerning
vers	towards (both time and position)
via	by way of, via
vu	seeing, considering

note: a few obsolete prepositions have been omitted. **Note**: also most of the above prepositions can also be used as adverbs and, sometimes, as adjectives: their meaning may differ when so used.

2. The preposition governed by a French verb may **not** be the equivalent of the English preposition, eg: English 'to buy **from**' in French is '*acheter à*' (see *acheter*): and an English transitive verb may be intransitive in French, eg: 'I obey the law', is '*je obéis à la loi*', **or** vice versa, eg: 'he has paid **for** the dinner', '*il a payé le dîner*' – intransitive English, transitive French. Those verbs which differ in usage from their English equivalents in such ways, or which may cause an English speaker similar difficulties, will be found listed in the Reference Section. See examples in *acheter*, *obéir*, *payer*.

3. The preposition governing an infinitive following another verb is normally 'to' in English, eg: he wants **to** work; he likes **to** read: in French sometimes there is **no** preposition: *il veut aller*, he wants to go: sometimes it is *de*: *il essaye de comprendre*, he tries to understand: sometimes *à*: *il consentit à partager*, he consents to share. Verbs likely to cause problems for an English speaker are in the Reference Section.

4.   For *en* = 'while', 'in the course of', followed by the present participle used as a gerund (verb noun), eg: while talking, *en parlant;* by helping, *en aidant,* see VERBS ¶43 below. For other ways to translate 'in' see *à* iii, *dans* and *en,* preposition, in Reference Section.

5.   The verb noun that follows **all** prepositions other than *en* is the infinitive: without thinking, **sans** *penser;* he finished by speaking, *il finit **par** parler;* she shuts the door before leaving, *elle ferme la porte **avant de** partir.* See VERBS ¶36.

6.   Following *après* (= after) the verb is normally in the **perfect infinitive** (ie: the infinitive of the auxiliary + past participle), eg: after writing = after having written, *après avoir écrit;* after having washed (herself), *après s'être lavée.* See VERBS ¶36.

PRONOUNS

1.   **Personal pronouns are**:
       i.   **conjunctive personal pronouns**: those used together with a verb either as subject **or** as direct **or** indirect object, coming either before the verb (the auxiliary in compound tenses) **or** after the verb (**or** auxiliary), and when following the verb linked to it by a hyphen
       ii. **disjunctive personal pronouns**: used when separated from the verb, **or** coming immediately after *être* as its complement, **without** hyphen.

2.   **Table to show position of conjunctive pronouns**: (See ¶3 and ¶4 for explanation of the following table.)

1		2	3	4	5	6		7
subject		object: direct or indirect or reflexive	direct only	dative	it some there			
je		*me**						past
tu		*te***				verb		participle
il/elle	*(ne)*	*se*	*le,la*	*lui*	*y, en*	or	*(pas)*	if
nous		*nous*				auxiliary		compound
vous		*vous*						tense
ils/elles		*se*	*les*	*leur*	*y, en*			

3.   In a normal sentence **all** conjunctive pronouns **precede** the verb. In a **negative** the pronoun objects come between *ne* and the verb (or auxiliary: see **Negative** in Reference Section). If there is more than one pronoun object, direct or indirect, **these must be in the order shown in the table above**, eg: *il nous le donne,* he gives it to us; *il m'en parle,* he speaks to me about it. Only one pronoun from any one column can be used with any one verb, **but** as *nous* and *vous* appear in two columns they can each be used as subject and direct or indirect object in the same sentence, eg: *nous vous parlons,* we speak to you;

vous vous lavez, you wash yourself. A pronoun in column 2 **cannot** be used with *lui* or *leur:* one **cannot** say *'vous me leur présente'* for 'you present me to them': the pronoun for 'to them' **must** be a disjunctive pronoun following *à* after the verb: *vous me présente à eux* (**or** *à elles* if 'them' is feminine). Two **direct** object pronouns **cannot** be used together, **but** pronouns from column 2 used indirectly precede direct objects from column 3. (For further details of *le, la, les* as pronoun objects see **him, her, them** and **it** ii in Reference Section.) For pronouns with the **imperative** see below ¶8 – 10.

4.　　**Notes on conjunctive pronouns**

　　i.　　**Singular**: *je* = I, is used **only** as subject of a verb, either before the verb, from which it can be separated only by *ne* and other conjunctive pronoun objects, or after the verb with a hyphen (see **I** in Reference Section). **Elision of *je***: see ¶5 below: *me* = 'myself', 'me' or 'to me' (*when replaced by *moi,* see ¶9): *tu* = you addressing one person in familiar manner (subject only: does **not** elide: *tu as*): *te* = 'yourself' ('thyself') 'you' ('thou'), 'to you' ('to thee'), when speaking to one person in a familiar manner (**for use of *toi* see ¶9 (**reflexive** direct or indirect object)): *il* = 'he' or 'it' (masculine thing, or impersonal: as subject): *elle* = she, or 'it' referring to a feminine thing (as subject): *se* = 'himself', 'herself', 'itself', 'oneself' or 'to himself,' 'to herself', etc (**reflexive** direct or indirect object): *le* = 'him' or 'it' referring to one masculine thing (as object): *la* = 'her' or 'it' referring to one feminine thing (as object): *lui* = 'to him', 'to her', 'to it' (when it means 'giving to', dative, but **not** motion towards or 'place to which')

　　ii.　　**plural**: *nous* = 'we', 'us', 'ourselves', 'to us', 'to ourselves' (subject, object, reflexive, direct or indirect): *vous* = 'you', 'yourself', 'yourselves', 'to you', 'to yourself' or 'to yourselves', whether speaking to several people or to one politely (subject, object, reflexive, direct or indirect): *ils* = 'they', masculine persons or things, or both genders mixed (subject **only**): *elles* = 'they', female persons or things of feminine gender (**and** some animals which have special feminine forms: subject only when used as a conjunctive pronoun): *se* = (in plural) 'themselves', 'to themselves' (reflexive direct or indirect object). *les* = 'them', of either or both genders, persons and things (direct object): *leur* = 'to them', either or both genders (invariable) (Dative only, giving to, speaking to, etc: **not** motion towards: see *y* below.) (**Note**: some of these pronouns are also used, sometimes with different meanings, as **disjunctive pronouns**: see ¶15, ¶16 below.)

　　iii.　　*y* = 'there', 'to that place', 'in it', or 'to it' if implying **motion** towards (**not** 'giving to' or 'speaking to'): see entry *y* in Reference Section

　　iv.　　*en* = 'of it', 'about it', 'of them', 'some', 'there from' (**distinguish from preposition *en*** = in): see entry *en* in Reference Section. (**Note**:

when motion to and from is implied *y* and *en* are, strictly speaking, adverbs.)

5. **Elision of pronouns**

je is elided (becomes *j'*) before a verb starting with a vowel or *h*-mute, but is **not** elided after the verb, eg: *ai-je eu?* have I had? *me, te, se, le, la* are **all** elided before a vowel or *h*-mute, after the verb when coming before *en* or *y* (**but** *le* and *la* **cannot** be used together with *en*), eg: *donnez-m'en*, give me some; *jette-t'y*, throw yourself into it; *mène-l'y*, lead him/her/it there. See ¶9 below and see also **Elision** in Reference Section.

6. **Conjunctive pronouns in compound tenses**

When the verb is in a compound tense, the position of the pronoun remains the same, coming directly before the auxiliary. The past participle will then agree with *le, la* or *les* because they are direct objects before the verb, eg: *voilà la maison, il l'a achetée*, here is the house, he has bought it. The past participle agrees with the reflexive pronoun if it is a direct object: *elle s'est lavée* (object **herself**): but *elle s'est lavé les mains*, she ('to herself') washed her hands (object *mains*); *elle s'est dit*, she said to herself (reflexive pronoun indirect object).

7. **In the interrogative form the object pronouns retain their position, and the subject pronoun moves** to a position after the verb or auxiliary, to which it is attached by a hyphen, with *-t-* inserted after a vowel before *il, elle* or *on*, eg: *l'a-t-il achetée* (*l'* is fem)*?* has he bought it? *s'est-elle lavée?* has she washed (herself)? *lui a-t-il parlé?* has he spoken to him/her? *l'a-t-on vue* (*l'* is presumably fem)*?* has one seen it? *y obéit-il?* does he obey it? *en avez-vous mangé?* have you eaten any of it/them?

8. **Conjunctive pronouns in imperative**

A true imperative has **only** the 2nd person singular and 1st and 2nd persons plural: the 3rd persons singular and plural are part of the present subjunctive. In the imperative proper, pronoun objects follow the verb, linked with a hyphen, and if there are two pronouns the direct object precedes the indirect, eg: *donnez-le-lui*, give it to him. **But** if the direct object is a pronoun in column 2 of the table in ¶2, instead of using another pronoun from the same column as indirect object, a disjunctive pronoun **must** be used: *confiez-vous à nous*, entrust yourself to us (**not** '*confiez-vous-nous*').

9. **The two pronouns *me* and *te* become *toi* and *moi* after the verb**, both as direct object: *aidez-moi*, help me: and when reflexive: *tais-toi*, keep quiet, **or** as an indirect object: *parlez-moi*, speak to me: **but** before *y* and *en*, they are elided to *m'* and *t'*: *donnez-m'en*, give me some; *jette-t'y*, throw yourself into it.

10. **In a negative imperative** the pronoun objects come between *ne* and the verb in the same position as for an ordinary statement: *ne me les donnez pas*, do

not give them to me; *n'en parle pas*, don't speak about it; *n'y touche pas*, don't touch (= don't put your hand on it).

11.   **The third persons of the imperative** (sing and plur), are formed from the **present subjunctive**, and pronouns keep the order described in ¶2 and ¶3, eg: *qu'il ne me le donne pas*, let him not give it to me.

12.   **Conjunctive pronouns with infinitive**
Pronoun objects of an infinitive coming after another verb precede the infinitive: *il veut le lui donner*, he wants to give it to him; *il pense d'y aller*, he thinks of going there. **But** when the infinitive follows *écouter, entendre* (sometimes *envoyer*), *faire, laisser, mener, regarder, sentir* and *voir*, the pronoun object of the following infinitive **precedes the first verb**: *je le ferai prendre*, I shall have it taken; *voilà ma maison: je l'ai fait bâtir*, there is my house: I have had it built; *je l'ai envoyé chercher*, I sent for him (to be looked for – **but** this could also mean: 'I sent him to look for': to avoid ambiguity, *le* could be placed before *chercher*).

13.   **When personal pronouns** are the object of a main verb followed by an infinitive, they come before the main verb: *je les voir venir*, I see them coming; nous *l'avons entendu chanter*, we heard her sing (*entendu* does **not** agree with *l'* (= *la*) because it is the singing that was heard): if each verb has an object pronoun, each precedes its own verb: *il m'a entendu lui parler*, he heard me speak to him: **but** if the object of the infinitive is *le, la* or *les*, it is also possible to put both pronouns before the first verb: *cette lettre, ils nous l'ont laissé* lire*, this letter, they have let us read it = 'they us it have allowed to read'. (*See note at end of paragraph.) In this case the *le, la* or *les* come **after** an indirect (dative) object pronoun in the first and second persons, singular and plural (*me le, nous le, vous le*): but **before** an indirect object pronoun in third person (eg: *le lui, la leur*, etc), although in whichever order the pronouns are placed, the **direct object** is the *le, la* or *les*, and the **indirect object** the other pronoun, *me, te, lui, nous, vous, leur*, eg: *il me les donne*, he gives them to me; *ils les leur donnent*, they give them to them. (***Note**: in the example above the past participle *laissé* does **not** agree – it is the 'to read the letter' not 'the letter' to which the past participle refers, a direct object following the verb, and genderless. It **is** possible to write: *ils nous ont laissés lire la lettre*, with '*nous*' considered the direct object of *ont laissés*, and '*la lettre*' the direct object of *lire*, in which case *laissés* may agree with '*nous*', **but** usage differs.)

14.   **Reflexive pronouns – omission**
If the infinitive of a reflexive verb comes after the verb *faire*, and at times **also** after: *emmener, envoyer, laisser*· or *mener*, the reflexive pronoun may be omitted: *il m'a fait asseoir*, he made me sit down; *voici un savon pour faire en aller les taches*, here is a soap to make stains vanish; *on a laissé échapper le chien*, the dog has been allowed to escape; *nous les mènent coucher*, we take them to bed. This, however, is **not** always done: *la faim l'a fait se décider*,

hunger made him decide; *on a envoyé les enfants se laver*, the children have been sent to wash. After other verbs the reflexive pronoun goes before its own verb: *je vais me promener*, I am going for a walk ('I go to walk myself'); *allons nous promener*, let's go for a walk ('let us go to walk ourselves').

15. **Disjunctive personal pronouns** corresponding to the conjunctive personal pronouns (**but** not normally used for things), are used when separate from a verb, after a preposition **or** after *que* = 'than' in comparisons, **or** as the complement of *être*. These pronouns are: *moi* – I, me; *toi* – thou, thee (you, sing); *lui* – he, him (**as a disjunctive pronoun *lui* does not mean 'to him'**); *elle* – she, her; *nous* – we, us; *vous* – you (plural or polite singular); *eux* – they, them (masc persons or things); *elles* – they, them (fem persons or things) **and** the impersonal pronoun: *soi* – oneself (see ¶18 below). **Although some of these are identical in form with the conjunctive pronouns they do not necessarily have exactly the same meaning**: note particularly *lui* and *elle*. Disjunctive pronouns may be strengthened by adding *même* (= self): *je le ferai moi-même*, I shall do it myself (see *même*, **he, her, them** in Reference Section).

16. **Disjunctive pronouns are used apart from the verb:**
    i. **to add emphasis to the subject**: *lui, il ne dort jamais pendant l'après-midi*, as for him, he never sleeps during the afternoon; *Jean aime bien sa femme, lui!* John loves his wife very much, he does; *–Qui est là? – Moi!* 'Who is there?' 'Me!'; *moi, je le ferais s'il c'était à moi à faire*, as for me (for my part) I would do it if it were for me to do
    ii. **after prepositions**, eg: *avec elle*, with her; *sans lui*, without him; *après moi*, after me; *malgré eux*, in spite of them; *chez vous*, at your place/home
    iii. **after the adverb *comme*** = as, like: *faites-le comme moi*, do it like me
    iv. **after *que*** = 'than' in **comparisons**: *vous êtes plus riche que moi*, you are richer than I am (than me); *j'y vais plus souvent qu'elle*, I go there more often than she does; *nous allons plus vite qu'eux*, we go faster than they do
    v. **disjunctive pronouns are also used after the verb *être***: *c'est elle qui l'a fait*, it is she who has done it; *ce sont eux que j'ai vus hier*, it is they whom I saw yesterday; *c'était toujours nous qui devions le faire*, it was always we who had to do it; *c'est moi*, it's I (me); *c'est lui*, it's he (him); *c'est nous*, it's we (us); *c'est vous*, it's you; *ce sont* eux*, it's they (them, masc); *ce sont* elles*, it's they (them, fem) (*note verb in plural for third person plural only).

17. After '*être à*' (= to belong to) the disjunctive pronouns can be used instead of possessive pronouns: *c'est à moi*, it's mine. **Neither** the possessive pronoun nor the possessive adjective shows the gender of the possessor, eg: *la maison est la sienne* = the house is his/hers and *sa maison*, his/her house. If it is necessary to show that the house belongs to 'her' and not to 'him', the disjunctive pronoun can be used: *la maison est à elle*. Other

disjunctive pronouns can be similarly used: *la maison est . . . à moi, à toi, à lui, à elle, à nous, à vous, à eux* and *à elles* = the house is . . . mine, yours (thine), his/its, hers/its, ours, yours, theirs (masc) and theirs (fem).

18.   *on* (pronounce with rounded lips): **pronoun**: masculine singular: invariable = 'one' (as in 'what does one do now?'):

    i.   can be used **only** as subject of a verb, in the third person singular: *on mange bien ici,* one eats well here; *on est né, on travail, on souffre, on meurt – c'est la vie,* one is born, one works, one suffers, one dies – that's life

    ii. **the reflexive form of *on* is *se*** – as used for other third person pronouns, and when so used means 'oneself': *on se demande,* one asks oneself; *on doit se laver chaque jour,* one must wash oneself each day: its corresponding **possessive adjective** (as in '**one's** name') is *son, sa, ses: on demande ses droits,* one demands one's rights: its **possessive pronoun** is *le sien, la sienne,* the same as for **his, hers, its**: its **disjunctive pronoun** (for use after prepositions) = *soi,* oneself: *on ne doit pas parler de soi,* one must not speak of oneself; *prendre sur soi,* to take upon oneself; *un soi-disant docteur de la loi,* a self-styled doctor of law (*soi-disant* is invariable): *soi* is often used together with ***même*** (self), which gives it emphasis: *il faut le faire soi-même,* one must do it oneself: *on* is **also** frequently used for the impersonal 'they' as in: *on dit que,* they say that: *on* is used more in French than 'one' in English, often to avoid the passive: *on m'a dit,* I have been told = 'it is said that'; *on a répondu à la lettre ce matin,* the letter was answered this morning; *on a réparé mon auto,* my car has been repaired; *ici on parle français,* French is spoken here: *on* **also** translates an undefined 'somebody', etc: *on fait un bruit dans la rue,* someone's making a noise in the street: **and** for the general 'you' as in: *d'ici on peut voir les montagnes,* from here you can see the mountains; *ici on vous donne à manger,* here you are given something to eat (or here one is given something to eat).

19.   **Demonstrative pronouns**
    celui: this one/the one, referring to some person or thing of known number and gender, with which it agrees, having the following forms: *celui* = masc sing; *celle* = fem sing; *ceux* = masc plur; *celles* = fem plural. Used as follows:

    i.   **before a relative pronoun** (such as *qui,* who; *que,* which; *de qui,* of whom; *dont,* of whom or of which), referring back to the noun with which they agree, eg: *j'ai lu tous les livres, y inclus celui qui est sur la table,* I have read all the books, including **the one** which (or **that** which) is on the table: **or** in the plural: *ceux qui sont,* **the ones** (or those) which are; *des deux roses, celle que vous m'avez donnée,* of the two roses, that which (the one which) you gave me; *ceux dont je parle,* those of whom I speak

    ii. **before a phrase introduced by a preposition**, eg: *j'ai vos chemises, mais où se trouvent **celles** de votre ami?* I have your shirts but where are those of your friend? *il arriva sans **celui** sur la table,* he arrived without the one on the table

    iii. **at the beginning** of a sentence provided it is known to whom or to what it refers: *j'ai visité les deux maisons hier; **celle** que j'ai trouvée la plus belle était celle sur la colline,* I looked at the two houses yesterday; **the one** which I found the most beautiful was the one on the hill: *je n'aime pas vos pommes; **celles** de votre frère sont magnifiques,* I don't like your apples; **those** of your brother are magnificent

    iv. **the antecedent of *celui*** need not be mentioned provided it is known to whom or what reference is made in order to establish the gender and number to be used: ***celui qui** ne veut pas aller peut rester ici,* **he (the one – anyone)** who does not wish to go can stay here (referring to males or persons of mixed gender): **if all** 'those' had been female: '***celle qui*** . . .', (she who) would be used. If there are more than one who might opt out, the speaker would probably use the plural: ***ceux qui*** . . . ***celles qui*** . . . those who . . . **or** possibly: *tous ceux* qui* . . . **or** *toutes celles* qui* . . . all (those*) who . . . . *Note: the demonstrative pronoun **cannot** be omitted in French as it may be in English. If speaking of something of **unknown gender** see ¶21.

20.   *-ci* and *-là*. **The invariable suffixes *-ci* and *-là*** can be added to any of these forms to distinguish between **this** (one) and **that** (one), or between these and those: *lequel est le vôtre, celui-ci ou celui-là?* which is yours, **this** one or **that** one? *celui-ci est pour moi, celui-là est pour vous,* this (one here) is for me, that (one there) is for you: if 'the one' is something **feminine**: *celle-ci est* . . . *celle-là est* . . . : **plurals**: *ceux-ci, ceux-là, celles-ci, celles-là.* ***Celui-ci*** and ***celle-ci*** can also mean the **latter** (the 'nearer') and ***celui-là/celle-là*** can also mean the **former** (the farthest away): **beware of confusing** the *-là* with the '*la* . . .' of latter, and **beware of thinking *-ci*** is masculine and *-là* feminine, eg: *ils s'appellent Jean et Marie: celle-ci est ma tante et celui-là est mon oncle,* they are called (their names are) John and Mary: the latter is my aunt, the former is my uncle.

21.   *ceci* and *cela* = 'this' and 'that', act as **demonstrative pronouns** when reference is made to something of unknown number and gender – an idea, an action, etc, or to something which has not been named – when **no** agreement is possible.

    i. Normally *ceci* refers to something yet to be said or produced: *écoutez bien ceci, on doit payer ce qu'on doit,* listen carefully to **this,** one must pay what one owes; *ceci est ce que je pense,* this is what I think (the explanation then follows); *regardez ceci,* look at this (the invitation precedes the demonstration); *ceci est l'entrée,* this is the entrance (**but** *voilà* or *voici l'entrée* = here is the entrance, can be used equally as well): *ceci* can **also** refer to something here and now: *ceci m'amuse* *toujours,* this always amuses me; *ceci ne me plaît pas,* this does not please me

ii.   *cela* refers to something already mentioned (**but** of no given gender): *on doit payer ses dettes – cela va sans dire,* one must pay one's debts – that goes without saying; *il a fait de son mieux, cela est certain,* he has done his best, that is certain; *il a essayé de le faire, mais cela ne lui était pas possible,* he tried to do it, but that was not possible for him; *je l'ai rencontré à Paris – il y a cinquante ans de cela,* I met him in Paris – that was fifty years ago ('there are fifty years from that')

iii. **when a general idea is expressed by itself,** eg: *on doit payer ce qu'on doit,* without reference to any specific occasion: **either** *ceci* **or** *cela* **can be used**: *les riches doivent aider les pauvres – ceci/cela est vrai,* the rich must help the poor – this/that is true

iv.   *ça* **is the abbreviated form of** *cela* as usually used in conversation: in familiar speech it may occasionally refer to persons as well as things, **but** this should not be copied

v.   *ça* is **not elided** before a vowel: *ça a bien marché?* did it go all right? **Distinguish from** *ç'* **which is** *ce* **elided**: see ¶23.

22.   *ceci* and *cela* before verbs other than *être* may be used for 'it': *cela me plaît à faire ce que vous voulez,* it pleases me to do what you want; *je peux vous donner un autre tournevis si cela vous aidera,* I can give you another screwdriver if **it** will help you: **and** *cela* may be used before *être* instead of *ce* to translate 'it' for emphasis: *cela c'est vrai!* **that's** true!

23.   *ce* – **neuter demonstrative pronoun**
      ce, **pronoun,** must be **distinguished from**: *ce, cet, cette, ces,* – the demonstrative adjective. **The pronoun** *ce* **is invariable except** when elided to *c'* before a vowel (*ç'* before *a*). Its most usual meaning is 'it', and it is used most frequently as the subject of *être,* **but** can **also** be used for 'this', 'that' and 'what': see ¶35, ¶36. *ce* at times must, at times may, be used pleonastically, ie: without adding any additional meaning, and where no corresponding word is used in English.

24.   *c'est*: 'it is' **with adjective complement**: when the complement of *être* is an adjective referring back to what has already been mentioned, 'it is' is usually translated by *c'est,* eg: *il m'a montré comment il faut le faire: c'est très facile,* he has shown me how it must be done: **it** is very easy; *les bombes m'ont éveillé: ç'a a été effrayant,* the bombs woke me up: **it** was frightening.

25.   *c'est* = **with non-adjective complement**: *ce* is the subject of the verb *être* when followed by a **complement that is not an adjective** (though an adjective may form part of the complete complement) referring back to a statement or idea already mentioned (and which is the real subject): *le plus grand de tous les biens, c'est d'avoir assez d'argent,* the greatest good of all is to have enough money; *nous y allons demain, c'est une bonne idée, je crois,* we're going there tomorrow, it's is a good idea, I think.

26.   *ce* = **subject of verbs other than** *être:* *ce* can also be the subject of ***aller***, ***devoir*** and ***pouvoir*** followed by *être*, eg: *ce doit être vrai*, that (**or** it) must be true; *ce peut être vrai*, that (**or** it) can be true; *ç'allait être amusant*, it was going to be amusing/entertaining ('it looked as if it would be amusing'); *la cirque arrive demain, ce doit* être *un beau spectacle*, the circus arrives tomorrow, it's said to be a fine sight.

27.   *c'est* = **in answer to questions**: in response to a question or statement implying a question, *c'est* usually introduces the reply: *–Il y a un bruit dans le jardin.–C'est le chien*, 'There is a noise in the garden.' 'It's the dog.' *–Qui est là? –C'est nous*, 'Who is there?' 'It's us': **but** if the complement is in the **third person plural** the verb should be plural: *ce sont eux, ce sont mes amis*, it's **them***, it's **my friends** (*ce* is invariable) (*strictly should be 'they', but rarely is).

28.   *ce* **pleonastic* between differing subject and complement**: *ce* **must** be inserted before *être* if its subject and its complement differ in number or person from each other: *mon seule amie, **c'est** vous*, my only (girl) friend, is you (third person subject, second person complement); *trois soldats seulement, **ce** n'est pas une armée* (plural subject, singular complement), only three soldiers, that is not an army; *ma plus grande joie, ce sont vos gâteaux*, my greatest joy is your cakes (singular subject, plural complement) (***pleonastic = not adding to the meaning**).

29.   *ce* **pleonastic between infinitives**: when the subject and complement of *être* are **both** infinitives *ce* **must precede** *être* if the infinitive complement is positive: *voir c'est croire*, to see is to believe: **but** *ce* is **not** so used before a negative infinitive complement: *croire n'est pas savoir*, to believe is not to know and it is **not** so used if an infinitive subject of *être* has a complement which is **not** another infinitive: *pouvoir bien écouter est une grande vertu*, to be able to listen well is a great virtue.

30.   *ce* **pleonastic or emphatic between equal phrases**: when two phrases of equal value (which can be changed round without altering the sense) are linked by the verb *être*, *ce* **may** be used or omitted: *le malheur le plus grand (c')est une vie sans l'amour* **or** *une vie sans l'amour (c')est le malheur le plus grand*, the greatest misfortune is a life without love **or** a life without love is the greatest misfortune (the choice is a matter of style and, in some cases, euphony). If *c'est* is placed first, *que* (or sometimes another conjunction such as *comme, si, quand*) **must** link the two clauses: *c'est une belle fleur, que la rose*, it's a beautiful flower, the rose is; *vouloir combattre l'ennemi (c')est une chose admirable*, to wish to fight the enemy is an admirable thing: when reversed, coming only after *admirable*, with *c'est* coming first, becomes: *c'est une chose admirable, que de vouloir combattre l'ennemi* **or** *si on veut combattre* **or** *quand on veut combattre*, it's an admirable thing to wish to fight the enemy **or** if one wishes to fight **or** when one wishes to fight. The use of *ce*, here, adds emphasis.

31.   **If *être* is followed by a pronoun, *ce* must be used**, eg: *mon meilleur ami, c'est vous*, my best friend is you (see ¶27).

32.   *ce* = **introducing a qualifying clause**:
   i.   when the subject of *être* is a clause starting with any form of *celui qui*
        or *celui que* (= he who, she who, they who, that which, the one(s)
        which), *ce* pleonastic is inserted **before** *être*, eg: *celui qui travaillait
        là,* * c'était le portier,* he (the one) who worked there was the door-
        keeper; *celles que j'aime le mieux,* * *ce sont les bleues,* those which I
        like best are the blue ones; *celui que j'ai trouvé,* * *c'est à* moi, the one
        which I found is mine
   ii. *ce* should preferably be similarly used after a clause beginning with *ce
        que* = 'what', eg: *ce que vous dites,* * *(c') est vrai,* what you say is true:
        but *ce* may be omitted if the speaker wishes to be succinct
   iii. if a qualifying preceding phrase or clause is linked by *que,* used as a
        conjunction, to the clause it qualifies, this phrase introduced by *que*
        should, by preference, be preceded by *ce,* eg: *une chose triste,* * *c'est
        qu'il est parti,* a sad thing, that he has left (* = qualifying clause or
        phrase acting as the real subject of *être* in the clause that follows).

33.   *c'est* = **he is a . . . (profession)**: *ce* = 'it' or 'they' when describing what is
      some person's or persons' profession or status: *c'est un professeur* * *qui était
      dans la salle,* it was a schoolmaster who was in the room: **or** when putting
      persons or things into a category: *il y avait beaucoup de garçons dans la cour
      de récréation: c'étaient des enfants de dix ou onze ans,* there were a lot of
      boys in the playground: they were children of from ten to eleven years old.
      (*But *il* or *elle* are used to state the fact that he or she is a doctor: *il est
      médecin,* he is a doctor.)

34.   *c'est* = **before days** and **dates**: *ce* also translates 'it' when speaking of the
      day/date: *c'est aujourd'hui jeudi,* it is Thursday today; *c'est le vingt juin,* it is
      the twentieth of June.

35.   *ce* = **that which, what**: *ce qui, ce que*: when a clause following the verb is
      introduced in English by 'that which' (or 'what'), either as subject or object,
      or by 'that to which' **or** by 'that of which' (or equivalents) – 'that' is
      translated by *ce,* eg: *ce qui me plaît,* that which (what) pleases me; *ce que je
      crois,* that which (what) I believe; *ce que vous dites,* that which you say (what
      you say); *ce à quoi je pense,* what I'm thinking about ('that about which I
      think'); *ce dont j'ai peur,* what I'm afraid of ('that of which I am afraid'); *ce
      dont nous avons besoin est ce à quoi nous avons droit,* what we need ('that of
      which we have need') is that to which we have a right.

36.   *ce* = **this, that (pronouns)**: *ce* translates the pronouns 'this' and 'that' in a
      number of phrases, such as: *ce disant,* saying this (so saying); *sur ce,* on this
      (thereupon); *ce faisant,* on doing this/that; *de ce non content,* not content with
      that; *pour ce* **or** *pour ce faire,* to that end, for that purpose.

37.   *il*, **not** *ce*, normally translates 'it' before an impersonal verb (see **Impersonal
      Verbs** and **it** in Reference Section). This includes asking and telling the time:
      quelle heure est-il? il est trois heures, what times is it? it is three o'clock.

38. **Possessive pronouns** = mine, yours, his, theirs, etc. These pronouns take the number and gender of the thing possessed, **not** of the possessor:

POSSESSIVE PRONOUNS	BEFORE A MASC SING	BEFORE A FEM SING	BEFORE A MASC PLUR	BEFORE A FEM PLUR
SINGULAR				
mine	*le mien*	*la mienne*	*les miens*	*les miennes*
yours	*le tien*	*la tienne*	*les tienes*	*les tiennes*
his, hers, its	*le sien*	*la sienne*	*les siens*	*les siennes*
PLURAL				
ours	*le nôtre*	*la nôtre*	*les nôtres*	*les nôtres*
yours	*le vôtre*	*la vôtre*	*les vôtres*	*les vôtres*
theirs	*le leur*	*la leur*	*les leurs*	*les leurs*

note: although *leur* has **no** feminine form, the definite article shows the gender of the thing possessed: *la maison est la leur*, the house is theirs. The -ô- (with circumflex) appears **only** in the possessive pronoun, **not** in the corresponding adjectives: *notre*, our; *votre*, your. **Examples of the use of the above:** *cette maison est plus petite que la mienne*, this house is smaller than mine; *j'ai mes amis, et vous avez les vôtres*, I have my friends and you have yours; *Marie aime son mari et Jeanne aime le sien*, Mary loves her husband and Joan loves hers (*le sien* agrees with *le mari*); *donnez-moi celui-là, c'est le mien*, give me that one, it's mine; *la tienne est sur la table; j'ai déjà trouvé la mienne**, yours is on the table; I have already found mine (*something feminine – *une lettre* perhaps).

39. **To emphasise the owner rather than the thing possessed,** a disjunctive pronoun after *à* is often used to replace the possessive pronoun: *c'est à moi*, it is **mine**. See ¶17v above.

40. **Relative pronouns are:**
   i. **simple forms:** as verb subject:

	PERSONS: MASC AND FEM		THINGS: MASC AND FEM	
SUBJECT SING AND PLUR	*qui*	who	*qui*	which
DIRECT OBJECT	*que*	whom	*que*	which
INDIRECT OBJECT*	*(à) qui*	(to) whom	*(à) quoi*	(to) which
POSSESSIVE	*dont*	of whom	*dont*	of which

* after *parmi*, among, in 'among whom' and 'among which', *lequel*, and not *qui*, must be used: *les gens parmi lesquels il se trouve . . .* , the people among whom he finds himself: see ii below and ¶43. See entry in Reference Section for *que!* in exclamations

   ii. **composite forms:** (combining definite article with *quel, quelle, quels, quelles*) as both subject and direct object, persons and things (= who, whom, which): masculine singular = *lequel;* feminine singular = *laquelle;* masculine plural = *lesquels;* feminine plural = *lesquelles*. (See ¶43 below.)

41. *qui,* when used as a **relative pronoun**, introduces a relative (or adjectival) clause qualifying its 'antecedent' – that is, a noun or phrase in the preceding clause (see ¶42). The relative pronoun *qui* changes to *que* when it is a direct object: it is assumed to have the gender and number of its antecedent if that is a noun **or** to be masculine singular if there is **no** gender to agree with: it remains *qui* after a preposition, **but** when so used can refer **only** to persons (or personified animals and things).

42. i. **The antecedent preceding a relative pronoun can be a noun**: *j'ai vu un **homme** que je connais et (un homme) **qui** demeure tout près,* I saw a **man whom** I know and **who** lives quite near by; *voici les fleurs **que** je vous ai achetées,** here are the flowers **which** I have bought you (* the past participle agrees with *que,* which stands for *les fleurs,* fem plur, **and** which is the direct object before the verb: see VERBS, ¶44); *l'homme encore malade, **de qui** (or **dont** or **duquel**) je vous ai parlé, est arrivé,* the man, still ill, of whom I spoke to you (whom I spoke to you about) has arrived. The antecedent (*l'homme* in the above example) does **not** always come directly before the relative pronoun: ***l'homme sans chapeau avec** qui **vous travailliez,*** the man without the hat with **whom** you were working (or **whom** you were working with*). *Prepositions **must** precede the relative pronoun *(avec qui)* – they **cannot** be put at the end of a phrase or sentence as in English

ii. **the antecedent of a relative pronoun can also be a personal pronoun or a demonstrative pronoun**, eg: ***nous,** qui croyons* . . . , **we who** believe . . . ; ***ceux,** que j'ai achetés* . . . , **those, which** I have bought . . . ; ***celle à** qui je parlais était **celle avec** qui j'ai voyagé,* **she to whom** I was speaking was **she** (the one) **with whom** I travelled

iii. **the antecedent of a relative pronoun can be a number or quantity**: *la douzaine (de gens) pour qui il a trouvé une chambre* . . . , **the dozen** or so (people) for **whom** he has found a room . . .

iv. **the antecedent of a relative pronoun can be a statement**, the relative pronoun then being preceded by *ce*: *vous l'avez tué, ce que je trouve terrible,* you have killed it, which I find terrible

v. **the antecedent of a relative pronoun can be an adjective**: *à moitié **morte** qu'elle était* . . . , **half dead that** she was/as she was. In such cases *que* (**not** *qui*) is used, referring to the state the person is in, **not** to the person: *toutes* **honteuses** *qu'elles soient* . . . , all ashamed that they may be (very ashamed though they be . . .) (**toutes* is really an adverb, and should be invariable, **but** in usage it agrees in gender and number before a feminine word beginning with a vowel or *h*-mute (see *tout*))

vi. **the antecedent of a relative pronoun can be an adverb**: *je reste ici **où** je suis,* I stay here where I am (*où,* is an adverb acting as a relative pronoun: see *où*).

43. *lequel,* **relative pronoun** = who, whom, which: fem = *laquelle;* masc plur = *lesquels;* fem plur = *lesquelles.* The prefixed definite article combines with *à* and *de* as if it were separate: *duquel, de laquelle, desquel(le)s, auquel, à*

laquelle, auxquel(le)s. As a relative pronoun *lequel* is mainly a literary form, **but** it is also used in speech, mainly to avoid ambiguity, eg: in 'he has two children, a boy and a girl, of whom I have just spoken': if 'of whom', refers to both the boy and the girl, the clause would be: '*desquels je viens de parler*': if 'of whom', refers to the girl alone, the clause would be: '*de laquelle je viens de parler*'. **In**: '*le toit de la maison, lequel était en ardoises*', the roof of the house which was of tiles: *le toit* is masculine, therefore *lequel* refers to the roof, not the house. **In**: '*l'homme, avec sa femme, duquel je parle*', the man, with his wife, of whom I speak: 'of whom' clearly refers to the man, masc sing. **In**: '*l'homme, avec sa femme, de laquelle j'ai parlé*', the man, with his wife, of whom I spoke: *laquelle* indicates that I spoke of the wife. Ambiguity **cannot** always be avoided – **in**: '*l'homme, avec son fils, duquel j'ai parlé*', *duquel* could refer to either; in such a case, if 'the man' is referred to, one could say: '*l'homme duquel (dont, de qui) j'ai parlé et son fils*': **or** alternatively, reference to 'the son' can be indicated by making the necessary pause: *l'homme – et le fils duquel je parlais – sont tous les deux arrivés*. The context may clarify ambiguity. If the context does not make the meaning clear, when it could refer to two different nouns of the same number and gender, *lequel* is assumed to refer to the first: in '*une amie de ma mère, laquelle était arrivée hier*', a friend of my mother who arrived yesterday: *laquelle* refers to *une amie*. The English, however, remains ambiguous. When *lequel* has **no** antecedent noun with which to agree it remains masculine in form: *il voulait prendre le train du soir, lequel était une meilleure idée*, he wanted to take the evening train, which was a better idea (the antecedent is 'the wish to take the evening train').

44.   *dont*, **invariable relative pronoun** = 'of whom' and 'of which'

    i.   *dont*, requires no agreement and, being so simple, is frequently used as an alternative to: *duquel, de laquelle, desquel(le)s*, when there is **no** danger of ambiguity: *dont* may be used for both persons and things, eg: *les hommes/livres dont je parle*, the men/books of which I speak

    ii.   *dont* **must** be used if the relative pronoun is immediately preceded by *ce*, *cela*, or *rien*, eg: *ce (*or *cela) dont il parle*, that of which he speaks; *il ne fait **rien** dont il doit avoir honte*, he does nothing of which he ought to be ashamed

    iii.   *dont* **cannot** be used if its antecedent is governed by a preposition: thus, 'the man **in** the house of whom (**in whose** house)' **cannot be translated as**: '*l'homme **dans** la maison dont . . .*': the correct construction is: '*l'homme dans la maison **duquel** . . .*': similarly, to translate: 'the man **whose** house I saw' as: '*l'homme dont (la) maison j'ai vu*' **is not correct**: it should be: '*l'homme, dont j'ai vu la maison*' = the man of whom I saw the house. If *dont* is thought of as meaning 'of whom' or 'of which' (and **not** as 'whose') the construction presents no difficulty

    iv.   *dont* **cannot be used** in the interrogative, **but** elsewhere it can replace, or be replaced by, both *duquel* and *de qui*, the latter normally for persons only, unless an animal or thing is personified.

45.   **Interrogative pronouns**: in form interrogative pronouns are the same as the relative pronouns, **but,** besides asking questions, they are somewhat different in meaning:

  i.   *qui?* = who? **and** whom? and is used **only** for persons: see ¶46

  ii.   *que?* = what? and refers to things, both as subject and as object: see ¶47

  iii. *quoi?* also = what? usually after a preposition: see ¶48

  iv.   *lequel?* = which? see ¶49.

46.   *qui?* = who? whom? when interrogative are used only for persons or for personified animals and things. For animals and things *qui est-ce qui* (subject) and *qu'est-ce que* (object) are used: see *qui est-ce qui?* ii in Reference Section. In questions, *qui?* is normally treated as masculine **but** it can be either **singular**, eg: *qui est venu?* who **has** come? **or,** if several persons are referred to, **plural**: *qui sont venus?* who have come? (of any gender): *qui d'entre vous a vu ce film?* who from among you (which of you) has seen this film? **But** when the reference is clearly exclusively feminine: *qui?* will be feminine for agreement purposes: *qui est venue?* who (ie: which female person) has come? As a direct object, *qui?* remains unaltered: *qui voyez-vous?* whom do you see? **And** it also remains unaltered after a preposition (as indirect object): *pour qui a-t-il acheté ce livre?* for whom has he bought that book? *avec qui parle-t-il?* with whom is he speaking? *avec qui d'autre peut on le faire?* with whom other (with whom else) can one do it? *à qui?* is used in asking 'to whom?' something belongs: *à qui est cette maison?* to whom is this house? = whose house is this? See also *qui est-ce qui?* in Reference Section.

47.   *que?* **neuter interrogative pronoun** = what? As subject: *que* (usually with *-il* after the verb): *que faut-il?* what is needed? **and** as object: *que voyez-vous?* what do you see? *que voulez-vous?* what do you want? *que deviendra-t-il?* what will become of him? ('what will become he?') After a preposition, 'what' = *quoi?* see ¶48. In speech in the extended form *qu'est-ce qui?* is usual: see *qui est-ce qui?* and also **Interrogative** in Reference Section.

48.   *quoi?* = what? (**cannot** refer to persons) may be used:

  i.   **elliptically** (in abbreviated sentences), eg: *Quoi?* – used to ask, not too politely, 'What?' (for 'what's that you said?') **or** *quoi de plus belle qu'un jardin anglais?* what more beautiful than an English garden? *quoi de nouveau?* what's new?

  ii.   *quoi* can be the object of a verb: *tu deviendras quoi?* you will become what? *quoi répondre?* what to reply? (how can one reply?)

  iii. **the most frequent use of *quoi* is after a preposition**: *avec quoi allez-vous manger la viande?* with what are you going to eat the meat? *à quoi sert cette cuillère?* 'to what end serves this spoon?' = what is this spoon for? *en quoi peut-on vous aider?* in what can one (can I/we) help you?

49.   i.   *lequel?* = which? (see ¶43 above) when used as an interrogative pronoun agrees with whatever it stands for, whether mentioned or 'understood': *laquelle des sœurs est la plus jeune?* which of the sisters

is the youngest? *lequel* (*'le livre'* understood) *voulez-vous lire?* which do you want to read? *dans laquelle* (*'la maison'* understood) *habite-t-il?* in which does he live?

ii. *lequel?* is especially useful in questions where a choice has to be made: *–J'ai un fils et une fille.* 'I have a son and daughter.' *–Lequel* aimez-vous le mieux?* 'Which do you love most?' (*Masculine if genders are mixed.) *–J'ai trouvé une des tasses perdues.* 'I've found one of the lost cups.' *-Laquelle?* (**gender is known**) 'Which one?' *–J'ai trouvé un des enfants perdus.* 'I have found one of the lost children.' *–Lequel?* (**gender not known***) 'Which one?' *lequel remains masculine: **but** if all were girls the question would have been *laquelle?*

50. **Indefinite pronouns** refer to **no** specific person or thing: the most used = *on*, see ¶18, above. Others, which may also function as other parts of speech, include: *aucun, autre, autrui, certain, chacun, grand-chose, le même, nul, personne, peu de chose, plusieurs, quelque chose, quelqu'un, quiconque, rien, tel, tout*. These will be found entered separately in the Reference Section.

VERBS

1. **Conjugations**. French verbs are divided into **four conjugations** according to their infinitive endings:

i. **those ending in** *-er* **like** *parler*
ii. **those ending in** *-ir* **like** *finir*
iii. **those ending in** *-re* **like** *vendre*
iv. **those ending in** *-oir* **like** *recevoir*. (**Note**: some Grammars reverse the order of iii and iv.)

i. The only really irregular 1st conjugation verbs are *aller*, to go and *envoyer*, to send (with *renvoyer*, to send back): **but** verbs ending in *-ayer, -oyer, -uyer, -ger, -guer, -cer*, e + consonant = *er* (like *mener, jeter, appeler*) and a few with *é* in the final syllable of the stem **all present spelling difficulties**: each is listed separately in the Reference Section. Verbs in *-er* (example: *parler*), form by far the largest and most regular group, and new verbs normally belong to this group.

ii. *-ir* verbs, the second largest group, like *finir*, has many which are irregular, and **two** sub-groups, those like *ouvrir (couvrir, offrir, souffrir)* and those like *partir (dormir, mentir, sentir, servir, sortir)*.

iii. *-re* verbs, form a less numerous group, many of which are irregular, the most irregular being *être*, to be. The example for regular verbs used here is *vendre*, to sell.

iv. **Verbs ending in** *-evoir* are **all** like *recevoir*, to receive: the example used for this small group. Verbs ending in *-oir* **without** *-ev-* are irregular, most of them important, eg: *avoir*, to have; *devoir*, must, to owe; *savoir*, to know; *pouvoir*, can, to be able; *vouloir*, to wish.

Regular verbs which present no problems are not listed, and are conjugated like the examples given in ¶13ff below: but regular verbs presenting problems of usage (generally use of prepositions), of spelling or translation will be found in the Reference Section.

2. **Voice.** Verbs are said to have two 'Voices'
   i. **the active voice**: in which the subject of the verb performs the action described, eg: **the man** eats the bread, **the man** walks
   ii. **the passive voice**: in which the subject undergoes the action of the verb: see ¶7 below.

3. **Moods.** The tenses of French verbs are grouped into three 'Moods'
   i. **the indicative mood**: those tenses the action of which is stated as a fact in the past, present or future
   ii. **the imperative mood**: expresses a command or a wish: see ¶19
   iii. **the subjunctive mood**: expresses something considered in the mind as speculative, used mainly in dependent clauses, see ¶33 = subjunctive, below.

4. **Tense**: the word means 'time': in French **both** 'time' and 'tense' are the same word: *le temps*. Tenses are grouped basically into **past, present** and **future**, indicated by their endings **and** sometimes by stem changes as well. For their meaning and use see 13ff below.

5. **Transitive and intransitive verbs.** A **transitive** verb takes a direct object, eg: 'I read a book': an **intransitive** verb has either no object, eg: 'I work' **or** an indirect object, governed by a preposition, 'I work **with** a spade'. Most intransitive verbs can take an indirect object, and the preposition required – often *à* or *de*, less frequently *avec, en, pour* or some other preposition – **note**: it may not be the preposition an English speaker would expect; moreover, some verbs are transitive in English **but** intransitive in French, and vice versa. French grammars distinguish between verbs which are ***intransitif*** = unable to have an object (eg: *dormir*, to sleep) and ***transitif indirect*** = having only an indirect object, taking a preposition before the object (eg: *aider à*, to help) and possibly transitive in English. Verbs differing from English usage will be found individually listed in the Reference Section.

6. **Number and Person.** The form of the verb, mainly its ending, changes with the 'Number' and 'Person' of the subject. **There are two 'Numbers': singular and plural;** and **three 'Persons' in each 'Number'. The first person is**, or includes, the speaker. **The second person is** the person or persons addressed. And **the third person is** the person, persons, thing or things about which the verb makes a statement. The **personal pronouns** used as the subject for the verbs are set out and explained in PRONOUNS ¶2 – 4. In **tenses** shown below, the pronouns *je, tu, il, nous, vous, ils* (or, in the third persons, some noun or nouns) **must** be 'understood' for each line respectively.

7. **Passive conjugation**. **The passive** of a French verb is formed, as in English, by using the appropriate tense of the verb 'to be', *être*, with the **past participle**: thus *aimer*, to love (**active**), has the **passive** – *être aimé*, to be loved, eg: I am loved, *je suis aimé(e):* similarly: she will be sent, *elle sera envoyée;* they (fem) have been found, *elles ont été trouvées*. **In all passive tenses** the past participle (in these examples *aimé, envoyé, trouvé*) acts as the complement of the verb *être*, and agrees in gender and number with the subject as an adjective. The **present participle passive** is formed from the present participle of *être* plus the past participle of the verb, eg: *étant aimé(e)(es)*, being loved, the past participle element agreeing with the person or thing referred to. The **past participle passive** is formed from the present participle of *avoir* (the auxiliary of *être*) with the past participles of **both** *être* and the verb, the latter again agreeing: *ayant été aimé(e)(s)(es)*, having been loved. To have a passive form a verb **must** normally be capable of having a direct object, **but** *obéir, désobéir*, and *pardonner*, though intransitive, may be used in the passive, eg: *il sera obéi*, he will be obeyed; *elle a été désobéie*, she has been disobeyed; *il est pardonné*, he is forgiven.

8. **The French often prefer to avoid the passive** by using the pronoun *on* and an active tense, eg: *on me dit*, one tells me (for 'I am told'). **Except** for those verbs given above this construction **must** be used if the verb does **not** take a direct object, eg: 'he is spoken to', is changed to: 'one speaks to him', *on lui parle*. **Alternatively** a reflexive verb can be used, eg: the door was opened, *la porte s'est ouverte* (literally, 'the door opened itself') **or**, as another alternative, subject and object can be reversed: 'the door is opened by the concierge' becomes: *le concierge ouvre la porte*, the concierge opens the door.

9. **Reflexive verbs** are those in which the action of the verb 'reflects' back upon the subject, eg: I wash myself, I say to myself. **Note**: verbs which are not reflexive in English are often reflexive in French, eg: in English we say 'I sit'; the French is *je m'assieds*, I seat myself. In French the reflexive pronoun follows the subject (pronoun or noun), and is **only** separated from the subject by *ne* if negative: *je me lave, je ne me lave pas*. There is **no** difference between reflexive pronouns which are direct objects (as in: *je me lave*, I wash myself) and those which are indirect objects (as in: *je me dis*, I say to myself). In **compound tenses** the auxiliary is **always** *être*, and the past participle agrees with the reflexive pronoun if it is a direct object, as in: *elle s'est lavée, ils se sont lavés*, but it does **not agree** if the reflexive pronoun is an indirect object, eg: *elle s'est dit*, she said to herself; *elle s'est lavé les mains*, she has washed her hands = she has to herself washed her hands – 'the hands' is the direct object, and follows the verb, so there is **no** agreement. See PRONOUNS ¶3, ¶4, ¶9, in this Section (above).

10. **Reciprocal verbs** are conjugated like reflexive verbs, **but** the action is 'mutual', as in: *se battre*, to fight 'each other'; *se regarder*, to look at 'each other'. Some verbs can be reflexive **or** reciprocal as the sense demands: the context shows which meaning is intended.

11.   **Auxiliary verbs** are those used to form **compound tenses**. In English 'to have' is the **only** auxiliary; in French *avoir* and *être* are both used. See **Auxiliary Verbs** in Reference Section, and also **compound tenses**, see ¶20 – 27 below.

12.   **REGULAR CONJUGATION, MEANING AND USAGE OF TENSES**
Tenses are divided into **simple tenses** and **compound tenses**. Simple tenses consist of one word – the stem plus the ending for the tense and person. Compound tenses are composed of a tense of the auxiliary (either *avoir* or *être*) with the past participle of the verb. There are both simple and compound tenses in the **indicative mood** and **subjunctive mood**. The **imperative mood** consists of one simple tense only.

13.   **SIMPLE TENSES**
Present tense: *le Présent.* The one French present tense translates, for example, English 'I speak', 'I am speaking', 'I do (not) speak'. There is **no** continuous present or emphatic 'I do speak' form in French. The following are **examples** of the present tense of regular verbs of each of the four conjugations, and of the two **irregular verbs** *avoir* and *être*.

	PRESENT					
	REGULAR VERBS				IRREGULAR VERBS	
	PARLER	*FINIR*	*VENDRE*	*RECEVOIR*	*ÊTRE*	*AVOIR*
	SPEAK	FINISH	SELL	RECEIVE	BE	HAVE
*je**	*parle*	*finis*	*vends*	*reçois*	*suis*	*ai*
tu	*parles*	*finis*	*vends*	*reçois*	*es*	*as*
il	*parle*	*finit*	*vend*	*reçoit*	*est*	*a*
nous	*parlons*	*finissons*	*vendons*	*recevons*	*sommes*	*avons*
vous	*parlez*	*finissez*	*vendez*	*recevez*	*êtes*	*avez*
ils	*parlent*	*finissent*	*vendent*	*reçoivent*	*sont*	*ont*
*in other tenses the pronoun subjects are the same						

14.   **Imperfect tense**: *l'Imparfait,* translates 'I was talking', 'I used to talk', 'I talked' (continuously or repeatedly) or 'I would talk' meaning 'I was accustomed to talk'. See also **used to** in Reference Section. The imperfect **cannot** be used for 'would' = 'insisted on'.
    All imperfects have the endings: *-ais, -ais, -ait, -ions, -iez, -aient.* In all but a very few cases the **stem** is that of the present participle and of the 1st person plural of the present.

	IMPERFECT				
parler	*finir*	*vendre*	*recevoir*	*être*	*avoir*
parlais	*finissais*	*vendais*	*recevais*	*étais**	*avais*
parlais	*finissais*	*vendais*	*recevais*	*étais*	*avais*
parlait	*finissait*	*vendait*	*recevait*	*était*	*avait*
parlions	*finissions*	*vendions*	*recevions*	*étions*	*avions*
parliez	*finissiez*	*vendiez*	*receviez*	*étiez*	*aviez*
parlaient	*finissaient*	*vendaient*	*recevaient*	*étaient*	*avaient*
* the imperfect stem of *être (ét-)* is that of the present participle. The present has **no** stem					

15.   **Future tense**: *le Futur,* translates the English 'I shall speak', 'you/he, etc, will
       speak', etc. French frequently uses the future where English uses the present,
       though the future is implied, eg: 'You will speak when my friend **arrives**'
       ('arrives' is present, **but** means 'when he in the future arrives') this becomes:
       *vous parlerez quand mon ami **arrivera*** (future) and: 'when I **am** (= at some
       future date) in London . . .' becomes: *quand je **serai** à Londres . . .* and: 'I
       shall give you back this book when I **have** read it' (= 'when I shall have read
       it') becomes: *je vous rendrez ce livre quand je l'**aurai** lu.* But the future is **not**
       used after the conjunction *si,* meaning 'if', though it may be used when *si* =
       'whether': I shall do it **if** you come, *je le ferai **si** vous venez* but: I do not
       know whether you are coming, *je ne sais pas si vous **viendrez**.* See *si* i in
       Reference Section.

16.   **All future stems end in the letter *-r-*,** the **stem** being formed from the
       infinitive of *-er* and *-ir* verbs without alteration, of *-re* verbs by dropping the
       final *-e* and of *-evoir* verbs by dropping the *-oi-*.

       **All future endings, <u>with the final *-r-* of the stem</u>, are: *-rai, -ras, -re, -rons,
       -rez, -ront*. No exceptions.**

FUTURE					
parler	*finir*	*vendre*	*recevoir*	*être*	*avoir*
parlerai	*finirai*	*vendrai*	*recevrai*	*serai*	*aurai*
parleras	*finiras*	*vendras*	*recevras*	*seras*	*auras*
parlera	*finira*	*vendra*	*recevra*	*sera*	*aura*
parlerons	*finirons*	*vendrons*	*recevrons*	*serons*	*aurons*
parlerez	*finirez*	*vendrez*	*recevrez*	*serez*	*aurez*
parleront	*finiront*	*vendront*	*recevront*	*seront*	*auront*

**Some important irregular future tenses, besides those of *avoir* and *être*
are**: *aller = irai; envoyer = enverrai; falloir = faudrai; faire = ferai; mourir
= mourrai; pouvoir = pourrai; savoir = saurai; voir = verrai; vouloir =
voudrai.* See these and other verbs listed in Reference Section.

17.   **Past historic** (past definite **or** simple past): *le Passé Défini* or *Passé Simple,*
       translates English 'I spoke' (once, at one definite time in the past). But it is
       not used in everyday speech, being replaced in practice by the **perfect** (see
       below). Its use is confined to narrative in literary French or formal speech
       (perhaps a sermon, dissertation or oration) and possibly in a very formal letter.
       The form of the 1st person singular and both 3rd persons, singular and
       plural, of the past historic is **somewhat different** in *-er* verbs from that of
       other conjugations, **but** otherwise the differences are in the vowel only: *a*
       for *-er* verbs, *i* for *-ir* and *-re* verbs and *u* for regular *-evoir* verbs and a
       number of irregular *-ir* verbs. Note: *tenir, venir* and their compounds have
       -n- inserted into their endings (*tins, tînmes,* etc) and *croître* retains the
       circumflex throughout: see these, and other irregular verbs, in the Reference
       Section.

PAST HISTORIC					
parler	*finir*	*vendre*	*recevoir*	*être*	*avoir*
a	*i*	*i*	*u*	*u*	*u*
parlai	*finis*	*vendis*	*reçus*	*fus*	*eus*
parlas	*finis*	*vendis*	*reçus*	*fus*	*eus*
parla	*finit*	*vendit*	*reçut*	*fut*	*eut*
parlâmes	*finîmes*	*vendîmes*	*reçûmes*	*fûmes*	*eûmes*
parlâtes	*finîtes*	*vendîtes*	*reçutes*	*fûtes*	*eûtes*
parlèrent*	*finirent*	*vendirent*	*reçurent*	*eurent*	
*note the accent on *parlèrent*					

18.   **The conditional**: *le Conditionnel*, translates English 'I should speak', 'he would speak', etc, the action depending upon something else happening. It is **not** used to translate 'should' when this means 'ought to', 'must', etc (see *devoir*): and it is **not** used to translate 'would' if it means 'wish', 'would like' (see *vouloir*) or 'used to be' (see imperfect, ¶14). Further explanation of usage is given in the entry **Conditional** in the Reference Section. The conditional is **always formed from the stem of the future + imperfect endings**. If the future stem is known so is that of the conditional.

CONDITIONAL					
parler	*finir*	*vendre*	*recevoir*	*être*	*avoir*
parlerais	*finirais*	*vendrais*	*recevrais*	*serais*	*aurais*
parlerais	*finirais*	*vendrais*	*recevrais*	*serais*	*aurais*
parlerait	*finirait*	*vendrait*	*recevrait*	*serait*	*aurait*
parlerions	*finirions*	*vendrions*	*recevrions*	*serions*	*aurions*
parleriez	*finiriez*	*vendriez*	*recevriez*	*seriez*	*auriez*
parleraient	*finiraient*	*vendraient*	*recevraient*	*seraient*	*auraient*

19.   **The imperative** is the mood and tense that gives a command or expresses a wish. There is **no** first person singular, and the third persons singular and plural are borrowed from the **present subjunctive**. In the case of -*er* verbs (and irregular verbs which have -*er* type imperatives) there is normally **no** -*s* in the second person singular; however, **before** -*en* and -*y* the -*s* is retained, unless an infinitive follows. **For example** *offrir*, to offer. Present: *tu offres*. Imperative: *offre!* offer! **But**: *offres-en*, offer some. Similarly: *vas-y*, go there, **but** *va y mettre*, to go and put there, with **no** hyphens (the *y* being complement of *mettre*). The meanings are as shown: the conjunction *que* is not part of the verb, **but** it is frequently put before the he third persons: thus *qu'il parle* = 'that he may speak' = let him speak.

IMPERATIVE	
parler	*Parle!* speak! *qu'il parle*, let him speak; *parlons*, let us speak; *parlez!* speak! *qu'ils parlent*, let them speak
finir	*finis!* finish! *au'il finisse*, let him finish; *finissons*, let us finish; *finissez!* finish! *qu'ils finissent*, let them finish

vendre	*vends!* sell! *qu'il vende*, let him sell; *vendons*, let us sell; *vendez!* sell! *qu'ils vendent*, let them sell
recevoir	*reçois!* receive! *qu'il reçoive*, let him receive; *recevons*, let us receive; *recevez!* receive! *qu'ils reçoivent*, let them receive
être	*sois!* be! *qu'il soit*, let him (it) be*; *soyons*, let us be; *soyez!* be! *qu'ils soient*, let them be
avoir	*aie!* have! *qu'il ait*, that he may have; *ayons*, let us have; *ayez!* have! *qu'ils aient*, let them have

* *qu'il soit* can mean: that he may be/let him be! that it may be/let it be! *soit!* alone is often used for 'so be it!' (= the subjunctive). The imperative is **often** used in such phrases as: *vive le roi!* long live the king!

20. **COMPOUND TENSES**

Compound tenses are formed with the **auxiliary** – either *avoir* or *être* – and the **past participle** (see **Auxiliary Verbs** in Reference Section). Verbs which make their compound tense with *être* are those the action of which essentially results in a change of position or condition, eg: *aller*, to go; *devenir*, to become. **All** reflexive verbs are conjugated with *être*. The past participle of verbs conjugated with *être*, other than reflexive verbs, agrees in gender and number with the subject; in reflexive verbs agreement occurs **only** when the reflexive pronoun is a direct object (see ¶9 above, ¶23 and ¶44 below): *vous* can be singular or plural. **The compound tenses,** including those of the subjunctive, are listed below: references are to the paragraphs which give their use and meanings.

21. **Indicative mood (compound tenses):**

The **perfect** *(le Parfait)*, using present of auxiliary, eg: *j'ai parlé*, I have spoken; *je suis allé(e)*, I had gone (see ¶24 for use of this tense).

Pluperfect *(le Plus-que-parfait)*, with imperfect of auxiliary: *j'avais parlé*, I had spoken; *j'étais allé(e)*, I had gone (see ¶22 – 23).

Past anterior *(Passé Antérieur)*, with past historic of auxiliary: *j'eus parlé*, I had spoken; *je fus allé(e)*, I had gone (see ¶25 for use of this tense).

Future perfect *(le Futur Antérieur)*, with future of auxiliary: *j'aurai parlé*, I shall have spoken; *je serai allé(e)*, I shall have gone.

Conditional perfect *(le Futur Antérieur du Passé)*, with conditional of auxiliary: *j'aurais parlé*, I should have spoken; *je serais allé(e)*, I should have gone.

Subjunctive mood (compound tenses) (see ¶38 – 32):

The **perfect subjunctive** *(le Passé du Subjonctif)*, with present subjunctive of auxiliary: *j'aie parlé*, I may have spoken; *je sois allé(e)*, I may have gone.

The **pluperfect subjunctive** *(le Plus-que-parfait du Subjonctif)*, with imperfect subjunctive of the auxiliary: *j'eusse parlé*, I might have spoken; *je fusse allé(e)*, I might have gone.

22. **The perfect** (**or** past indefinite), *le Parfait (Passé Composé).*
Strictly speaking, the French perfect corresponds to the English perfect, as in
'I have spoken': but **in everyday speech** it is also used to translate the simple
past, 'I spoke' when this means 'I spoke at that time, on the one occasion'
(**not** if it means 'I used to speak, I often spoke,' etc, which requires the
imperfect). It is composed of the present of the auxiliary + past participle. All
verbs used in a sense which can take a direct object have *avoir* as auxiliary:
verbs which imply a change of state or condition, and all reflexive verbs, use
être. Some verbs take **both** auxiliaries according to their meaning.

PERFECT TENSES OF REGULAR VERBS CONJUGATED WITH *AVOIR*	
parler	*j'ai parlé,* I have spoken; *tu as parlé; il (*or *elle) a parlé; nous avons parlé; vous avez parlé; ils (*or *elles) ont parlé*
finir	*j'ai fini,* I have finished; *tu as fini; il (*or *elle) a fini; nous avons fini; vous avez fini; ils (*or *elles) ont fini*
vendre	*j'ai vendu,* I have sold; *tu as vendu; il (*or *elle) a vendu; nous avons vendu; vous avez vendu; ils (*or *elles) ont vendu*
recevoir	*j'ai reçu,* I have received; *tu as reçu; il (*or *elle) a reçu; nous avons reçu; vous avez reçu; ils (*or *elles) ont reçu*

23. In verbs of change of position or condition conjugated with the auxiliary *être,*
the past participle agrees with the subject, as its complement, **but** in the case
of **reflexive verbs** the past participle agrees **only** if the reflexive pronoun is a
direct object (see ¶9 and the second column below).

PERFECT TENSE CONJUGATED WITH *ÊTRE*		
AGREES		DOES NOT AGREE
I have gone; you have gone . . .	I have washed (myself); you have washed (yourself) . . .	I have said to myself; you have said to yourself . . .
je suis allé(e)	*je me suis lavé(e)*	*je me suis dit*
tu es allé(e)	*tu t'es lavé(e)*	*tu t'est dit*
il est allé	*il s'est lavé*	*il s'est dit*
elle est allée	*elle s'est lavée*	*elle s'est dit*
nous sommes allé(e)s	*nous nous sommes lavé(e)s*	*nous nous sommes dit*
vous êtes allé(e)(s)	*vous* * *vous êtes lavé(e)(s)*	*vous vous êtes dit*
ils sont allés	*ils se sont lavés*	*ils se sont dit*
elles sont allées	*elles se sont lavées*	*elles se sont dit*
* *vous* is treated as singular when only one person is addressed		

24. **Pluperfect**: *le Plus-que-parfait,* usually translates 'I had spoken' (**but** see also
next tense). It is composed of the imperfect of the auxiliary + the past
participle, agreeing as in the perfect:

PLUPERFECT (EXAMPLES)			
elle avait parlé	she had spoken	*ils avaient parlé*	they had spoken
elle était allée	she had gone	*ils étaient allées*	they had gone
elle s'était lavée	she had washed	*ils s'étaient lavées*	they had washed
elle s'était dit	she had said to herself	*ils s'étaient dit*	they had said to themselves

25. **Past anterior**: *le Passé Antérieur*, also translates 'I had spoken', etc, but in a time clause (that is, one introduced by a conjunction of time such as *quand*, when; *après que*, after, etc) following a main clause in the past historic. It is formed with the past historic of the auxiliary + the past participle (thus a past historic in the main clause takes a past historic auxiliary (see ¶21) in the dependent clause):

PAST ANTERIOR (EXAMPLES)	
j'eus parlé	I had spoken
je fus allé(e)	I had gone
je me fus lavé(e)	I had washed
je me fus dit, etc	I had said to myself.

26. **Future perfect**: *le Futur Antérieur*, translates the English 'I shall have spoken', etc, and is composed of the future of the auxiliary (see ¶21) + the past participle of the verb itself:

FUTURE PERFECT (EXAMPLES)	
j'aurai parlé	I shall have spoken
je serai allé(e)	I shall have gone
je me serai lavé(e)	I shall have washed
je me serai dit	I shall have said to myself.

27. **Conditional perfect**: *le Futur Antérieur du Passé*, translates 'I should have spoken' and is composed of the conditional of the auxiliary (see ¶21) + the past participle:

CONDITIONAL PERFECT (EXAMPLES)	
j'aurais parlé	I shall have spoken
je serai allé(e)	I should have gone
je me serai lavé(e)	I should have washed
je me serai dit	I should have said to myself.

28. **SUBJUNCTIVE MOOD AND TENSES**
Whereas tenses of the indicative mood express something that has actually happened, is happening or will happen, the tenses of the subjunctive are used to express what may happen, what it is hoped will happen, what it is feared might happen, or what one regrets having happened although there may be the possibility that it might have been avoided or could have been otherwise – something about which there is an element of doubt as to its inevitability or actuality. In English we now rarely use the subjunctive: it is still regularly used in French. See rules and examples in ¶33 below.

29.   **There are four subjunctive tenses: two simple tenses:** the present
subjunctive and the imperfect subjunctive, and **two compound tenses** formed
from the simple subjunctives of the auxiliary + the past participle.

30.   **Present subjunctive,** *le Présent du Subjonctif,* usually translated as 'I may
(speak)'. **Except** for *avoir* and *être,* the endings are **always -e, -es, -e, -ions,
-iez, -ent,** and with a few exceptions (including *avoir, être, faire* and *savoir*)
the stem is that of the present participle (modified as in the present tense of
the verb). The following are the present subjunctive tenses of regular *-er, -ir,
-re, -evoir* verbs, and of *être, avoir, aller, faire* and *savoir* (other irregular
verbs and those which modify their stem are in Reference Section):

PRESENT SUBJUNCTIVE								
parler	finir	vendre	recevoir	être	avoir	aller	faire	savoir
parle	finisse	vende	reçoive	sois	aie	aille	fasse	sache
parles	finisses	vendes	reçoives	sois	aies	ailles	fasses	saches
parle	finisse	vende	reçoive	soit	ait	aille	fasse	sache
parlions	finissions	vendions	recevions	soyons	ayons	allions	fassions	sachions
parlies	finissiez	vendiez	receviez	soyez	ayez	alliez	fassiez	sachiez
parlent	finissent	vendent	reçoivent	soient	aient	aillent	fassent	sachent

In **regular verbs** the 1st and 2nd plural of the present subjunctive is identical
with the same persons in the imperfect indicative, and the 3rd plural is
identical with the 3rd plural of the present indicative. Where the present
singular ends *-e, -es, -e* the present subjunctive is the same. This does **not**
always apply to irregular verbs.

31.   **Imperfect subjunctive,** *l'Imparfait du Subjonctif,* is usually shown as
translating 'I might speak'. In all conjugations and in the two auxiliaries
(which differ only by their initial letter) all are constructed in exactly the same
way, with the vowel of the past historic dominant:

IMPERFECT SUBJUNCTIVE					
parler	finir	vendre	redevoir	être	avoir
a	i	i	u	u	u
parlasse	finisse	vendisse	reçusse	fusse	eusse
parlasses	finisses	vendisses	reçusses	fusses	eusses
parlât	finît	vendît	reçût	fût	eût
parlassions	finissions	vendissions	reçussions	fussions	eussions
parlassiez	finissiez	vendissiez	reçussiez	fussiez	eussiez
parlassent	finissent	vendissent	reçussent	fussent	eussent

The 3rd singular of the imperfect subjunctive is **always** identical with that of
the past historic of *-ir, -re,* and *-oir* verbs: **but with the addition of a
circumflex:** (*croître* has a circumflex in both tenses and *haïr* has **no**
circumflex): in *-er* verbs ^t is added: *il parla, il parlât.* The other endings,
following the vowel of the stem, are **always** the same: the imperfect
subjunctive can thus **always** be deduced if the past historic is known.

32.   The two compound subjunctive tenses, the **perfect subjunctive**, *le Subjonctif Passé*, and the **pluperfect subjunctive**, *le Plus-que-Parfait Subjonctif*, are formed, like the indicative compound tenses, using the present subjunctive and imperfect subjunctive of their auxiliary:

PERFECT SUBJUNCTIVE WITH *AVOIR*		PERFECT SUBJUNCTIVE WITH *ÊTRE*		PLUPERFECT SUBJUNCTIVE WITH *AVOIR*		PLUPERFECT SUBJUNCTIVE WITH *ÊTRE*	
j'aie parlé	I may have spoken	*je sois allé(e)*	I may have gone	*j'eusse parlé*	I might have spoken	*je fusse allé(e)*	I might have gone
tu aies parlé	you may have spoken	*tu sois allé(e)*	you may have gone	*tu eusses parlé*	you might have spoken	*tu fusses allé(e)*	you might have gone
il (or elle) ait parlé	he may have spoken	*il (or elle) soit allé(e)*	he may have gone	*il (or elle) eût parlé*	he might have spoken	*il (or elle) fût allé(e)*	he might have gone
nous ayons parlé	we may have spoken	*nous soyons allé(e)s*	we may have gone	*nous eussions parlé*	we might have spoken	*nous fussions allé(e)s*	we might have gone
vous ayez parlé	you may have spoken	*vous soyez allé(e)(s)*	you (sing or plur) may have gone	*vous eussiez parlé*	you might have spoken	*vous fussiez allé(e)(s)*	you (sing or plur) might have gone
ils (or elles) aient parlé	they may have spoken	*ils (or elles) soient allé(e)s*	they may have gone	*ils (or elles) eussent parlé*	they might have spoken	*ils (or elles) fussent allé(e)s*	they might have gone

33.   **USE OF THE SUBJUNCTIVE**

The subjunctive is used:

i.   in a subordinate clause introduced by one of the subordinating conjunctions (listed in CONJUNCTIONS ¶5) which **must** be followed by a subjunctive clause, eg: *j'attendrai jusqu'à ce qu'il vienne*, I shall wait until he comes. The clauses may be reversed, with the conjunction coming first: **bien qu**'il ne soit riche, il mange bien, although he is not rich, he eats well

ii.   **after** verbs expressing a wish that something may be: *je veux que vous le fassiez*, I wish you to do it (= that you may do it – but it may not happen)

iii. **after** a verb expressing a negative wish: *je veux que je ne fusse jamais né!* I wish I had never been born (pluperfect subjunctive using *être* in imperfect subjunctive as auxiliary)

iv.   **after** a verb expressing a prayer that someone may do something or something may happen: *que Dieu vous pardonne!* may God forgive you! (No certainty that He will.) *que Dieu ne plaise*, God forbid (= may

God not please)! *vive le roi!* long live the king (= may the king live). Exceptionally, ***espérer***, to hope, takes the subjunctive **only** in the negative: *je n'espère* pas *qu'il le fasse*, I don't hope he'll do it **but**: *j'espère qu'il viendra*, I hope he will come (future indicative), a factual statement of what I hope. In the **interrogative**, the indicative or subjunctive may be used according to the meaning: *espérez-vous qu'il meure?* do you hope that he may die (that there may exist a possibility of his dying)? *espérez-vous qu'il mourra?* do you hope that he will die? (a simple wish that such may be the case)

v.   **after** a command or prohibition that someone is supposed to obey (there is **no** certainty it will be obeyed), eg: *il a ordonné que les prisonniers soient liés*, he ordered that the prisoners be bound; *je défends que vous le fassiez*, I forbid you to do it (= that you do it)

vi. **after** an order not to do something: *j'ai défendu qu'ils le fasse*, I have forbidden them to do it (forbidden that they do it)

vii. **after** expressions of feelings, emotions, eg: *je regrette qu'il soit mort*, I am sorry that he is (= that he be) dead: similarly with expressions such as: *je suis content que*, I am pleased that; *je suis heureux que*, I am happy that; *je suis déçu que* (from *décevoir*), I am disappointed that; *je suis ébahi que*, I am amazed that; *je suis fâché que*, I am annoyed that; *je suis triste que*, I am sad that

viii. **after** verbs of fearing, eg: *je crains qu'il ne le fasse*, I fear that may do it, lest he do it (see ***ne***, ***craindre*** and **fear** in Reference Section)

ix. **after** verbs expressing an opinion, belief, uncertainty that something may be, eg: *il supposa qu'elle l'eût fait*, he supposed that she had done it; *je doute/conteste/nie qu'il ait raison*, I doubt/dispute/deny that he is right (= 'that he may have reason')

x.   **after** impersonal verbs such as 'it is possible', 'doubtful' 'impossible', 'necessary', eg: *il est possible/impossible qu'il sache la vérité*, it is possible/impossible that he knows* the truth (* English subjunctive = know). (**But** where there is no element of doubt, but the simple statement of a fact, the indicative is used, eg: *il semble que je l'ai déjà vu*, it seems (certain) that I have (in fact) already seen it.)

xi. in a **relative (adjectival) clause** qualifying a superlative, or similar expression, such as: *dernier*, last; *seul*, only; *suprême*, supreme; *unique*, unique, etc, eg: *c'est la seule place qu'il puisse prendre*, it is the only position he could take

xii. in a relative clause qualifying a negative statement, eg: *je n'ai jamais su s'il l'ait payé*, I never knew if he paid it (I have never known whether or not he has paid it); *je ne connais personne qui ne* veuille être heureux*, I know no one who does not wish to be happy (*in a negative relative clause in the subjunctive following a main clause which is also negative there is **no** *pas:* see ***vouloir*** in Reference Section)

xiii. in a relative clause which describes a characteristic which may or may not exist: *où est l'homme que puisse le faire?* where is the man who can do it (ie: the man with the necessary qualifications, if such a man

exists)? *je cherche quelqu'un qui ait l'argent,* I'm looking for someone
who has the money (= someone who may be rich enough).

34. **SEQUENCE OF TENSES**
     Rules for the correct sequence of tenses are:
     i.   **in the indicative**
          a. when a dependent 'had' clause is linked to a main clause by a
              conjunction of time (such as *quand,* when; *aussitôt que,* as soon as)
              and if the main clause is in the **past historic**, the **past anterior** is
              used in the dependent clause, eg: *il l'acheta dès qu'il l'eut essayé,*
              he bought it as soon as he had tried it. **Note** that the same applies if
              the two clauses are reversed, putting the main clause *(il l'acheta)*
              after the dependent clause (This sequence results in the use together
              of **two** past historics: that of the verb of the main clause and that of
              the auxiliary of the verb in the dependent clause.)
          b. similarly, if the verb of the main clause is in the **imperfect**, the verb
              of the dependent clause is in the **conditional**, thus both verbs use
              imperfect endings, eg: *ils voulaient manger dès qu'ils seraient
              arrivés,* they wanted to eat as soon as they arrived
          c. for tenses in *si* clauses: see *si* i in Reference Section
     ii. **sequence of tenses in a subjunctive clause coming after** *que* (or a
          conjunction including *que*)
          a. if the main clause is in the present, future **or** perfect, the subjunctive
              present **or** subjunctive perfect is used, eg: *j'attendrai jusqu'à ce
              qu'il le fasse,* I shall wait until he does it (present), **or** *jusqu'à ce
              qu'il l'ait fait,* until he has done it (perfect – the choice of tense
              depending on the intended meaning)
          b. if the main clause is in any other tense the imperfect or pluperfect
              subjunctive is used. These rules for the sequence of tenses are **not**
              absolute, and circumstance or niceties of meaning may require that
              they be ignored.

35. **THE INFINITIVE**
     The infinitive is the **verb noun**, eg: *voyager,* **c'est apprendre,* to travel is to
     learn. *When one infinitive is used as subject and one as complement, as in
     this example: *ce* (or *c'*) **must** be placed before the connecting verb.

36. **The infinitive after a preposition**: the infinitive is the part of the verb which
     in French follows a preposition or prepositional phrase, whereas in English
     the present participle (ending in **-ing**) is used, eg: *sans parler,* without
     speaking; *pour aider,* for helping (in order to help); *avant de monter,* before
     going up; *au lieu de venir,* instead of coming. When *après* is used, the **perfect
     infinitive** (= the infinitive of the auxiliary + past participle) is normally used,
     eg: *après avoir parlé,* after speaking (after having spoken); *après être
     arrivé(e),* after arriving. **Except**: after the preposition *en* = on (= subsequent
     to), the present participle is used as in English: *en arrivant,* on arriving. See
     ¶43vi.

37.   The **negative infinitive** takes both elements of the negative before the verb: *ne pas travailler n'est pas sage*, not to work is not wise; *ne rien dire serait mieux*, to say nothing/saying nothing would be better. See **Negative** in Reference Section (last few lines).

38.   Some **infinitives** are used as normal nouns, eg: *le devoir*, duty; *le dîner*, dinner; *un être*, a being; *le rire*, laughter, the laugh; *le souvenir*, the memory, etc. These are **always** masculine.

39.   The **infinitive** can at times be used as a **finite verb** (that is, used as if it were a tense in a sentence) especially in the interrogative: *que faire?* what is to be done? *où aller?* where shall we go? *pourquoi ne pas espérer?* why (should we) not hope? **Or** it may be used in exclamations: *Moi, pleurer! jamais!* Me, cry! never! **and** sometimes also to make a description more vivid or lively, following *de*: *quelques garçons de voler et de disparaître*, several boys who would steal and disappear.

40.   The **infinitive** is sometimes used in notices as an **imperative**: *ne pas se pencher en dehors*, don't lean out (of the window) (used on French railway trains); *prendre deux fois par jour*, take twice a day (as on a medicine bottle); *s'adresser au concierge*, apply to the door-keeper/porter.

41.   **Many verbs can govern an infinitive**, eg: *envoyer: envoyez chercher un médecin*, send for a doctor (= send to seek a doctor); *espérer: j'espère venir demain*, I hope to come tomorrow; *pouvoir: vous pouvez monter*, you can go up; *savoir: il sait lire*, he knows how to read; *sembler: ils semblaient dormir*, they appeared to sleep/be sleeping; *vouloir: il veut ne pas le faire*, he wants not to do it. This is indicated in the Reference Section entries of these verbs, with *'faire'* ('to do') shown following the verb without any preposition, eg: see *pouvoir*.

42.   **PARTICIPLES**
        Formation: the **present participle**, with very few exceptions, can be formed by cutting off the *-ons* of the 1st person plural of the present tense, and adding *-ant*, eg: *parler, nous parl(ons), parlant*, speaking; *finir, nous finiss(ons), finissant*, finishing, etc. **Past participles** are not formed according to any general rule; those of regular *-er* verbs are like *parler = parlé*: of *-ir* verbs, like *finir = fini*: of *-re* verbs, like *vendre = vendu*, and of *-evoir* verbs, like *recevoir = reçu*. Irregular past participles are shown in the separate entry for each verb. For use of participles, and agreement of present participle, and of past participles in a compound tense, see below ¶43 – ¶44. For **passive participles** see ¶8 above.

43.   **Uses of the present participle**
        i.   although the French present participle corresponds to the present participle in English, **it cannot be used** to make a continuous present tense as in the English "he is **talking**'; this must be translated by the simple present, 'he talks', *il parle*

ii. **as a verb**, a present participle is used to describe an action simultaneous with that of the main verb, eg: the crowd, amassing in the square, awaited the arrival of the king, *la foule, s'amassant sur la place, attendait l'arrivée du roi:* as the participle here acts as a verb there is **no** agreement

iii. when 'while' is meant, whether stated or understood, *en* normally precedes the participle: the soldiers sing while marching, *les soldats chantent en marchant.* See ¶36

iv. if the action of the main verb takes place as the result of, or after, that of the participle: *en* is omitted, eg: opening the door, he went out (the one action **must** follow the other), *ouvrant la porte, il sortit*

v. 'having done something' is expressed by using the present participle of the auxiliary, whether *avoir* or *être,* with the past participle of the verb being used, eg: having spoken, *ayant parlé;* having arrived, *étant arrivé(e)(s)*;* having washed, *s'étant lavé(e)(s)** (*the past participle agreeing)

vi. some present participles can be used as an **adjective**; they then follow, and agree in gender and number with, the noun qualified: *une horloge parlante,* a speaking clock; *une jeune fille charmante,* a charming (young) girl; *des bruits agaçants,* irritating noises

vii. some present participles can be used as **nouns**, eg: *les vivants,* the living.

44. **Uses of the past participle**

i. the past participle is used to form compound tenses, see ¶20 above. In compound tenses, when a verb is conjugated with *être,* the past participle, acting as complement of the verb *être,* agrees with the subject in gender and number, as set out in ¶23 above. **But** in reflexive verbs it agrees with the reflexive pronoun **only if the reflexive pronoun is a direct object**, as explained above, at the end of ¶9. In verbs conjugated with *avoir,* the past participle agrees with **a direct object before the verb**: this may be a conjunctive pronoun, *le, la, les,* as in: *je les ai achetés,* I have bought them: or if *les* is feminine: *je les ai achetées.* The **direct object** before the verb may also be a relative pronoun, eg: *voici la maison, que j'ai achetée: achetée,* feminine, agrees with *que,* which in turn agrees with *la maison,* feminine, in the preceding clause

ii. some past participles can be used as **adjectives**, eg: *une lettre bien écrite et souvent lue,* a letter well-written and often read. Unless invariable they agree like other adjectives

iii. some past participles are commonly used as **nouns**, eg: *un fait,* a fact; *un mort,* a dead man; *une morte,* a dead woman. Referring to a feminine noun the past participle will normally be in the feminine, unless it is invariable

iv. **an attitude of the body**, which in English is described by the present participle, is described in French by the **past participle** used as an adjective, eg: she is sitting, *elle est assise;* they were lying down, *ils étaient couchés.* See also **while**.